A CRITIQUE OF THE NEW
NATURAL LAW THEORY

REVISIONS

A Series of Books on Ethics

General Editors:

Stanley Hauerwas and Alasdair MacIntyre

A CRITIQUE OF THE NEW NATURAL LAW THEORY

Russell Hittinger

UNIVERSITY OF NOTRE DAME PRESS
NOTRE DAME, INDIANA

paperback edition 1989
ISBN 0-268-00775-6

Library of Congress Cataloging-in-Publication Data

Hittinger, Russell.
    A critique of the new natural law theory.

    (Revisions ; v. 7)
    Bibliography: p.
    Includes index.
    1. Natural law. 2. Law—Philosophy. 3. Finnis,
John. 4. Grisez, Germain Gabriel, 1929–
I. Title. II. Series: Revisions (Notre Dame, Ind.) ;
v. 7.
K474.F562H57   1987   171'2   87–40344
ISBN 0-268-00766-7

Manufactured in the United States of America

CONTENTS

v

INTRODUCTION

Despite John Rawls's much celebrated effort in *A Theory of Justice* (1971) to tame the utilitarian tradition of ethics, and to wed together deontological ethics with the contractarian tradition, ethicists have grown increasingly weary of conducting ethical analysis within the context of the utilitarian-deontological debate. Rather, what has emerged in the past two decades is an interest in recovering what could be called "premodern" ethics—or at least those facets of ethical analysis which predate the utilitarian-deontological stalemate, and which promise to furnish grounds for some forward moves, whether they comprise diagnostic reflections on the state of contemporary ethics or systematic and constructive proposals.

Perhaps the most important, and certainly the most controversial, of these recoverists is Alasdair MacIntyre, whose *After Virtue* (1981) was a bombshell thrown in the sandbox of contemporary ethicians. MacIntyre offered a historical and critical diagnosis of what he termed the "interminability" of contemporary moral discourse and, in Nietzschean style, announced that moral discourse is paralyzed, if not dead. The Enlightenment and its heritage, he argued, destroyed ethics, and no one is willing to acknowledge, much less to avow, the deed. As is well known by now, he proposed that the problem should be seen in the light of two alternatives: either the way of Nietzsche or the way of Aristotle. A rejection of the former, he argued, requires a willingness to reconsider those elements in Aristotelian ethics which lend themselves to coherent moral discourse

1

and practice, and which ought to be recovered. For MacIntyre, the principal element to be recovered is an ethics of virtue, understood not within the context of a "metaphysical biology," but rather in terms of societal narratives which give specificity and a meaningful teleology to the virtues. All of this, he proposed, requires a narrative of how we reached the point of paralysis in the first place.

The recoverist project, however, has included other theorists. For example, Alan Donagan, in *The Theory of Morality* (1977), wishes to recover the "common morality" of the West which, in large part, has been ignored by "academic philosophers." The "traditional morality of the Western world," he observed, "must remain largely unintelligible to anybody unwilling to investigate its philosophical and religious foundations."[1] Donagan, however, has focused upon that part of the "common morality" which is separable from the religious or theistic elements—namely, the Kantian emphasis upon the value of human persons which, in his estimation, constitutes the main ingredient of the morality of the West which pre-dates the Enlightenment. In a more recent article, he has gone so far as to argue that "if we scrutinize the structure of St. Thomas's theory of natural law, we shall find that the teleology underlying it is not a Christianized version of eudaimonism, but an anticipation of the very same teleology Kant was to arrive at a little more than five hundred years later."[2]

It is important to bear in mind that this effort to recover one or another facet of a premodern ethics, much less *the* common morality, is not of one piece or mind. In a very important essay of nearly thirty years ago, entitled "Modern Moral Philosophy" (1958), Elizabeth Anscombe contended that the notion of a "law conception of ethics" is derived exclusively from Christianity. Here Anscombe goes against the grain of Donagan's ambition to recover the common morality without its theological context. Indeed, Anscombe herself went so far as to argue that the lexicon of "law," "duty," "norms," and "obligation" ought to be "put on the

Index" until the Christian premises are recovered.[3] For Anscombe, the problem of contemporary moral discourse —its "interminability," to use MacIntyre's term—is due to the fact that modern theorists wished to retain the accoutrements of "ought" terminology without the theological and religious contexts which would make sense of such an ethics.

Anscombe anticipated at least two lines of thought which would later emerge among the so-called recoverists. In lieu of the theological context, she reasoned that moral theorists must recover the classical emphasis upon an ethics of virtue, which underscores the excellence of actions rather than rules. To this extent, she set the stage for MacIntyre's work twenty years later. Her insistence upon the importance of the specific religious tradition of Christianity also anticipated the work of Stanley Hauerwas. An interesting figure among the recoverists, Hauerwas first stressed the importance of an ethics of virtue and character. For instance, in his early book *Character and the Christian Life* (1975), he provides an astute analysis of Aquinas's theory of moral character which, he argued, had been overlooked not only by the Protestant tradition but by Thomists as well. However, in more recent works, such as *The Peaceable Kingdom* (1983), he has moved decisively toward the opinion that an account of a common morality is mistaken, and that a distinctively Christian ethics requires a recovery of what is specifically *Christian* about such an ethic. Moral virtue and character continue to play a role, but now within the specific context of Christian moral theology. The story of Jesus provides a school for training in moral character that allows communities to live "amid the fragments" of the so-called common morality.[4]

It is worth noting, too, that the recoverists of various stripes are not simply within the orbit of Anglo-American thought. Ernst Bloch, for example, has argued from a Marxist perspective that the "tricolor" of the revolutionary tradition must be recovered in tandem with a sympathetic reconsideration of natural law—"purged," as he says, "of bourgeois illusions."[5] In *Natural Law and Human Dignity* (posthumously translated and published in 1986), we find Bloch observing that the revolutionary tradition of rights is still in search of a normative theory of nature that would allow the "tricolor" to avoid the reefs of positivism and orgiastic revolutionary action. Whether or not Bloch manages to locate and appropriate those elements of the older tradition "that are unclaimed" is a matter that goes beyond the remarks we wish to make at this point. His massive work, *The Principle of Hope,* that sets the groundwork for the reclamation project, has only recently been translated and made available to the English reading public.[6]

Among the recoverists mentioned, we can discern a general outline of those elements in the premodern tradition(s) of ethics which need to be reclaimed. For MacIntyre, the key is virtue, within the context of coherent social narratives. For Donagan, the value of the person is the central component. For Anscombe, the missing link is religion. For Hauerwas, it is not the religious context in general, but rather specific ecclesial communities which constitute schools of Christian virtue and practices. From the other shore, Bloch stresses the need to reclaim natural law for the purpose of rescuing rights from the grip of statism, positivism, and irrational currents of revolutionary movements.

It would not be unfair to say that what Donagan has called the "common morality" would include *all* of the foci taken by these various theorists. After all, if one were to examine the main lines of the common morality, one would find the presence of communal narratives, a teleological conception of nature, an emphasis upon virtues, the idea of dignity of the human person, and the notion that certain rights precede social and political conventions, as well as specific ecclesial traditions. How one might put all of these elements together (theoretically, and especially practically) is a serious question. The fact that none of the

theorists mentioned thus far has done so should indicate
the inherent difficulty of attempting such a project.

For this reason, among others, it is important to consider
the work of Germain Grisez and John Finnis. For lack of a
better term, their work constitutes a new natural law
theory. Finnis's *Natural Law and Natural Rights* (1980)
has done as much as any other single work to bring the
subject of natural law back to the forefront of scholarly
attention. The importance of their work is at least threefold. In the first place, Grisez and Finnis claim to have
recovered Aquinas's natural law theory in a way that
avoids the standard objections which have beset such a
theory since the Enlightenment. Moreover, they contend
to have rescued Aquinas's natural law theory from the
problems inherent in the rest of Aquinas's work. In the
second place, they claim a systematic and comprehensive
status for their position. In other words, they are not
about the business of recovering an isolated strand of a
premodern ethics; nor does their work involve mere sorties
into the history of premodern ethics. Rather they contend
to have retrieved the systematic core of natural law theory
in a way that is congruent with the older tradition *and* in a
way that is persuasive to contemporary ethicians. In the
third place, with the publication of *Christian Moral Principles* (1983)—the first volume in what is intended to be a
new *summa* of moral theology—Germain Grisez has undertaken the application of this new natural law theory to
moral theology.

Grisez makes no bones about the fact that his work is
meant to realize the Second Vatican Council's call for a
renewal of moral theology. Since the Roman Catholic
Church historically has been the principal locus for premodern ethics, and the main agent of the natural law
legacy, the significance of Grisez and Finnis's project cannot be overlooked. Since the Council, moral discourse
within the Roman Catholic community has come to
resemble wide-ranging skirmish lines, along which nearly

every item of moral theology is under contention. Grisez purports not only to have put the issues back together systematically, but to have done so in such a way that he is able to arrive at "orthodox" conclusions. Indeed, *that* he arrives at orthodox conclusions has attracted as much, or more, attention than the manner by which he makes his arrival.

If the Grisez-Finnis natural law system is coherent, then it surely has profound implications for Catholic ethicists, as well as for the recoverists. Since the flourishing of neo-Scholasticism around the time of the Second World War, natural law theory has been relatively quiescent. The systematic ambition and scope of the Grisez-Finnis project makes one sit up and take notice. If, however, the system does not work, then it still has important implications. In this regard, we can agree with Henry Veatch's recent observation that "successful or not, I think this Grisez-Finnis position is singularly illuminating, and its failure can be most instructive."[7] In this book we shall argue that the position does have serious deficiencies. But we need to locate precisely where it falls short, and for what reasons.

We will focus especially upon the relationship between religion and their natural law method. The theme is not extrinsically imposed upon their project, for as we will show in detail, religion is the lightning rod for a number of problems—even contradictions—in this new natural law theory. It bears upon axiological issues concerning goods or values and the moral principles whereby goods are chosen. Moreover, it precipitates certain other problems: whether there exists a hierarchy of goods prior to choice; the teleological question of whether there exists an end for human beings; and the methodological issue of how one is to undertake the transition from philosophical ethics to moral theology. We need to understand why religion is a natural good, how it should entail moral obligations, whether it is a superordinate good, and how the introduction of revealed data held by faith, and regulated by divine and ecclesial positive laws, fits with the natural law account of practical rationality.

The first chapter provides an interpretive exposition of the main lines of the Grisez-Finnis system, first in terms of their critique of rival systems, and then in terms of their account of practical reason and human goods. They adopt a rather unusual method of distinguishing between the premoral and moral facets of natural law method. Our concern is not whether they have the words, but whether they have the music of an authentically natural law method. In the first chapter we will explain the premoral facet. Then, in the second chapter we will examine their understanding of the specifically moral facet of natural law, particularly as it involves the question of teleology and hierarchy. These two chapers constitute a critical summary and exposition of the system.

In chapter three we will move to the relationship between religion and natural law: first, as religion functions as one of the goods which, according to natural law, requires moral respect; and second, as religion involves revelation and the norms derived from divine and ecclesial positive law. Here we shall argue that religion is not adequately treated in either mode, much less in the transition between them.

Finally we shall critically examine the precise points where the system proves insufficient. We will introduce a distinction between foundational and implicational approaches to the relationship between religion and practical reason. A foundational approach would include religion in the foundation of one's account of practical reason, and would perhaps assign to theology the task of elaborating what specific difference revelation makes. An implicational approach, on the other hand, would not place religion in the foundation, but would reserve it, in a way similar to Kant's method, for issues which arise after the foundation has been established. The Grisez-Finnis method straddles these two approaches. While they avow a natural law method, and thus include religion in the foundation, we shall argue that they do not give good reasons why it should be included. For reasons which we will explain in due course, their system inclines toward a Kantian-like implicational approach that does not square with the other aspects of their natural law system. Here, and in the conclusion, we shall point out why the failure of this new natural law theory holds, as Veatch says, some "illuminating" implications for ethics and for the various recoverist projects in particular. As we will observe later, the problem lies in a failure to interrelate systematically practical reason with a philosophy of nature. The problem not only derails the Grisez-Finnis reclamation of natural law, which obviously requires a commitment to law as in some way "natural," and nature as in some way normative; the problem also crops up in the works of the other recoverists.

Before we go on, it is necessary to explain our use of the hyphen when referring to the Grisez-Finnis position. There are differences between them. Finnis, for example, does not press the system into the domain of moral theology. Also, he takes a slightly different position on the relationship between religion and practical reason. Moreover, his list of the modes of moral responsibility is slightly different than Grisez's. Wherever there is a significant difference between the two, it will be explicitly noted and discussed. Nonetheless, Finnis explicitly relies upon Grisez's natural law theory. Throughout *Natural Law and Natural Rights,* and in other writings, Finnis refers his reader to Grisez, or states that his own theory is but an elaboration of Grisez's.[8] It should also be noted that Grisez and Finnis have co-authored an article in response to critics, and have thus publicly identified their common stake in the system.[9] Our use of the hyphen, therefore, is both fair and convenient.

Grisez and Finnis argue that Aquinas's understanding of the first principle of practical reason is exactly the same as their own. Yet neither wishes to be called a Thomist. In their skirmishes with various Thomists on the issue of whether or not they have correctly interpreted Aquinas, they have rejected the cogency of any critique that confuses the historical, interpretive issues regarding texts with the substantive and systematic aspects of their own position. One who would exposit and critique the Grisez-Finnis system is faced with a problem. On the one hand, their system proceeds from a far-reaching reinterpretation of Aquinas. Aquinas is frequently cited, especially by Grisez, in support of one or another aspect of his position. One would be remiss if one completely avoided the questions regarding their interpretation of Aquinas. On the other hand, they claim that the natural law theory is, in any event, their own. We will have to address both angles of the problem, but we will focus principally upon the substantive and systematic issues set forth and avowed by Grisez and Finnis.

Special thanks are due to Professors James Marsh, Vincent Punzo, and Richard Blackwell, who guided the research done during my graduate work at St. Louis University. I should also express my gratitude to those who have critically read the manuscript and who have offered suggestions: Henry Veatch, Ralph McInerny, Stanley Hauerwas, Fathers Leonard Kennedy and Victor Brezik, William Marshner, and Damian Fedoryka. The work, and any deficiencies found herein, are of course my own. Finally, I would like to remember the late Professor James Collins, who always encouraged scholarly care and fairness in philosophical inquiries which inevitably come to involve some polemical edges.

1

THE GRISEZ-FINNIS ACCOUNT OF PRACTICAL REASON AND HUMAN VALUES

This chapter is an interpretive exposition of the Grisez-Finnis account of practical reason. It is expository, first, in the sense that we will outline the basic criteria of the system and the intent of these criteria with regard to alternative systems. In the second place, we wish to provide a general exposition of their understanding of the first principle of practical reason and its relationship to human goods. This relationship between the first principle of practical reason (hereafter *Fppr*) and the human goods constitutes, for Grisez and Finnis, the premoral facet of their natural law theory. The distinction between premoral and moral facets of natural law is apt to prove confusing to those familiar with the more conventional moral meaning of the term *natural law*. It can prove all the more confusing because Grisez and Finnis understand both facets as constituting a natural law method for morality. As we proceed in these next two chapters, the Grisez-Finnis way of construing and applying the term *natural law* should become clearer.

If we are to give an exposition of the overall framework, some interpretation is required. First, it is necessary to draw together an enormous amount of published material from these two ethicists in order to give a synoptic view. Second, during the course of our exposition we shall highlight those aspects of the Grisez-Finnis position which bear especially on the relationship between religion and practical reason. In some instances we will simply note, or tag, as it were, an issue for future consideration in subsequent chapters which deal forthrightly with the relation between religion and practical reason. There are problematic implications for this relationship within the overall frame of the system which we must defer for the time being. It would be prudent first to see whether we can understand what Grisez and Finnis themselves understand about their own system.

At this juncture, it would be worthwhile to outline what could be called system criteria. They represent the intent of Grisez's account of practical reason. First, they are the criteria he uses in his critique of the adequacy or coherence of other systems. Second, they constitute the standard that Grisez wants to meet with regard to his own theory. The meaning of these criteria will become clearer as we proceed into Grisez's treatment of the substantive issues. Although they are not discussed explicitly as "system criteria" by Grisez, they can be found in the first chapter of *Christian Moral Principles,* where he delineates the general lines of his project.

1) *An adequate moral theory must account for the practicality of practical reason.* For Grisez, this means that, at a minimum, the nature and work of practical reason must not be reduced to being a mere tailpiece of theoretical reason on the one hand, nor reduced to being a mere extension of human desire on the other hand. Set in larger terms, this criterion demands that we justify what is distinctive about practical rationality itself, in contrast to theoretical or descriptive sciences. There must be something for practical reason to do. Unless human persons "have possibilities which are not yet defined," he argues, "there is no room for them to unfold themselves through intelligent creativity and freedom."[1]

In this regard, Grisez is critical of conventional natural law theory, which allows practical reason "an extremely limited role" in that moral conclusions are viewed as practical only insofar as they refer to "practical subject matter."[2] Moreover, to the extent that some species of conventional natural law theory were compelled to invoke the will of God as a determining condition for an obligation to follow the natural order, the creative practicality of human reason becomes subsumed under the will of a superior. When such is the case, according to Grisez, conventional natural law theory tends to reduce practical reason to the confines of a theoretical description of nature, and to the will of a superior without an intervening principle.

2) *An adequate theory of practical reason must account for our relationship to, and interest in, concrete goods.* For Grisez, it is not enough if we account for the unique role of practical reason, unless we also understand its interest and work within the world. Here, Grisez is critical of a certain tendency to reduce the scope of nonhypothetical goods, which attends deontological theories of ethics. He is critical of any theory that locks practical reason into itself by reducing the good of the moral life exclusively to it. Thus, in his evaluation of Kant, Grisez argues that Kant is not so much mistaken about the radical practicality of practical reason as he is mistaken in restricting the range of morally relevant human goods to the good of practical reason itself. Grisez wants to restore a eudaimonistic content in ethics—content drawn from a wide range of human inclinations. He hopes to show why these goods can serve as *prima principia* of practical reason.

On this subject, once again, he is no less critical of scholastic natural law theory which, in conjunction with a certain strain of popular religious piety, reinforced the notion that since man's unique end is beatitude in heaven, practical reason must concern itself exclusively with this supreme good. Whereas the Kantian position lends itself to an *a*cosmic view of practical reason, the extreme form of otherworldliness in popular piety tends to construe ethics as a task of being relieved of the finite, human world altogether.

Finally, in this same vein, Grisez is critical of the utilitarian or consequentialist tradition. While the conventional religious piety "considers the whole of life a test which must be passed only in order to get an extrinsic reward," the utilitarian tradition is prepared to disrespect human goods in order to achieve an extrinsic, though this-worldly, future consequence. Neither "type of theory," Grisez observes, "considers material goods to be intrinsically related to the ultimate good of man."[3]

3) *A theory of practical reason must show both the distinctions, and interrelations, between values and specifically moral norms.* Grisez argues that although practical reason is able to grasp goods as possibilities, and thus as values, this only generates a "field of possibilities in which choices are necessary."[4] There is a need, then, for moral norms which govern choices. According to Grisez, Thomas Aquinas was able to provide a natural law account of the first part of this scheme, viz., practical reason's grasp of goods as possibilities for action; but he failed sufficiently to distinguish between the practical orientation towards goods and the norms of morality which govern choices. As we mentioned earlier, Grisez seeks to distinguish, within practical reason, between the "first principle of practical reason" as premoral (that the good(s) ought to be pursued) and the "first principle of morality" (that they should be chosen in a way that respects the integrity of human well-being). In making this distinction, Grisez wants to differentiate clearly between natural law as involving material principles of practical rationality, and natural law as involving specifically moral principles governing choice.

4) *A Catholic moral theology must meet all the above requirements, as well as show what specific difference revelation makes for morality.* This criterion arises from Grisez's explicit effort to achieve a consistent and unified account of basic moral principles and Catholic moral theology. The specifics of this criterion depend, of course, upon just what Grisez means by "Catholic" and by "theology." We will deal with these details in later chapters.

Here, however, we can note that, at the very least, he understands his own project as that of providing a post-Vatican II system of ethics which avoids the problems inherent in both the conventional natural law tradition and the contemporary method of proportionalism. With respect to this criterion, our main concern is the consistency between the principles of practical reason, as philosophically explicated, and how these principles are affected once revelation is introduced into the picture.

1.1. Grisez's Critique of Alternative Theories

In *Christian Moral Principles* Grisez often examines in tandem what he calls "scholastic natural-law theory" and "classical moral theology."[5] It is important to understand exactly what he means by these terms. By "classical moral theology" he means the "moral theology which developed after Trent and persisted until Vatican II." For Grisez, its distinguishing characteristics were: "rationalism," "voluntarism," "legalism," "otherworldliness," and "minimalism."[6] Those who are familiar with Grisez's vigorous defense of the church's teachings on controversial subjects are liable to be surprised (should they wade into his thousand-page *summa*) by what a dim view he takes of preconciliar philosophy and theology. In his view, these characteristics were intimately related to what he calls either "scholastic" or "conventional" natural law theory.[7] This relationship was due, in large part, to the way this natural law theory shaped the manuals of ethics and moral theology prior to Vatican II. Grisez does not include the thought of Thomas Aquinas in either of these categories, even though, as we will show, Grisez is critical of many of the most central tenets and presuppositions of Aquinas's natural law theory.[8]

The fusion of "classical" moral theology and "scholastic" natural law theory, according to Grisez, can be traced to the natural law theory developed by Francisco Suarez and his followers. Our concern is not Grisez's historical point, but rather the substantive features of what he criticizes; for he wants to contrast this position with the "more adequate account of natural law" that he himself holds, and which we will examine subsequently.[9]

The rationalism of conventional natural law theory is rooted in the theory's understanding of human nature as a standard for moral judgment. He writes: "On this view, essential and unchanging human nature is the standard of human goodness. This nature is open to rational observation; good acts conform to it, while bad acts do not. Judgments of fitness are, however, purely speculative."[10] Practical reason, therefore, is viewed as a mere footnote to the conclusions of the speculative disciplines, which are principally interested in the invariant essences and structures of nature. By "rationalism," then, Grisez means an overly theoretical determination of human nature, which leaves little or no place for understanding how reason operates creatively in a practical mode. We have a kind of Eleaticism stomping in the vineyards of practical reason.

Grisez observes that this theory found it difficult to avoid a mitigated or "limited voluntarism." It avoided the full-fledged voluntarism found in some divine command theories of moral obligation, because it left at least a subordinate role for human reason to grasp the requirements of nature. Thus, it did not fall into "blind obedience." Nevertheless, he claims, it was "permanently in danger of falling into the illusion that practical knowledge is merely theoretical knowledge plus force of will"—such as what Suarez proposes in *De Legibus* where natural law is described as natural goodness plus preceptive divine law.[11]

As Grisez explains, the voluntarism arises because of a logical deficiency within the system itself:

> . . . to become aware of one's obligations it is not enough to observe the conformity or nonconformity between the action and one's nature. More than this

theoretical knowledge, one needs a basic requirement. According to the theory, this can be expressed in various ways: *follow reason, act in accord with nature,* or *do good and avoid evil.* However formulated the demand's full meaning is grasped only when one sees it to be a message to the created subject from God's sovereign will. And one sees nature itself as an effective moral norm only when one sees it as a sign of God's will.[12]

In other words, the theory requires a divine command in order to tie together the natural law as propositions concerning teleological functions and relationships and the natural law as a set of moral injunctions.[13]

He points out that once this theory is fused with ecclesiastical positive law, the net result is not only less attention paid to the intrinsic reasons for accepting moral norms, but also a concomitant tendency to "treat moral norms as laws which members of the Church must obey because the Church insists upon them with divine authority."[14] This, in turn, encourages a kind of "legalism," by which moral norms are regarded as the "decision of a supreme court." The church, regarded as the deputy of God, discharges the role of mediating natural teleology and moral norms. Taken to its extreme, one comes to believe that the moral doctrines can be changed simply by the fiat of authority. Grisez (rightly in our view) suggests that much of the confusion in postconciliar Catholic ethics has its origins in this preconciliar attitude. Once the mediation of the authority is called into question, the deficiency of this particular brand of natural law theory becomes quite apparent, for the relationship between natural teleology and moral norms appears to lack its authoritative "middle." Thus, those on different sides of ethical disputes find themselves wrangling over which authority ought to provide the mediating function. To this extent, the problems of preconciliar moral theory are still being played out and have not been superseded. One cannot help noticing that, in the main, postconciliar disputes have tended to involve debates over authority and power, and that the specifically moral issues are frequently reduced to questions of assent or dissent.

Moreover, even apart from the post-Suarezian emphasis upon the preceptive force of divine commands, scholastic natural law theory uncritically accepted, according to Grisez, the Augustinian and Thomistic teaching that man's end consists "more or less exclusively in the vision of God after death."[15] Grisez holds that Aristotle and Augustine "pointed St. Thomas in the direction of an overly definite conception of the natural end of human persons."[16] This likewise reinforced a popular piety which not only demoted the value of this-worldly goods but also confused nature and supernature.[17] For Grisez, in its most extreme form the position amounts, at least implicitly, to a kind of theological consequentialism.[18]

Finally, Grisez regards the conventional natural law theory as involving an ethical "negativism and minimalism." What does not conform to human nature can be forbidden absolutely, but what does conform to human nature proves difficult to specify in moral terms. Understandably, this puts an enormous burden upon casuistry. "Thus, scholastic natural-law theory," he says, "is far more adept at issuing a few prohibitions than at directing people's lives toward growth and flourishing."[19] In accord with the second and fourth criteria outlined above, Grisez concludes: "Against scholastic natural-law theory, [moral theory] must provide us with guidance toward goods which fulfill human persons more and more abundantly."[20]

Thus far we have indicated in a rather broad way Grisez's objections to scholastic natural law theory. We would be remiss if we failed to indicate the way in which his critique pertains to the moral issue of contraception. His book *Contraception and The Natural Law* (1964) contains his earliest systematic critique of conventional natural law theory. In what follows, we will briefly outline his thinking on this matter, but only as it pertains to his criticism of conventional natural law theory; we will examine his positive doctrine on the issue of contraception in the next chapter.

First, let us consider what Grisez calls the "syllogism of conventional natural-law theory":

Major: To prevent any act from attaining its natural end is intrinsically immoral.

Minor: Contraception prevents sexual intercourse from attaining its natural end.

Conclusion: Contraception is intrinsically immoral.[21]

He correctly points out that this conclusion follows only if the "natural end" is something one is morally obligated to seek. Even if the major premise is changed to read "the prevention of the realization of an end which one ought to seek is immoral," it is still not revealed why "the natural teleology of human functions requires absolute moral respect."[22] Moreover, he adds, if human nature is considered to the extent that it is already an object of moral knowledge, the "determination that a certain kind of action would not agree with it is prejudiced by the moral knowledge that is assumed."[23]

An appeal, at this point, to the argument that the integrity of human functions must be respected because God instituted the function falls short, because, so far as Grisez is concerned, "it is not evident that God requires that this design always be respected."[24] The failure of conventional natural law theory to advance its case on this issue without begging the question illustrates the problem with the system as such. It is unable to coherently interrelate three components in the argument: the theoretical knowledge of a natural necessity; the awareness of moral obligation; and the command of a divine will. The position ends in a series of negative prohibitions, under the auspices of divine sanctions, with little or no positive understanding of the value that practical reason is either affirming or denying.

Lest there be any mistake, Grisez does not defend the licitness of contraception. We are dealing here only with his criticism of conventional natural law theory which, according to his assessment, is unable to show what is morally wrong with the practice of contraception. The following passage from *Christian Moral Principles* nicely summarizes his position for why "scholastic natural law theory must be rejected":

> It moves by a logically illicit step—from human nature as a given reality, to what ought and ought not to be chosen. Its proponents attempt to reinforce this move, from what is to what ought to be, by appealing to God's command. But for two reasons this fails to help matters. First, unless there is a logically prior moral norm indicating that God's commands are to be obeyed, any command of God considered by itself would merely be another fact which tells us nothing about how we ought to respond. Second, even leaving this problem aside, the difficulty remains that human persons are unlike other natural entities; it is not human nature as given, but possible human fulfillment which must provide the intelligible norms for free choices.[25]

As the passage indicates, Grisez contends that in between the *is* of nature as given, and the *ought* of moral commands, there must be a scope for practical reason to grasp values which it, itself, can bring into being through its own free agency. Therefore, Grisez's critique not only focuses upon the problem of how one is to derive an *ought* from an *is* but also is aimed at what he takes to be an inadequate appreciation of practical reason in the first place.

Before we turn our attention to Grisez's criticism of consequentialism, it would be useful to take note of two things which ought to be kept in mind for future reference. First, Grisez's dissatisfaction with the problems inherent in conventional natural law theory inclines him to the view that divine commands have little or no positive role in ethics—insofar, that is, as we understand ethics apart from divine revelation. Indeed, as we will see later, he holds that the obligation to obey a divine command depends solely upon the posture of faith. Any other sense of a divine command can be reduced to what is already known and assented to by unassisted practical reason. Yet, as we will also see later, Grisez does *not* hold that unassisted reason can demonstrate the existence of God as an object of religion; nor does he subscribe to a metaphysics of final causality by which it would be at least theoretically possible to interrelate divine positive law (e.g., the Decalogue) with norms derived from a scheme of natural teleology. Obviously, this will hold important implications for how he understands the moral nature of religion, and for whether divine commands, once introduced, bring therewith the problem of heteronomy or, at least, systematic inconsistencies within the main frame of the natural law theory.

His criticism of the older theory's heavy-handed emphasis upon theoretical reason also inclines him to the view that speculative reason, including its metaphysical mode, is able to affirm little, if anything, concerning God as an end of human striving. Although he doesn't count Augustine or Aquinas among the conventional natural law theorists, Grisez is at best ambivalent about their arguments concerning the moral teleology of the "restless heart." On this basis, Grisez is prepared to separate question 94 of the *prima-secundae* of the *Summa theologiae*—in which Aquinas articulates the first principle of practical reason—from the preceding questions which set forth Aquinas's understanding of the teleological principles governing man's natural end.

Grisez's critique of consequentialism is well known. Both in his books and in published articles he has maintained a steady debate with the proponents of various philosophical and theological species of consequentialism—or, as it is more recently termed, proportionalism—namely, the position that, prior to choice, the agent is to consider the range of options available to choice and is to choose that option which promises the greater net sum, or proportion, of good consequences. Of particular importance is his lengthy essay, "Against Consequentialism," which was published in the *American Journal of Jurisprudence* (1978).[26] It would not be unfair to say that Grisez's system is a sustained criticism of, and alternative to, consequentialist ethics.

As we will see in due course, there are several features of Grisez's ethics which cannot be sufficiently appreciated without understanding why, and how, he wants to avoid the assumptions of the consequentialist or utilitarian tradition. Suffice it here to say that this is important because Grisez wishes to root his moral theory in a eudaimonistic pursuit of goods. It is therefore crucial for him to distinguish his own position from that of consequentialism (just as he wishes to distinguish his own natural law method from the Augustinian and Thomistic notions of man's natural finality). A complete account of Grisez's critique —especially as it involves his ongoing debate with different theorists—would require an essay in its own right. Here we shall have to be content with a distillation of his thought on the matter.

Although different theorists distinguish between consequentialism, proportionalism, and utilitarianism, Grisez holds that the logic is essentially the same, differing only by denomination. Insofar as he engages in a normative critique, the terms for Grisez are interchangeable. In his earlier writings he uses the term *consequentialism,* while in his most recent writings he uses the term *proportionalism.*[27] Since our objective in this section is to distill the core of Grisez's thought, we will use the terms in the same way Grisez does.

Grisez is not altogether unsympathetic to proportionalism. It has "some plausibility" because it "does relate morality to some aspects of human fulfillment—namely, to the goods of persons which are affected by human actions."

"Proportionalists," he emphasizes, "are certainly right in thinking that the fulfillment of persons has to settle what is morally right."[28] It is interesting that Grisez finds proportionalism superior to scholastic natural law theory, at least to the extent that it takes into account the "important truth" that ethics must be rooted in choices which bring about "human fulfillment."[29] Grisez himself holds that moral justification of actions must be undertaken with explicit references to human goods. Whereas scholastic natural law theory tends to reduce practical reason to the goal of reaching an other worldly beatitude, and thus pays insufficient attention to human goods, proportionalism "tries to base moral judgments on human goods, [but] it provides no workable method for doing so."[30] This lack of a "workable" method, rather than the concern to maximize goods, is the focal point of Grisez's critique.

For Grisez, the proportionalist method is unworkable because, as a theory of moral choice, it requires that two incompatible conditions be met. He explains:

> The two conditions are: first, that a moral judgment is to be made, which means both that a choice must be made and a morally wrong option could be chosen; second, that the option which promises the definitely superior proportion of good to bad be knowable. If the first condition is met and the morally wrong option could be chosen, then its morally acceptable alternative must be known. Otherwise, one could not choose wrongly, for one chooses wrongly only when one knows which option one ought to choose and chooses a different option. But when the first condition is met, the second cannot be. The option which promises the definitely superior proportion of good to bad cannot be known by a person who chooses an alternative which promises less. If the superior option were known as superior, its inferior alternative simply could not be chosen.[31]

Hence, Grisez concludes that "proportionalism is not false but absurd, literally incoherent."[32]

One could respond by saying that a person faced with a morally good and a morally bad option is always free to choose the latter. This, however, is not the point at issue. Rather, to the extent that proportionalism is meant to be a method for assessing prior to choice the superior versus the inferior mix of net goods, and since one knows prior to choice which is the superior option, then the inferior simply could not be chosen. In other words, Grisez is arguing that proportionalism requires real alternatives which could never be given to choice, and that the method of weighing alternatives is, from a moral perspective, "meaningless."[33] Proportionalism has invalidated all but one of the potential options in such a way that no intelligible motive could prompt one to choose any of the others.

Grisez's second problem with an ethics that tries to determine the rightness or wrongness of choice on the basis of assessing the "greater good" or "lesser evil" is that such a method assumes that "goodness is measurable and that diverse forms of it are commensurable" and, further, that the result of these calculations is able to settle moral issues.[34] Setting aside the additional problem of what range of future consequences we are obligated, and able, to consider in establishing differences of proportion, Grisez simply contends that there is no known standard by which to commensurate the goods.

Grisez has his own account of the incommensurability of the goods, which we will examine later. Here, in advance, we will point out that Grisez denies that there is, prior to choice, an objective hierarchy among human goods—either in terms of intrinsic differences of rank among the values, or in terms of the situational properties which set the context for choices regarding these values. Prior to choice, according to Grisez, we are only entitled to assume (1) that acting for goods in a moral way is superior to acting for them in an immoral way, and (2) that goods which are intrinsic to persons are superior to those which are merely instrumental.

In response to Richard McCormick's contention that any hierarchy requires "some kind of commensuration," Grisez agrees; but he goes on to state that "commensuration does occur once one adopts a hierarchy," *yet only* "in the choice." He points out that "choice does determine which good henceforth will be considered greater and which evil lesser, because the good with which one identifies in choosing becomes part of one's personal scale of value. But by locating commensuration in choice, McCormick implicitly admits that proportionalism has failed. It was to have been a rational method of moral judgment, and a rational method should determine what is right and wrong before one chooses."[35]

In making this point against McCormick, Grisez adopts what will later become a scorched-earth policy with regard to the matter of hierarchy, for he is forced to say that because there is no objective hierarchy by which to compare the relative goodness or badness of options, the adoption of an *order* of goods (which, after all, everyone must do if they are to determine their vocation, and arguably if they are to act at all with regard to a good) is left to one's personal tastes. Richard McCormick has pointed out that "Grisez does not seem to realize that his arguments bite back."[36] Concerning hierarchy, this denial of an objective *ordinatio* prior to choice is a central problem, which we shall carefully consider later.

We should hasten to add that Grisez does not mean that moral nature of the choice of goods is sheerly idiosyncratic, and that there are no objective moral norms governing our pursuit of the goods; but he *does* mean to say that the personal choice of a hierarchy is simply personal, and that one must establish moral norms on grounds completely independent of the choice by which one adopts a hierarchy. Simply put: "When it comes to making choices, there is no objective standard by which one can say that any of the human goods immanent in a particular intelligible possibility is definitely a greater good than another."[37] We will have more to say about his position later, for it is obviously a central issue not only in terms of general axiological criteria, but in particular for the status of religion as a good. His argument against consequentialism primarily rests upon the point that the calculus of options is absurd, since one must already know which is the best, and has therefore invalidated the others. Grisez, however, pushes the critique one step further on this matter of hierarchy, and burns his bridges in terms of any way to recover it.

To summarize what we have said thus far, Grisez argues that proportionalism only gives a simulacrum of a real choice situation; and beyond this problem, the method is defective because it must assume a common denominator by which to commensurate the goods in order to assess, prior to choice, the relative weight of values as consequences. The first involves a critique of the internal logic of the method, while the second presupposes Grisez's own argument that the goods are incommensurable. There are a number of other things that he has to say about consequentialism, and we should at least touch upon them before moving to the next section.

As we said, Grisez is sympathetic to the effort of consequentialism or proportionalism to stress the relationship between practical reason and its role in bringing about outcomes which are fulfilling to human beings. He points out, however, that the method reduces the good of choices to outcomes which are extrinsic to the choices. "Consequentialists," he argues, "overlook the self-creativity of choices by which persons, individually and in communion, constitute themselves as participants in goods which continue to unfold as they are responsibly pursued."[38] In effect, Grisez contends that consequentialism shortchanges the full scope of human goods by focusing more or less exclusively upon the states of affairs caused in carrying out choices" rather than on the concomitant, and equally important, "significance choices have apart from the tangible benefit or harm they lead to." The value of practical reason itself, for example, would be grossly distorted if it were viewed simply as a power by which future goods are maximized.

In Grisez's analysis, proportionalism usually omits from consideration the dimensions of value which inhere in choices and commitments. Goods are thought to exist only in the concrete instances of their realization, that is to say, subsequent to the choices which bring them about. It is understandable, then, that proportionalism tends to define the goods "which can be sacrificed for proportionate reasons entirely independently of moral specifications."[39] So, for example, an existential good such as marital friendship (existential, as involving choice or commitment), is redescribed in nonmoral, or premoral, terms. Overlooking the fact that the good in question cannot be adequately described without including the intrinsic good of the commitment itself, the proportionalist method would allow one to calculate the greatest net result of premoral goods which are effectuated by choice. One good can be sacrificed to another while the good of choice remains unscathed. This drives a wedge, Grisez observes, between moral goodness (viz., the choice to maximize goods) and the so-called premoral or ontic goods to which one is committed in one's choice. As we will see shortly, Grisez himself has a theory of the premoral status of the goods, and it will remain to be seen whether his account makes better sense.

Grisez also objects to proportionalism on the grounds that it is, at one and the same time, overly laxist and rigorist. It is laxist in the sense that anything can be rationalized. It is rigorist to the extent that "there is only one right act in any situation: the act which is likely to yield the greatest net good." In this way, the theory demotes the role of practical reason by conceiving of morality as composed "entirely of affirmative norms" which, Grisez reasons, verges on wanting to be told "precisely what to do."[40] If there is, *ex hypothesi,* only one right way to act in any situation, practical reason would seem to be as locked in to the given as the scholastic natural law theory makes it on entirely different grounds.

In Grisez's critique of consequentialism, there is at least one thing to be kept in mind for future reference. As we have already noted, Grisez explicitly denies that there is any rational and objective standard by which to commensurate the goods. In our view, this will have a significant impact upon his understanding of the manner in which practical reason is to deal with what he calls the "good" of religion. Moreover, as he moves into moral theology proper, it will also put a certain pressure on Grisez to explain, in light of his own system, the many scriptural passages and traditional ascetical injunctions having to do with sacrificing human goods to a superordinate divine reality.

Although early in his career he published an essay on "Kant and Aquinas" (1958), in which he compared the two thinkers in a most general fashion, Grisez has not written as extensively on Kantian ethics as on scholastic natural law theory and consequentialism. One reason, perhaps, is that Grisez does not believe that Kant's theory of practical reason is inherently flawed—not to the extent, anyway, that Kant identifies the nature of moral principles.

In the chapter of *Christian Moral Principles* entitled "Some Mistaken Theories of Moral Principles" (wherein Augustine is included among the mistaken theorists), his remarks on Kant are consigned to an appendix. Here he states that "Kant's view of moral principles is not so much false as grossly inadequate. Hence, it is not treated in this chapter as a mistaken theory."[41] It is not mistaken, he argues, because, in contrast to conventional natural law theory and consequentialism, Kant does not reduce practical reason, in its moral role, to a "mere technique" by which to achieve some ulterior goal. In other words, Kant refuses to shortchange the specifically moral domain of practical reason.

Nonetheless, the theory is "grossly inadequate," he argues, once it is seen in the light of the dualism of the *homo noumenon* versus *homo phaenomenon* scheme. This *does* shortchange the scope of practical reason in terms of its interests in material goods. In this respect, then, it is not unlike the distortions found in the older natural law theory (which spiritualizes the ultimate good of man as heavenly beatitude) and in consequentialism (which instrumentalizes material goods). Kant's particular position leads him to identify the moral good of human persons exclusively with the good of practical reason.

As we will see, Grisez himself advances at least seven basic goods as "non-hypothetical principles of practical reason"—goods, he adds, which "Kant wishes to discover."[42] All of Grisez's goods have content derived from inclination; and whereas Kant stipulates one norm for moral consistency, Grisez stipulates eight requirements governing choice, which are called "modes of responsibility." Grisez identifies the good of humankind not exclusively with practical reason, but with the miscellany of basic goods. In fact, he refuses to identify the good of man, *qua* man, as consisting in any particular power or end.

Both Grisez and John Finnis (who follows Grisez explicitly in this area) wish to retain the core of Kant's understanding of the moral dimension of practical reason while prying it loose from Kant's anthropology, which, they contend, limits the axiological scope of values which are morally relevant to practical reason. Thus far, Finnis has been more interested than Grisez in showing the consonance between Kant's second formulation of the categorical imperative (that persons should be treated as ends, and never as mere means) and the method which he and Grisez share.[43]   Finnis reformulates the imperative to read: "Respect every basic human good in every one of your acts," rather than "Treat humanity as an end and never as a means." Finnis observes that:

if we read 'humanity' as Kant explicitly meant it, we find those intermediate principles of ethics conceived only 'thinly' and with unjustified restrictions of content and scope. . . . When we fill out Kant's inadequate conception of the humanity that must be respected in every act, and identify basic goods intrinsic to humanity (and human perfection and happiness), we are not adulterating or diverging from the principle of respect for persons. We are simply treating persons in their non-dualistic wholeness.[44]

Now whether the essence of Kant's ethics can be retained after reformulating the imperative according to an emphasis upon human goods rather than human persons is, at the very least, a difficult hermeneutical question.

In *The Theory of Morality* Alan Donagan has noted, with regard to Grisez's position on the matter, that these two formulations "converge" but do not "coincide," for Kant's formula "takes the ends of actions to be human beings themselves, not the human goods that may be realized in them."[45] There is a difference, Donagan argues, between respecting the person of a criminal who attacks the life of another, and respecting goods in which he might otherwise participate were he not imprisoned or even harmed when restrained from attacking an innocent victim.

Shortly, we will more carefully examine Grisez's understanding of the relationship between moral principles and human goods. For the moment, we will only say that our interest is not so much in whether Grisez's formula is consonant with Kant's, but rather in the Grisez-Finnis position in its own right, viz., the meaning and implications of shifting one's focus from persons to goods. Does this not assume, or suggest, that goods and persons are strictly coextensive both ontologically and in terms of actions which bear upon them? Is moral agency, for instance, something more than the sum of the parts of the goods with which practical reason is interested? In other words, is there something of value in personhood that needs to be affirmed in terms quite different from merely our concern for goods which fulfill persons? These questions are intimately related to whether it is possible to give a convergent importance to eudaimonistic and deontological perspectives without diluting what is unique to either point of view—and to whether such a convergence can be made to fit with Aquinas's understanding of practical reason. The problem will crop up continually as we move further into the system.

1.2 The First Principle of Practical Reason and Human Goods

This section covers two major components of Grisez's moral theory. First we will examine his understanding of the first principle of practical reason—the Fppr, drawn from Aquinas, is the general directive that good should be done and pursued, and evil avoided. Then we will discuss the Fppr in relation to human goods or values. As we deal with this material, it is important to continue to bear in mind that Grisez distinguishes between the Fppr and what he terms the "first principle of morality." The latter will be treated in the next chapter. For Grisez, the Fppr is "premoral." It represents practical reason's innate capacity to grasp goods as "possibilities" of fulfillment, and, as such, it directs us to goods rather than specifying moral norms which guide choices.

The most important piece of writing that Grisez has done on the subject of the Fppr is his article "The First Principle of Practical Reason: A Commentary on the *Summa Theologiae,* 1-2, Question 94, Article 2" (1965). Its importance consists, first of all, in the fact that Grisez's interpretation of Aquinas's Fppr formula—"Good is to be done and pursued, and evil is to be avoided"—has influenced scholarly discussion of Thomistic ethics. John Finnis and

Alan Donagan, among others, base their understanding of Aquinas on Grisez's interpretation.[46] For our purposes, however, the article is important because Grisez has made his interpretation of Aquinas the foundation of his own theory that natural law method must distinguish between the premoral and the moral.

In his analysis of Aquinas's text, Grisez argues that while Thomas considers practical reason to be the mind exercising the "capacity in which it is 'directed to a work'," it would be a mistake to conclude that this is simply a matter of "knowledge sought for practical purposes."[47] In other words, practical reason is not theoretical reason caught up in what might be termed a practical moment. Its capacity of being directed to a work indicates that what is under consideration is not so much the given, but the mind charting what is to be. It is foundational in its own right.

Grisez explains that the "very first principle of practical reason is a grasp upon the necessary relationship in existential reality between human goods and appropriate action bearing upon these goods."[48] The relationship is not something that is already "in the world." If it were, then practical reason could be reduced to the first principles of other sciences which deal with the given (one notes the Kantian flavor of this formula). In contrast, the Fppr is unique in the sense that it pertains to what can be bestowed upon, or put into, the world by human action. Grisez hastens to add that "these tendencies are not natural law" in the moral sense of the term. Rather, "the tendencies indicate possible actions, and hence they provide reason with the point of departure it requires in order to propose ends. The precepts of reason which clothe the objects of inclinations in the intelligibility of ends-to-be-pursued-by-work—these precepts *are* the natural law."[49] Thus, the Fppr is neither a statement directly about principles of human nature (i.e., a theoretical description of capacities and tendencies) nor about moral principles governing choice; rather, given certain inclinations or tendencies, practical reason is able to grasp them as possibilities. The Fppr, therefore, simply stipulates, albeit in a general fashion, that action be brought to bear upon them as values.

For this reason, Grisez argues that the Fppr necessarily spawns a plurality of directives or "practical principles." There are as many practical principles as there are values grasped in the mode of "ends-to-be-pursued" by action. Each of the practical principles is a specification of the general Fppr formula. In the older scholastic parlance, he notes, these were known as the "primary precepts" of natural law.[50] In shaping action from within, the minimum condition for practical reason is that it "have some intelligible object toward which it can be directed."[51] As practical reason considers intelligible goods, the plurality of principles arises both from the range of inclinations as well as from the almost indefinite range of possibilities suggested. Grisez states:

> The general determinations of the first principles of practical reason are these basic precepts of natural law. They take the form: Such and such is a basic human good to be done and/or pursued, protected, and promoted. The practical principle which directs thinking to each basic human good is a self-evident truth. It proposes that particular good as something to be pursued and protected, while directing that what is contrary to it be avoided and prevented. For example, life is naturally understood as a good to be preserved, death as an evil to be prevented.[52]

He concludes that because "basic human goods have many distinct aspects," it is impossible to "make a simple, exhaustive list of the basic principles of natural law." The Fppr, as a general norm, does not commend any one of the essential goods more than another.[53] That the term *good* can be predicated analogously of a wide range of possibilities only indicates the creative and generative ability of practical reason to stimulate many points of departure for the development of "interests which lead to choices." At this juncture we have not yet outlined what Grisez means by an "essential" good. The axiological assumptions are crucial, because what he is calling the "first principles" of practical reason are basically specifications of the Fppr according to whether or not a value is "essential." We will take up the axiological issue shortly.

Before we discuss the premoral dimension of the Fppr, we should take note of Grisez's understanding of Aquinas's statement that the Fppr and its basic precepts are self-evident (*per se nota*) and indemonstrable. In the *Summa theologiae,* Saint Thomas states that "the precepts of the natural law are to practical reason, what the first principles of demonstrations are to the speculative reason: because both are sets of self-evident principles."[54] Just as the principle of noncontradiction necessarily falls within one's grasp of being, so too the good necessarily falls within the grasp of practical reason. In his interpretation of Aquinas's distinction between "objective self-evidence" and "self-evidence to us," Grisez points out that it is the latter that is especially important for practical reason.[55] Whereas objective self-evidence depends upon the lack of a middle term connecting a subject and predicate (and hence the reason for the truth of a self-evident principle is what is directly signified by it), subjective self-evidence is a recognition of its underivability, which is marked by the fact that one has "such an adequate understanding of what is signified by the principle that no mistaken effort will be made to provide a derivation for it."[56]

Grisez argues that this is precisely the case with the Fppr and its attendant plural principles. The Fppr cannot be deduced or otherwise inferred from theoretical statements, because the very core of the principle involves a grasp of a good or goods as possibilities. Simply put, the Fppr is self-evident because the starting point of practical reason is itself unique. "In thus deriving practical principles from given inclinations," Grisez reasons, "our practical intelligence is operating neither rationally nor irrationally.... It simply is working intelligently—that is, intuitively—using experience as a point of departure for forming its own fundamental insight."[57]

Building upon Grisez's interpretation of Aquinas on this matter, Finnis explains that "by a simple act of noninferential understanding one grasps that the object of the inclination which one experiences is an instance of a general form of good, for oneself (and others like one)."[58] Whereas Grisez sometimes uses the term "intuition," Finnis is careful to say that the Fppr involves "an insight which is not an 'intuition'," because it "is not made in the absence of data, nor by any 'noticeable' intellectual act."[59] Without any deduction or inference from one proposition to another, he goes on to say, "one understands some of those inclinations as inclinations towards *desirable* objects, and some of those possibilities as opportunities rather than dead-ends."

We will have more to say later about the intuitional aspects of Grisez's ethics. Here, we want to emphasize two cardinal points held by both Grisez and Finnis on the subject of self-evidence. First, the key term is the *noninferential* aspect of the Fppr. Hence, they wish to emphasize that there is no way to sidestep the unique standpoint of practical reason by making one's grasp of goods dependent (via inferential reasoning) upon theoretical descriptions about nature, or human nature. Second, both Grisez and Finnis include within the orbit of self-evidence not only the general principle of the Fppr, but also the attendant principles which express, in a more determinate form, practical reason's grasp of plural goods—goods which are equivalent (so long as we remember that we are in a premoral mode) to the scholastic understanding of the primary precepts of natural law. To put it succinctly: the content of the particular good which is grasped as a good to be promoted (e.g., life) shares in the self-evidence of the Fppr, and therefore we can speak of the practical and indemonstrable principle that life is to be promoted. Further remarks will have to await our consideration of Grisez's position on the "goods."

Grisez insists that the Fppr is a "directive for action, not a description of good and evil."[60] The term *good* in the Fppr refers to "whatever can be understood as intelligibly worthwhile," and the term *evil* designates whatever is understood as a "privation of intelligible goods." According to Grisez's interpretation, Saint Thomas's formulation of the Fppr does not involve the moral inperative, "Do good!" if one means by this exclusively, "Do the moral good!" To use older Scholastic terminology, the Fppr is a *lex indicans* rather than a *lex praecipiens*. Needless to say, this systematic distinction between the premoral and moral is an unusual interpretation of Aquinas and has generated a good deal of scholarly controversy.[61] Our interest is in the substance of the position, since regardless of the status of Saint Thomas's text, it is the position avowed by Grisez himself.

Grisez regards the Fppr as premoral for at least two reasons. In the first place, the extensive scope opened up by the Fppr cannot be reduced exclusively to moral value, for moral goodness does not exhaust the general meaning of the term *good* which is given in the formula. The question is over what is directly included or excluded by the Fppr. If the Fppr is understood strictly to mean "do good," or "be good," then it is primarily a principle (again, a very general one) of moral obligation. Grisez contends, however, that moral goodness can be taken as but one form of *bonum*; therefore, the more inclusive rendering of the principle is the more coherent. In our view, Grisez's argument is valid to the extent that the Fppr, so formulated, would have to include a wide range of goods, both moral and premoral (however one defines those); but the inclusion of premoral goods does not necessarily imply that the *principle* itself is premoral. In other words, neither the inclusive nor the exclusive focus regarding content is sufficient to nail down an answer to the question of the morally preceptive versus the merely indicative force of the Fppr *qua* principle. Without additional content and principles drawn from a philosophy of nature and, in particular, human nature, the very generality of the principle "good is to be done and pursued" would seem to lack what is needed to determine whether it is moral or premoral.

Grisez's second point is nearer to the heart of his position. He states: "Indeed, if evildoers lacked practical judgment they could not engage in human action at all. It follows that practical judgments made in evil action nevertheless fall under the scope of the first principle of the natural law, and the word 'good' in this principle must refer somehow to deceptive and inadequate human goods as well as to adequate and genuine ones."[62] Grisez's point is clear enough. As a minimal condition for an agent to act, one must be able to grasp a possibility under the formality of a good, and the Fppr is precisely what transparently underlies each and every such act of practical reason. This does not guarantee that the agent has grasped the good correctly and has a morally sound attitude, much less that the agent will go on to make a morally upright choice. It means only that the Fppr is so constitutive of practical reason that "no human action can violate it directly."[63]

Grisez admits that since the primary practical principles underlie everything we do, it would seem to "open the doors too liberally," for they "begin from every possible basic human good and they endorse every one of these goods indiscriminately."[64] Ralph McInerny, in his *Ethica Thomistica,* has argued that when mistaken judgments are brought under the scope of the principle, even those actions which are not perfective and fulfilling of the agent are sanctioned by the principle.[65] The Fppr will therefore have to speak with a forked tongue, being at one and the same time a *principium* directing us to the good(s) while sanctioning indiscriminately any action performed according to what appears to be good. This construal of the Fppr, McInerny argues, not only fails to "truly save the formality of goodness," but implies that the basic principles of the natural law are not "moral values."[66] McInerny, of course, objects to the manner in which Grisez has split the Thomistic formula into premoral and moral facets, as well as to Grisez's apparent unwillingness to treat the Fppr within the broader context of a philosophy of nature. We shall have more to say about this later, but it should be noticed that neither Grisez nor Finnis describes the practical orientation to goods in terms of "natures" or in terms of what could be called "proper completions." To borrow a term from Ernst Bloch, we are dealing with a "multiversum of open possibilities" rather than with "natures" governed by formal and final principles of causality.[67] It entails a more radical departure from Thomistic natural law theory than either Grisez or Finnis is willing to admit.

Another way to look at the problem is to see that Grisez's inclusive rendering of the Fppr runs into the problem of having to regard moral goodness as moral *and* premoral. It is *premoral* in the sense that it is one good, *inter alia,* to which the Fppr directs us as a possibility rather than as an obligatoin; and it is *moral* in the sense that moral goodness is a specific attitude or manner of choice whereby we choose this or that good under obligation.

In a coauthored response to McInerny's criticism, Grisez and Finnis have not altered their position:

> But the fact is that . . . Finnis is concerned to make the same point as Grisez, and both of us consider this to be the position of St. Thomas. The basic principles of practical reason do underlie and make possible the reasoning of good and bad people alike. The price paid for denying this is to say that the immoral are sheerly irrational, and thus free of moral responsibility.[68]

The terms of the debate between McInerny and Grisez come down to whether or not the Fppr has morally preceptive force; if it does, then Grisez's position is inconsistent, for such a principle could not command what it expressly forbids or excludes. Perhaps further light can be shed on the issue if we take two other considerations into account.

First, quite apart from the preceptive versus the indicative status of the Fppr, it is difficult to understand how one could be deceived about one's grasp of the goods or how we might debate the issue. As we recall, Grisez includes within the ambit of self-evidence not only the Fppr as a general principle, but also the primary principles dealing with our grasp of basic goods. Both form and content are given in this self-evidence. Recall that Grisez stated that the Fppr is a "grasp of the necessary relationship in existential reality between human goods and *appropriate* action bearing upon these goods."[69] Therefore, a mistaken conception of the goods, or the inappropriateness of an attraction, or even an action (at least in the premoral setting) cannot be the result of a mistaken inference. Grisez would probably say that insufficient experience would deter the adequate function of practical reason. Finnis concedes that a deficient theory of nature or of humanity might tend to "block" practical reason.[71] But insofar as the long arm of self-evidence encompasses the principle *and* experiential content (so long, that is, as we simply "know"—to use Finnis's expression—that some desirable things are "opportunities rather than dead ends"), how can we ever open for philosophical debate the important issue of what content is fitting—in Grisez's term, "appropriate"—or in accord with the principle? This will become especially acute in terms of the good of religion. Would it make sense, for example, to include religion within the intuitive ambit of the Fppr without availing ourselves of some independent criteria for deciding whether or not it is (whatever the *it* is), in fact, a good, rather than a dead end?

Second, as we alluded to earlier, the premoral status of the Fppr is troublesome if it requires us to grasp the good of morality in a premoral way. One of the strengths which Grisez claims for his theory of practical reason is its emphasis upon the difference between affirming a theoretical proposition and grasping the mode of the *is-to-be*. Given the requirements of his own distinction, it is dubious that a morally good action (or a state of being morally good) could ever be grasped as a possibility without containing an implicit consent to the value of morality *formaliter*. For example, if one has grasped the value of honesty as a possibility for one's action, and regards it simply within the premoral context, then it would seem to mean either that one has not really grasped the value or that one is rationalizing in a way that is already fraught with moral responsibility. This is precisely the *basso profundo* of Grisez's critique of the proportionalists. At the very least, to the extent that we are dealing with the good of morality, the Fppr as a *lex indicans* is already in the vestibule of the *lex praecipiens*.

To summarize, Grisez holds that the Fppr—that good is to be done and pursued, and evil avoided—is inherent in the very operation of practical rationality. It functions neither as a theoretical principle concerning human nature, nor as a moral principle governing choice. It is premoral. The primary principles of practical reason are specifications of the Fppr, for instance, that knowledge is a good to be pursued, and ignorance an evil to be avoided. Both the Fppr and its primary specifications are *per se nota*. However, as we noted, the primary principles include content which presupposes a theory of human goods or values. We will now turn to this facet of Grisez's system.

As indicated earlier, Grisez argues that "a sound account of normative existential principles must show how they are grounded in human goods." Without such grounding, there is "no adequate answer to the question, 'why should I be morally good?'" In our analysis, this is not a query in search of an answer; for the question already implies some knowledge of morality, as well as some level of responsibility inherent in the very asking of the question. In any event, Grisez states that the answer cannot be that God commands this, for the "moral obligation to obey divine commands, although rightly accepted by believers, is not self-evident."[71] Thus, he goes on to state that "nothing clarifies the force of moral norms except the relationship of morality to human goods." The statement concerning the evidence of faith prompts certain questions which we will have to consider later. Here, we need to know what exactly he means by "goods."

Throughout his writings, Grisez has employed more than one term for the "goods." They are variously called: "possibilities"; "purposes"; "values"; "sources of motivation"; "basic human needs"; "tendencies"; "basic inclinations"; and "ideals." Not infrequently, they are called "primary practical principles."[72] The terms are more or less equivalent, depending upon whether Grisez is emphasizing practical reason's grasp of the possibilities inherent in an inclination or emphasizing the way that the Fppr is directive of this grasp. Faced with this hodgepodge of terms, Finnis has distinguished between *good* as referring to some particular objective or goal that one is considering "as desirable," and *value* as a general form of the good that can be "participated in or realized in indefinitely many ways on indefinitely many occasions." A value is what the ancients called a *bonum honestum*.[73] Yet this is just what Grisez means by a "basic good."

Grisez and Finnis distinguish between goods which can be sought for their own sake, and which are properly called "ends," and goods which are instrumental, or "means." It is important to observe that all goods which are "ends" are likewise "final ends."[74] Although he rejects the notion of the existence of a determinate and objective Final End (insofar as we speak about human ends), he does hold the position that there are as many finalities as there are "basic goods." Therefore, the best term to use is that of "basic human goods," which is the one Grisez himself uses most consistently. By definition, then, a basic human good is an aspect of "what one might call human 'full-being'," or what Finnis calls "being all that one can be." [75] As definite possibilities of the fulfillment of human persons, these goods "have a real objectivity, even though they are not actual entities." [76] Again, Grisez is not speaking of "natures" with determinate and proper completions; rather, they are "definite possibilities" intuited independent of any other sort of knowledge.

Before we proceed to the ontological and epistemological facets of Grisez's axiology, it would be good to outline his list of the "basic goods." Over the years his list has undergone alterations. [77] We will focus upon the most current one, elaborated in *Christian Moral Principles.* Here Grisez divides the basic goods into those that are "reflexive" (sometimes called "existential"), which have to be defined in terms of human choice, and the "nonreflexive" or "substantive" goods, which provide "reasons for choosing which can stand by themselves." [78]

There are four reflexive goods: (1) *self-integration,* "which is harmony among all the parts of a person which can be engaged in freely chosen action"; (2) *practical reasonableness or authenticity,* "which is harmony among moral reflection, free choices, and their execution"; (3) *justice and friendship,* "which are aspects of interpersonal communion of good persons freely choosing to act in harmony with one another"; and (4) *religion or holiness,* "which is harmony with God, found in the agreement of human individual and communal free choices with God's will." [79] As a problem that we will take up later, it should be noted that religion is defined as an agreement of human choices with God's will. At the outset of this section we quoted Grisez as saying that the obligation to obey divine commands, although rightly accepted by believers, is not self-evident. Whether or not there is a contradiction here will have to be treated carefully later.

The "substantive" goods are threefold: (1) *life,* "including health, physical integrity, safety, and the handing on of life to new persons"; (2) *knowledge* "of various forms of truth and appreciation of various forms of beauty or excellence"; and (3) *activities of skillful work and of play,* "which in their very performance enrich those who do them."[80]

Finnis's list is slightly different,[81] but both he and Grisez contend that the list of basic goods is exhaustive in a threefold sense. First, no one of the goods can be analytically reduced to any one of the others.[82] Each is "irreducible" as a value, and therefore "incommensurable." Second, any other good that can be added to the list will, upon examination, turn out to be a facet of one of the basic goods contained in the list.[83] Third, each basic good is inexhaustible insofar as it can be participated in more and more, both in the extensive and intensive sense of participation.

Grisez's repertoire of the basic goods prompts a number of questions regarding the criteria for the distinction between basic and nonbasic, and between reflexive and substantive. This is not to mention the further issue of how we undertake the transition from grasping a value as a *bonum mihi* (a good for me) to predicating it of human beings at large (as a universal form of good).[84] Of course, in the older Scholastic system the criteria were derived from a philosophical anthropology that distinguished between essential and accidental properties. This philosophy of nature presupposed different levels of causality—particularly formal and final causality—which set the terms of participation with regard to the good, as well as the means for universalizing the good according to a *scientia moralis* that is distinct from the personal, and even intuitive, dimension of moral judgment in the sphere of action. Grisez does not hold to this kind of Scholasticism.[85] Be that as it may, the problem at hand is that Grisez insists that the grasp of these goods cannot be a matter of deduction or inference from prior principles. These basic goods are the same as what we earlier discussed as the primary practical principles, which are *per se nota*. Are we locked into an intuitive realm that cannot be further discussed or articulated?

Grisez does say that we are "conscious" of the basic human goods "by experience."[86] We are aware of our own inclinations, longings and delights. By practical intelligence, we grasp these facts not as a spectator, but as a "moulder and director" of them. The basic goods are, therefore, self-evident, not in the sense of being innate, but rather in the sense of being interpreted as potentials. If we ask, how can one understand on the basis of experience (refusing to avail ourselves of any philosophy of nature) what is not actual but only potential, and what is a good for me and a good for others as well, he answers:

> This question can be answered only if one realizes that human intelligence does not become practical merely by its subject matter, nor merely by being moved by will or inclination. Reason is practical by nature just as much as it is theoretical by nature. And just as theoretical thought by its very nature is thinking *that-it-is,* so practical thinking by its very nature is thinking *that-it-would-be-well-to-be.*[87]

In other words, the self-evident foundation of the basic goods is embedded in the very exercise of practical reason working on experience. No other explanation, much less demonstration, can be given. To be sure, if one were to sever the roots of experience, nothing would be self-evident; for although the practical capacity is innate, the principles are not *a priori.* Indeed, they cannot in principle be *a priori* for the reason that we are dealing, not with the merely given data of inclinations, but with a prospective and interpretive mode that can only operate within the field of the "possible." The simplest way to put it is to say that the evidence is given in the exercise of practical reason, and to look elsewhere is to miss the point.

This represents the main thrust of Grisez's answer to the question of what evidence exists for the basic goods. However, we would be negligent if we did not mention that he sometimes refers to what could be called indirect evidence. For example, especially in his earlier writings Grisez is quite prepared to consider the findings of any science that "would lend empirical support" to the list of basic goods.[88] In one of his earliest statements on the issue, Grisez writes: "The task of discovering all of man's basic inclinations may seem impossible of fulfillment. Indeed it is not easy, but it is by no means as difficult as the theoretical confusion in ethics might lead one to suppose." The question, he concludes, "requires and can be settled only by empirical inquiry."[89] In particular, he singles out the need for a "survey of psychological literature and a comparison with the categories of human activity found by anthropologists."[90] Given the self-evident, and purportedly universal, nature of these goods, it is not explained why we should have to consult anthropological surveys to be reminded of them.

Nevertheless, Finnis, too, speaks of research by anthropologists and psychologists which "parallel" the list of goods as discovered by the exercise of practical reason. These should not, he warns, be regarded as answering the question of values by "way of any 'inference' from universality or 'human nature'." Instead, they are to be taken as an "aid" by way of "an assemblage of reminders of the range of possibly worthwhile activities and orientations open to one."[91] In an article defending Finnis's position against those who would argue that it entails a decisive rejection of any role for speculative reason, Thomas Russman concedes that if "metaphysical discussion can sometimes be helpful or necessary [it] does not show that it is necessary per se." Rather, a "preliminary excursus into metaphysical issues" may be helpful "in order to persuade someone."[92] The use of theoretical rationality, as an "assemblage of reminders," appears to be principally one of apologetical value for a person who has lost, or is severely confused regarding, his practical rationality.

It is clear that the "empirical" approach (both Finnis

and Grisez frequently equate theoretical reason with propositions concerning "facts") is not a substitute for the mode of practical reason, and indeed cannot be if the Grisez-Finnis account of practical reason is to make sense. In the first place, the goods are discovered not as mere givens, but as values and possibilities. Arguably, even the substantive good of health, which has an irreducibly physiological character, is not merely empirical *qua* value; moreover, the existential or reflexive goods have a certain spiritual quality (since they are defined in terms of free choice) which must elude the methods of the exact sciences. Evidence here could only be indirect; for example, cultural historians can show that most human societies have placed a high value on justice. To the extent that the good of religion is described as a relationship to an unseen, supernatural being, the so-called empirical method would be of minimal value—except to say, once again, that anthropologists can confirm its (again, whatever *it* is) presence in most cultures.

The other indirect route is by "noticing the assumptions implicit in people's practical reasoning."[93] This method is one of operational self-consistency. Grisez has employed it in his writings against determinism, but less so in his discussion of the human goods.[94] Finnis, however, who has taken it over from Grisez, has made it central to his exposition of the basic goods.

In the chapter in *Natural Law and Natural Rights* devoted to the basic goods, Finnis begins by suggesting: "We should not begin our response by postulating any doctrine of truth or objectivity. Instead we should see what conception of truth and objectivity is implicit in the statements of the sceptics, and in their performance in putting forward these statements for our acceptance."[95] As an example, Finnis takes the basic good of knowledge. That knowledge is a general form of human well-being is "self-evident, obvious," and something that "cannot be demonstrated, but equally needs no demonstration."[96] The practical principle that truth is worth having and that ignorance is to be avoided is

not a moral principle. Moral scepticism, he argues, has
nothing immediately to do with the point at issue: viz.,
whether one can remain a sceptic about the value of knowledge. The statement that knowledge is not a basic good is
operationally self-refuting, for one who makes it is "implicitly committed to the proposition that he believes his
assertion is worth making, and worth making *qua* true; he
is thus committed to the proposition that he believes that
truth is a good worth pursuing or knowing."[97]

In the case of the good of knowledge, the self-referential
method is cogent; from a philosophical standpoint that
regards itself as a natural law method, it is certainly more
cogent than anthropological surveys. Nonetheless, it is significant that Finnis makes no effort to account for the
other six basic goods or principles in this fashion. Reason,
after all, is transparently present in any conscious pursuit.
And since, as Finnis points out, we are not yet speaking of
moral principles, it would be senseless to deny that knowledge is a good. But, in identifying himself with Aquinas's
position, Finnis puts his case even more strongly:

> It amounts to no more than saying that any sane
> person is capable of seeing that life, knowledge, fellow-
> ship, offspring, and a few other such basic aspects of
> human existence are, as such, good, i.e., worth having,
> leaving to one side all particular predicaments and
> implications, all assessments of relative importance,
> all moral demands, and in short, all questions of
> whether and how one is to devote himself to these
> goods.[98]

Unfortunately, it is not so clear that "sanity" requires a
consent to the goods other than knowledge, whatever good
sanity comes under in their roster of values.

Among the problems with affirming goods apart from
assessments of "relative importance" is that Finnis and
Grisez's notion of basic goods includes the judgment of
relative importance, that is, the self-evident perception that

some goods are basic and others not. The argument (which we have not yet examined) that each of the basic goods is irreducible, and hence incommensurable, still must presuppose a way to distinguish them from nonbasic goods. Furthermore, it is difficult to understand how a value judgment can be made apart from all "particular predicaments and implications" and apart from questions of how one is to "devote" oneself to the goods. For, by their own definition of practical reason, Grisez and Finnis contend that "interest in" goods as possibilities marks the distinctive work of practical reason. It is not consistent that the goods can be affirmed apart from the condition by which they are supposed to emerge as practical values in the first place. The matter of goods and "importance" would seem to be coimplicates, whether this is arrived at by intuition or by inferential reasoning—or both.

Turning to a good like religion, after the searching criticism of theoriests like Hume, Feuerbach, and Freud, is it philosophically advisable simply to posit religion as a basic good? Is the commitment to bring one's choices into conformity to the will of God such a transparent good that one operationally refutes oneself in the act of questioning the value? Once again, it is clear that this either presupposes or postpones certain principles established in a philosophy of religion, if not a natural theology. While one who uses reason to deny the value of reason can be said to contradict oneself, this is certainly not clear in the case of religion—unless, perhaps, Anselm's *insipiens,* who says in his heart there is no God, is caught primarily in an axiological inconsistency rather than in a metaphysical dilemma (which already presupposes a grasp of a rather definite God and religion as goods).

Because Grisez's moral norms will obligate us to respect, protect, and promote the basic goods, our methodological concern over the derivation and description of the goods is by no means idle. Each and every affirmation of a basic good necessitates an affirmation of that good as a practical principle. To demote one of the goods is to violate a fundamental principle of practical reason. In this sense, the deck is already stacked before we arrive at a specifically moral principle. That is to say, whatever morality turns out to be, it could not enjoin one to violate a principle of practical reason (whether or not it be described as premoral). Therefore, the Fppr with its attendant axiology has already set the guidelines for morality. Grisez's method of distinguishing between the premoral and moral facets of what he calls "natural law" is quite interesting. However, if the premoral facet has set the framework for morality by committing us to certain *prima principia* of practical rationality, then one is led to wonder whether this account significantly advances beyond the conventional natural law theory. Why not go on and admit that the Fppr includes foundational moral precepts? We will return to this question when we consider Grisez's own doctrine on contraception. First we must examine his understanding of the first principle of morality, which constitutes the second phase of his natural law method.

2

NATURAL LAW, MORAL PRINCIPLES, AND ENDS

Grisez understands the practical principles considered thus far as generating the "field of possibilities in which choices are necessary." The premoral facet of natural law theory clarifies the possibilities afforded to choice: "they [the principles] cannot of themselves determine why some choices are morally good and others morally evil."[1] There is a need, then, for an additional phase of the natural law method—for moral norms which guide choices.

In the Grisez-Finnis system, the first principle of morality is to the modes of obligation as the Fppr is to the practical principles. That is to say, just as the primary principles of practical reason are specifications of the Fppr, so too the modes of obligation are specifications of the first principle of morality (hereafter abbreviated *Fpm*). In this chapter we shall first examine the Fpm and its attendant modes of responsibility; then we will show how this bears upon the specific issue of contraception. We bring in the issue of contraception here not only in order to contrast the Grisez-Finnis natural law method with what they have called "conventional" natural law theory, but also in order to highlight certain weaknesses in their method which we have only alluded to thus far. Then we shall address what is the most important problem en route to our discussion of religion in the context of the Grisez-Finnis natural law method, namely, the problem of how we might move from the *ratio* of the goods to principles governing the *ordinatio* of the goods, in terms of both hierarchy and ends.

2.1 The First Principle of Morality

Grisez defines the Fpm as follows: "In voluntarily acting for human goods and avoiding what is opposed to them, one ought to choose and otherwise will those and only those possibilities whose willing is compatible with a will toward integral human fulfillment."[2] While the Fppr dictates that goods are to be pursued, and privations of those goods avoided, the Fpm introduces the morally perceptive rule that choices must be compatible with "integral human fulfillment." The extensive range of the good implicit in the Fppr is now given explicit force in the Fpm. Finnis clarifies this transition as "the 'natural law method' of working of the (moral) 'natural law' from the first (premoral) 'principles of natural law'."[3] Once again, it is necessary to stress that, whereas the older Scholastic ethicians derived the so-called premoral facets from a philosophy of human nature and its powers and inclinations, and thus reserved the Fppr for the beginning of moral reflection, Grisez and Finnis begin with the Fppr and a premoral axiology and then move to the Fpm.

The first thing to notice about the Fpm is its ideality. Grisez explains:

> In referring to human goods, the first moral principle envisages them not merely as constituting diverse possible fields of action but as together comprising the stuff of integral human fulfillment. The ideal of integral human fulfillment is that of a single system in which all the goods of human persons would contribute to the fulfillment of the whole community of persons.[4]

The Fpm is an ideal for at least three reasons. In the first place, Grisez holds that none of the basic goods is "absolute"; but on the other hand "none of them is so relative that it does not resist submergence."[5] Even considered in their premoral status, Grisez's axiology rules out reducing one good to another. The goods "represented by these different principles are equally basic and equally essential to the ideal of integral human fulfillment."[6] In terms of value, they are atomic wholes. Therefore, since no one of the goods provides a principle by which to subordinate the others unilaterally, the goal of human fulfillment is an ideal of their collateral realization. In this meaning of ideality, Grisez's Fpm is opposed to any utilitarian rule that guides choice by requiring that some goods be subordinated for the sake of a concrete "greater good."[7] To the extent that these basic goods are likewise principles of practical reason, none can be made subordinate (as a mere means) without violating the canons of practical reason itself.

In the second place, Grisez argues that the basic goods are not inert objects or things, but rather possibilities or objectives in which one participates. In human history, as well as in the course of a person's life, "new dimensions of human goods unfold and new possibilities of serving them emerge." Therefore, human participation in the basic goods is never finished or rounded off in a completed state. As Grisez puts it: "In other words, 'integral human fulfillment' does not refer to a definite goal to be pursued as a concrete objective of cooperative human effort."[8]

In the third place, Grisez holds that, "apart from faith, humankind cannot know that integral human fulfillment is possible, and faith teaches that this possibility can be realized only by the divine act of re-creating all things in Jesus."[9] In his transition from moral principles to moral theology, Grisez regards Jesus as the concrete good that annuls the ideality of the Fpm. Its ideality, therefore, makes room for (even requires) a move into moral theology. This will raise a host of questions with regard to the system as a whole; but the problem must be deferred until the next chapter on practical reason and religion.

Given the ideality of the Fpm, how is it derived? Grisez answers very simply that "reason does not exclude the possibility of integral human fulfillment."[10] It is important to note his insistence that "the first principle of morality cannot be proved directly by being deduced from prior truths."[11] If this is true, then there is no way for reason to exclude the possibility, for the intuition cannot be gainsaid anyway. However, its cogency is indirectly supported by the fact that the practical orientation to fulfillment is at least implicit in the Fppr. One could say that it is the specifically moral facet of what is already intuitively grasped in the Fppr. In acting in a way compatible with the ideal, there will be a "concretely expanding degree" of participation in the basic goods toward which we are already launched, as it were, by the Fppr. More to the point, however, the Fpm guides choice in the negative sense of enjoining one to avoid "unnecessary human self-limitation."[12] Grisez frequently reiterates this point:

> The guidance which the ideal of integral human fulfillment offers to choice is to avoid unnecessary limitation and so maintain openness to further goods. True, here and now one must pursue this or that; but one who chooses in a morally right way cares no less for the goods involved in the alternative not chosen.[13]

It stipulates that one should have an attitude of "constant openness" to the goods.

Under a premoral description, goodness is defined as a "realization of potentialities." "Moral goodness," he now explains "is in choices which not only lead to some participation in particular human goods—as all choices do—but which maintain a constant disposition toward all human possibilities."[14] Moral goodness, then, is the character of a choice that respects all the human goods, and moral badness is the characteristic of a choice in which freedom is used in a "self-limiting way." Obviously, one cannot choose every human good simultaneously. Moreover, even the wicked choose some good or goods. The Fpm simply enjoins us to choose with an "inclusivistic" attitude. If one chooses, for example, to devote one's life to scholarship (the basic good of knowledge), one must not demote or disrespect another basic good like play or health. Is the emphasis or focus of morality given to the goods, or to my own fulfillment? Expressed in a slightly different way, is the essence of the moral attitude a due respect for each basic human good, or is it a due respect for my own possibilities? Where is the categorical being placed? This is a complex issue for anyone who would study Grisez's thought. We will have much more to say about it later. Grisez's ethical theory aspires to give convergent importance to a Kantian-like emphasis upon respect as well as to a eudaimonistic and teleological emphasis upon the amplitude of goods and human fulfillment. Furthermore, Grisez often speaks in a way that appears to give the emphasis to one or the other. Thus, on the one hand he says, "moral goodness is characteristic of choices in which one avoids unnecessary human self-limitation"; on the other hand we can find him saying that "right choice is in accord with open-hearted love of all the basic human goods."[15] The first statement underscores moral respect for the good as a *bonum mihi,* while the latter suggests not only that what is good for me is good for others, but that I am morally obligated to respect and promote it among others.

Consider what Grisez has to say about love, and about Aquinas's position on the matter:

> Abstract as it may seem to call love a disposition toward a fulfilling good, we do use the word this way: People "love" steak and they "love" truth. Even more often we speak of loving people, ourselves and others. But the two things, loving something and loving somebody, are not separate; they are different aspects of the same thing. Thus to be disposed to a fulfilling good is to be disposed to the person fulfilled by that good. St. Thomas distinguishes between these two aspects of love, calling the disposition to that which is good "love of concupiscence" and the disposition to the person "love of friendship." This

terminology misleads if it is mistaken to mean two different kinds of love—for example, selfish love and love which is altruistic.[16]

Grisez is correct in saying that, for Aquinas, the *amor concupiscentiae* is not necessarily morally bad, in the sense of being selfish. However, Aquinas *does* argue that the *amor concupiscentiae* is morally deficient if the object of one's love is a being of equal or greater ontological rank than oneself. To love another person, or God, in such a way that one principally loves one's own delight rather than the other for his or her own sake is morally deficient. It is true, of course, that either mode of love can be fulfilling in one way or another, but Aquinas introduces the distinction in order to make a point much different than Grisez's. For Aquinas, the issue is not merely the good as objectively fulfilling, but rather the morally appropriate kind of love with regard to various kinds of entities being loved. The appropriateness of love with regard to its objects sets the criteria for what is appropriately fulfilling, and, by nature, what is most fulfilling. In short, right reason requires attention not only to a good as it promises to fulfill the self, but also to the status of the beloved. Aquinas presupposes that the agent is situated in a world of hierarchical settings, and a recognition of this is crucial to the operation of right reason in a practical mode.

Setting textual questions aside, there is an important substantive issue involved in whether or not Grisez's axiology, in not distinguishing between different kinds of love with regard to the differences between persons and things (either of which may be fulfilling in some respect or another), thereby becomes one-dimensional, with the emphasis weighted toward goods characterized simply as one or another *bonum mihi*.[17]

For the purposes of our investigation in this chapter, we can give an accurate and fair interpretation of the matter if we keep two things in mind. First, Grisez surely understands the Fpm as including *both* the pole of respect for goods and the pole of respect for the fulfillment of one's own person. He explicitly mentions both features. Properly described, human fulfillment is respect for the human values, among other reasons because the value of morality and human fulfillment are reciprocally entailed. Thus, for instance, to regard the value of morality as a mere instrument for achieving the fullness of other goods is to disrespect the good of morality (this is his critique of consequentialism); at the same time, however, to construe morality as the sole nonhypothetical value is to disrespect the other goods, and in effect to limit arbitrarily human possibilities (which is the substance of his critique of deontological "thin" theories of the goods). This helps to make more sense of the situation; but, since all of the goods are defined as actions which are attractive to the agent, there is still a distinction missing that would allow us to speak of "respect" for something more than ourselves.

Having said this, it is nevertheless true to say that the system as a whole, prior to his introduction of theological tenets, tends to emphasize a moral respect for basic human goods (insofar as these goods are defined within the method which, as we pointed out above, is still problematic in terms of how the "respect" comes to include anything or anyone other than oneself). It is worth recalling our earlier discussion on Grisez and Finnis's understanding of Kant, where we pointed out that they wish to understand the "humanity" in the second formulation of the categorical imperative as "human goods." Stronger evidence is given in Grisez's understanding of the modes of responsibility (to be treated shortly) which are specifications of the Fpm. Each mode of responsibility is a rule enjoining certain attitudes which must be adopted toward the various goods if one's will is to be in conformity with the ideal of integral human fulfillment. Moreover, each of the modes is negative; they stipulate what cannot be done if the goods are to be respected. In conclusion, then, it is our interpretation that if the Fpm is taken in isolation from the modes of responsibility, morality will appear weighted toward self-fulfillment: accordingly, the prohibition against self-limitation will assume a particularly well-defined profile. If, however, the Fpm is seen in the light of its modal specifications (especially, as we will see, the seventh and the eight modes), the emphasis will shift to prohibitions against disrespecting the goods—including those which are not immediately chosen for the sake of fulfillment. As we will indicate shortly, the modal specifications are really more important than the Fpm when it comes to guiding concrete attitudes and choices.

This does not iron out every difficulty in Grisez's understanding of the Fpm. It only represents our effort to make sense of Grisez's position from within his own system—again, as it is laid out prior to moral theology. There remains a tension between the Fpm's moral emphasis upon self-realization and the specific moral norms which enjoin a "decent respect" for the human goods in their irreducible and disparate status. In subsequent chapters we will show how the tension finally becomes resolved in favor of the eudaimonistic quest for self-fulfillment. This part of the puzzle must await our analysis of Grisez's moral theology. Our next task, though, is to examine the modes of responsibility.

The principles of practical reasoning which flow from the Fppr (e.g., life is a good) do not specify the Fpm, "for each," Grisez explains, "refers only to one basic human good, not to integral human fulfillment."[18] While the Fpm is a general moral norm to act in accord with the ideal of integral human fulfillment, more specific moral norms are required as a bridge between the Fpm and concrete choices. The primary specifications of the Fpm are "intermediate principles" which serve as this bridge. They are called modes of responsibility because they "shape willing in view of the moral responsibility inherent in it."[19] (Once again, we must remember that, all the way along, these categories have been derived from the original practical insight or intuition).

Although Grisez contends that morality is not itself negative, the modes of responsibility take the form of negative propositions: "Each mode of responsibility simply excludes a particular way in which a person can limit himself or herself to a quite partial and inadequate fulfillment." As propositions, the modes generate "judgments of conscience prior to choice."[20] The modes are as follows:

1) *One should not be deterred by felt inertia from acting for intelligible goods.* One who violates this mode fails, without any real reason, to act for some human good and so does not proceed in a manner consistent with integral human fulfillment.

2) *One should not be pressed by enthusiasm or impatience to act individualistically for intelligible goods. . . .* Unnecessary individualism is not consistent with a will toward integral human fulfillment, which requires a fellowship of persons sharing in goods.

3) *One should not choose to satisfy an emotional desire except as part of one's pursuit and/or attainment of an intelligible good other than the satisfaction of the desire itself. . . .* in deliberately settling for mere emotional satisfaction, one's choice is not that of a will toward integral human fulfillment.

4) *One should not choose to act out of an emotional aversion except as part of one's avoidance of some intelligible evil other than the inner tension experienced in enduring that aversion.* Violations occur when one chooses to refrain or desist from acting, or changes a reasonable course of action, because of repugnance, fear of pain, or other concerns about obstacles which involve nothing intelligibly bad.

5) *One should not, in response to different feelings toward different persons, willingly proceed with a pref-*

erence for anyone unless the preference is required by intelligible goods themselves. . . . Instead of proceeding in a manner consistent with a will toward integral human fulfillment, one who acts with partiality settles for an unnecessarily limited fulfillment of certain people.

6) *One should not choose on the basis of emotions which bear upon empirical aspects of intelligible goods (or bads) in a way which interferes with a more perfect sharing in the good or avoidance of the bad.* Violating this mode means sacrificing reality to appearance, as is done, typically, by someone more interested in the conscious experience of enjoying a good or avoiding an evil than the reality.

7) *One should not be moved by hostility to freely accept or choose the destruction, damage, or impeding of any intelligible good.* Violations occur when people deliberately will out of anger or hatred (or milder feelings of the same sort, such as distaste or resentment) the destruction, damaging, or impeding of any instance of any intelligible human good. . . . they reduce human fulfillment without reason, and so proceed in a manner which is inconsistent with a will toward integral human fulfillment.

8) *One should not be moved by a stronger desire for one instance of an intelligible good to act for it by choosing to destroy, damage, or impede some other instance of an intelligible good.* . . . Thus one subordinates some possible elements of human fulfillment to others, even though there is no reasonable basis for doing so.[21]

Grisez adds that since one's personality is formed by choices in accord with these modes, the "virtues embody the modes."[22] The virtue associated with the fifth mode, for instance, is that of justice; while the vice associated with the first mode is sloth. In point of fact, however, neither Grisez nor Finnis (whose list of modes is slightly different) makes a sustained effort to interrelate an ethics of virtue with the modal "propositions."[23] It is significant that neither the virtues nor the moral attitudes are included among the list of basic goods; the Fpm and its modes are propositions governing how various attractions are to be selected, and hence the virtues are not constitutive of the attractions, or goods, themselves. The virtues are an afterthought, and play second, if not third, fiddle in this natural law method.

Our principal interest is in the seventh and eighth modes. These indicate most clearly the absolute prohibition, in Grisez's system, against subordinating one good to another. They represent, in essence, rules against proportionalism. This is not to suggest that the other modes are superfluous extras. The second and fifth modes appear to be particularly important for issues of social justice. Indeed, the fifth mode appears to presuppose not only a distinction between goods and persons, but also some way to universalize the categorical of respect—viz., that the good is something good not only for me, but for others, and that one is morally obligated to promote it among others. Here, and elsewhere in Grisez's work, this is not justified but simply posited or implied. In any case, one can expect the seventh and eighth modes to carry much of the load in terms of disputed issues which have occupied Grisez's attention. As an example, let us turn to the issue of contraception.

With the Fpm and its modes at hand, more specific moral norms, Grisez says, can be derived, "first, by considering the voluntariness involved in the kind of action under consideration in relation to relevant basic human goods, then considering the moral determination which the first principle of morality and the modes of responsibility indicate for such volition; from these two premises one deduces the moral determination of that kind of action."[24] In the case of contraception, the relevant value is the basic good of life, which, for Grisez, includes the procreative good.[25]

As he explains in his book *Contraception and the Natural Law,* the pertinent mode of responsibility is what he will later, in *Christian Moral Principles,* call the eighth mode:

> If the goods do not require that we always be acting toward them, they do require that we never act against them with direct intent. To act directly against any of the basic human goods is to spurn one aspect of the total possibility of human perfection, and it is freely to set the will at odds with its own principle of interest in the goods open to us.[26]

Following Grisez's method, we are to compare the relevant good with the mode of responsibility and arrive at a judgment of conscience prior to choice.

Earlier we discussed Grisez's rejection of the conventional natural law syllogism on the matter of contraception. Now we can examine his own syllogism:

Major: For one who has sexual intercourse to act in a way which presupposes an intention opposed to the procreative good is intrinsically immoral.

Minor: Contraception is an act—the prevention or lessening of the likelihood of conception by any positive deed directly willed for this purpose—of one who has sexual intercourse which presupposes an intention opposed to the procreative good.

Conclusion: Contraception is intrinsically immoral.[27]

If one grants the premise that the procreative good is a basic good, as well as the assumption built into the eighth mode of responsibility—that it is never right to subordinate a basic good for the sake of a greater good—then Grisez's logic appears valid. The components involved are these: (1) the Fppr orients us to pursue goods and to avoid evils; (2) procreation is a basic good and therefore a *primum principium* of practical reason; (3) the eighth mode of responsibility dictates that we are never to act against a basic human good. But we need to take a closer look at the assumptions.

Grisez contends that the malice of contraception is not in the violation of a general obligation to cause conception. Rather, "the malice is in the will's direct violation of the procreative good as a value in itself, as an ideal which never may be submerged."[28] Since basic goods, we recall, are exactly the same as the primary principles of practical reason, Grisez reasons that one who practices contraception "acts directly against one of the principles which make human action meaningful."[29] He puts it even more strongly in another passage, where he states that in directly willing against a principle of practical reason, one "puts himself in intellectual and volitional absurdity."[30]

Grisez explicitly maintains that his argument does not presuppose the "perverted faculty" argument of the older natural law theory. Not every frustration of a natural process is wrong. Once again, his system does not require one to tote around the baggage of a philosophical anthropology, much less a metaphysic, because he understands himself to be dealing, not with "given" natural teleologies, but rather with certain actions or possibilities which are attractive to the agent—in particular, those attractions which he calls "basic" goods. What is wrong with contraception is not that it violates the natural teleology of a physiological, or even more generally, a "human," function, but that it violates the value or practical principle regarding the procreative good. Whereas, according to Grisez, the older natural law theory held that the "given" function sets the norm (which seems to us to give the weakest rendition of the older system on this issue), Grisez proposes that the practical grasp of the given as an attractive possibility sets the norm. The distinction is suggestive, but it is unclear whether he avoids having to make at least some of the assumptions of the natural law system he wishes to replace.

The issue returns us to the problem of criteria by which procreation is placed among the basic goods, and *a fortiori* among the primary practical principles. How do we recognize that procreation is as irreducible a good as justice and fellowship, not to mention practical reason itself? What makes procreativity so attractive that it is a good that can never be submerged? As we have already said, Grisez maintains that these goods cannot be deduced or inferred from theoretical principles. For his part, Finnis baldly states that "any sane person" is capable of seeing that "offspring" are worth having. In any event, despite his position on the intuitive nature of the value judgment, in his *Contraception and the Natural Law* Grisez does make an effort to provide evidence for the basic nature of the good of procreativity.

He argues, in the first place, that the good of life must be judged as a whole rather than in relation to the end of each faculty or physiological power. Accordingly, respiration or nutrition cannot be said to be basic human goods. However, from a biological point of view, the "work of reproduction is the fullest organic realization of the living substance."[31] In other words, it differs from respiration in the sense that it bestows the good of life as a whole, and therefore ought to be included within the basic good of life. Second, he argues that we must not suppose that reflexive or spiritual goods contain in an "eminent mode" all of the organic perfections, for "the goods of organic life are not achieved by the spirit alone."[32] Unless we make the assumption that a substantive good depends as a value on some other condition, we "must consider the good of procreation as a determinant of a primary principle of practical reasoning."[33]

Regardless of whether one takes these arguments concerning biology as valid, our point is that Grisez does in fact directly rely upon anthropological, if not metaphysical, evidence for including procreation in the list of basic goods

—not as a mere "reminder" but as a "determinant" of the practical principle. His conclusion that contraception is "intrinsically immoral" clearly depends upon an antecedent argument that procreation is an intrinsic good, which itself depends upon a theoretical argument concerning what is essential or accidental to human organicity and how human organicity is related to the nature of being human. It looks very much like the older natural law argument except that it lacks the philosophical apparatus for making, justifying, and sustaining the series of theoretical moves which involve the relationship between the person and the body, the nature of life, and the relative importance of the procreative power in relation to human organicity in general.

Simply put, his use of this evidence (such as it is) is not consistent with his understanding of the inferential and deductive underivability of the basic practical principles, which are *per se nota*. In the very same book on contraception, for instance, he states that the "whole problem can be seen to come down to this one point" concerning first principles:

> If we are to use freedom meaningfully, we must judge what to do. But since we lack angelic intuition we must reason in order to judge, and reasoning either goes around in circles or it goes back to basic principles. Once it has gone as far as the very first principles, there is no place further to which it can reasonably go. First principles of themselves cannot be judged. Nor can they be played off against another, because by the very fact that they are many and yet primary it is clear that they are incommensurable with one another.[34]

This passage indicates why we suggested earlier that too much was being built into the original practical "insight." In effect, the insight includes the Fppr, the primary practical principles, the difference between basic and nonbasic values, the difference between reflexive and nonreflexive values, the Fpm, and the modes of responsibility.[35]

Another issue of some importance which we can touch briefly upon here is the relationship between the seventh and eighth modes of responsibility and the Fpm. In the case of contraception, does the Fpm really provide positive guidance? Setting aside the assumptions which we have questioned above, it is not clear that the ideal of integral human fulfillment immediately enters into the judgment concerning the malice of contraception. As Grisez says elsewhere in the book on contraception, none of the goods "satisfy man's potentiality for goodness as such." Therefore, "what reason requires is that all the goods be maintained in their irreducible but not absolute positions."[36] This is exactly what the seventh and eighth modes enjoin us to do. In other words, if a good is acknowledged as basic, I cannot directly act against it, whatever the ideal of integral human fulfillment might be. Hence integral fulfillment is not the immediate issue, though it might set the background, or a prospective ideal, for why one wishes to get married, engage in sex, or spawn a family.

What this means is that, in the case of contraception, we are urged by the system to move directly from a first practical principle (i.e., procreativity as a basic good) to the particular mode of responsibility, and thereby make a judgment; namely, I ought not to act against *this* good. The principle determining judgment rests not so much upon Grisez's notion of the ideality of the Fpm's directive to be open to integral fulfillment as upon his notions, first, that the basic goods are the *prima principia* of practical reason which cannot be abrogated without falling into volitional absurdity, and second, that these goods are irreducible and incommensurable. The problems in the division of the natural law method into premoral and moral are evident, for apparently we can bypass the Fpm altogether. This is why the seventh and eighth modes of responsibility will have to carry so much of the load, and why, ultimately, the modes are framed in the negative. So, in addition to the problem of criteria for including or excluding goods as "basic," we see that the other part of the puzzle is how we establish the principle of irreducibility and incommensurability. In our view, it is pivotal to Grisez's ethics because it bears upon all the other tangents of the system. At this point, then, we are prepared to move to the final section of this chapter where we hope to tie together the foregoing discussion.

2.2 End and Ends: Problems and Implications

In this final section we shall take up a cluster of related issues which, up to this point, have only been alluded to in passing. In one way or another, each of the issues has to do with the problem of *ends*. For example, we have seen that Grisez maintains that each of the practical principles (as premoral) represents practical reason's grasp of a good as a finality (something intrinsically worth participating in). We have also seen that the Fpm and its modal specifications involve the ideal of integral human fulfillment—an end that is morally obligatory, but only as an ideal guiding choice. What we now have to ask is, first, whether there is an objective order to the goods as independent finalities, such that we can speak of the good of humanity as being something more than the sum of the parts of these goods; and second, whether there is an ethically significant notion of transcendence in his system. By *transcendent* we do not necessarily mean supernatural, but rather an openness of practical reason to goods or values which are not simply immanent modalities of one's own fulfillment. For example, we can ask whether the good of friendship is merely the good of the realization of *my* capacity to have friends. Similarly, we can ask whether an act of injustice is merely a frustration of *my* capacity to be just, or whether we needn't take into account the harm done to someone other than myself.

To begin, we will examine what Grisez has to say about the unity of human being as a person and as a moral agent in order to see whether his moral anthropology provides any clues to the problem of hierarchy and ends. Then we will examine an extremely important matter that we have had to defer until this point in our investigation: namely, Grisez's doctrine on the irreducibility and incommensurability of the basic goods. In turn, we will have a few words to say about the concept of a life plan. Finally, we will discuss the problem of whether there is a transcendent nature to practical reason, with a special focus now upon the prospective problem of how religion is to be handled within the system.

Grisez has not published a work exclusively devoted to an ontology of human nature, or of the self. As we have already noted, in his book *Contraception and the Natural Law* he makes some remarks about the meaning of human organicity with respect to the procreative power. Quite clearly, he opposes any kind of dualistic anthropology. This theme surfaces throughout Grisez's writings. In the book on contraception, for instance, he states that of the many problems which hound contemporary moral theory, a "pseudo-religious personalism" is the most dangerous, because it confuses the "way in which human spiritual goods excel material goods and the way in which divine goodness transcends finite goods."[37] The appeal of such a "personalism," he believes, is the breeding ground for both religious and secular ethical theories which are prepared to sacrifice or subordinate substantive to reflexive goods—and, in the more extreme religious case, to sacrifice all of the human goods to an otherworldly state.

In addition to his remarks in the work on contraception, Grisez has a section in *Beyond the New Theism,* entitled "The Human Person and the Human Community," in which he offers a more sustained analysis of the concept of the person. Together with comments he makes in still other works, we can assemble the main lines of his position. First, though, let us take note of a few theories which Grisez rejects.

Grisez not only opposes the conventional natural law method on the grounds that it infers practical principles from metaphysics; he also is a sceptic regarding the prospects of resolving anthropological issues by means of any theory. In his book *Abortion: The Myths, the Realities, and the Arguments,* he eschews the notion that the ontological status of the unborn can be settled by anything other than "facts":

> In the first place, we saw that beyond doubt the *facts* show the embryo at every stage to be a *living, human individual.* To go beyond this is not a question of fact but a question of metaphysics. We should not expect and will never get a factual answer to the ulterior question. What our arguments revealed is that there is no compelling reason to deny that the embryo is a person. . . . Similarly, we cannot consider ourselves blameless if we are willing to kill what may or may not be a person, even if it is not. In being willing to kill the embryo, we accept responsibility for killing what we must admit *may* be a person. There is some reason to believe it is—namely, the *fact* that it is a living, human individual and the inconclusiveness of arguments that try to exclude it from the protected circle of personhood.[38]

"Anyone with sufficient ingenuity in metaphysical argument," he concludes, "should be able to construct some sort of plausible theory of personality according to which any one of us will turn out to be a non-person." Here, as in the passages we cited earlier concerning the list of the goods, Grisez prefers the support of an "empirical" approach, lest we become swamped in "theoretical confusion in ethics."[39]

Why anthropological surveys can help as an assemblage of reminders, but data derived from a philosophy of nature cannot, is not answered. Why, for instance, is the latter particularly subject to a deflective sort of rationalizing, when the empirical approach—which is as theoretical as any other theory—is not? There is more than one assumption here that is not brought to light.

Grisez is also directly critical of Aristotelian anthropology—or at least its heritage. In this regard, he rejects the hylomorphic theory which, he maintains, is "plausible for animals other than persons and for persons as natural bodies."[40] While the theory accounts for the unity of a sentient organism, it does not account for the self-constituting aspects of selfhood. Grisez argues that despite Aristotle's effort to avoid dualism, his hylomorphism required the existence of a "non-human agent" (i.e., the "agent intellect") in order to prevent reason from being limited by the materiality of the body.[41] Thus hylomorphism is to be rejected for its incipient dualism as well as for its inadequate account of the creative self-constitution of the person. It is interesting to note that although he frequently cites Aquinas in support for his own position on other matters, here he does not mention that Thomistic hylomorphism is significantly different from Aristotle's.[42]

In any case, he even more strongly opposes what could be called the unique *ergon* concept; that is, the Aristotelian notion that "persons have a single, well-defined goal or function." The concept of a "single goal" is to be rejected for the reason that, if "persons are ends in themselves, they cannot be ordered to a good as any part to a whole or any means to an end."[43] No argument is given to justify the inclusion of this Kantian doctrine within the framework of his natural law theory, which otherwise resists speaking of any determinate or unified end in this manner. As we have pointed out, according to Grisez's theory, the basic goods (as what attract and fulfill persons) are finalities in themselves, not persons.

The "single function" argument has to be set aside because it implies either a dualism, or a hierarchy in which self-evident basic goods intrinsic to persons are subordinated to merely one of the goods. Finnis characterizes the unique *ergon* concept as an "erratic boulder" that Aristotle has sent tumbling through the history of Western ethics. Indeed, he goes so far as to say that it was this that sent Kant himself off course.[44] Finnis contends that the whole range of goods are "the intrinsic point of one's autonomy," for they outline the worthwhile "self" that one may "constitute by one's self-determination."[45] Earlier we asked whether the Grisez-Finnis position implies that the good of the self is ontologically coterminous with the range of goods. Finnis suggests so. However, the problem with making the worth of the self coterminous with the basic goods is that to the extent that many of these goods are not realized the self would seem to be diminished, not just ontologically, but in terms of value (even if we are speaking only of the premoral value of the self, however one may go about justifying a premoral self).

For reasons similar to those he gives against the Aristotelian outlook, Grisez is suspicious of what he calls the "phenomenological" approach.[46] In the book on contraception Grisez examines the positions of theorists like Louis Janssens, who holds that a phenomenological analysis of conjugal love reveals that, in a marital context, the act of intercourse is a mode of mutual benevolence in which the partners wish to accomplish the most perfect possible expression of their love. Hence, contraception represents a deliberate limitation on mutual self-giving, and for this reason is an offense against the very meaning of the act; that is to say, it violates an "ought" already consented to in the performance of the act. Because the position does not rely upon a mere descripiton of the end of the sexual function, Grisez concedes that it has "a certain value." What interests us here, however, is Grisez's contention that the phenomenological approach "is connected with a very questionable philosophical theory of man." He explains: "The subjective and interpersonal life of the spirit is no more human than is the *humblest* of human functions. And it is a mistake to yield to the temptation to attribute superiority to the immanent value of marriage over the transcendent value of the procreation and education of children to which marriage is ordained."[47]

In contrast to Grisez's method, the phenomenological approach assumes the existence of an order and hierarchy of values; for conjugal love is understood as implicitly bearing within itself the norms by which the other values are ordered. Spousal love is therefore regarded as an inclusivistic end. While the theory entails a notion of a superordinate good, it certainly is not a proportionalist ethics. So described, the phenomenological account does not recommend one to act against a basic good in order to achieve a greater good. Rather, it understands the goods according to an order that is something more than the sum of its parts. Grisez's problem with the theory, when all is said and done, comes down to this: it assumes that there is an objective, hierarchical order among the values, which is discoverable within human activities, in this case by a phenomenological method. This runs against the grain of the Grisez-Finnis axiology, which they are prepared to defend at all costs (which well they should, for the axiology constitutes the basic principles of practical reason, and thus constitutes the spine of their natural law theory).

His resistance to speaking of an inclusive principle by which to understand the unity of the human being is made very clear in his own doctrine on the issue. Grisez employs, as a model for appreciating the diverse dimensions of human personhood, a remark that Aquinas makes at the outset of his commentary on Aristotle's *Ethics*. Aquinas states that "order is related to reason" in a fourfold way: (1) according to an order that reason does not establish but only beholds, such as the order of things in nature; (2) according to an order that reason establishes in the conceptual order, such as semiotics and logic; (3) according to an order that reason establishes in acts of the will, such as in moral deliberation and choice; and (4) according to an order that reason establishes in external things, such as art and culture.[48]

However, in citing Aquinas on this matter Grisez neglects to point out that, prior to his discussion of the *ordo ad rationem* outlined above, Aquinas prefaces the discussion by stating tht the *ordo in rebus* is twofold: first, the order of "parts of a totality", and second, the order of "things to an end," which is of "greater importance than the first."[49] In other words, Aquinas is careful to establish the two principles of order or unity in things before he outlines the four different ways reason is ordered to things. Grisez, who uses the fourfold schema in several of his works, never mentions the preceding sentences in Aquinas's text.[50] Once again, our chief concern is not one of scrutinizing in detail Grisez's rendering of Aquinas's texts, which strikes one as being rather fast and loose. He never claims that his use of Aquinas's schema is meant to be an interpretation of Aquinas. Nevertheless, it is interesting that he chooses (and Finnis follows suit in this regard) to emphasize Aquinas's fourfold strata of orders rather than the twofold principles of unity.[51] The two omitted principles mark the chief difference between Aquinas and the new natural law theory expounded by Grisez and Finnis.

Grisez argues that human persons "involve four distinct and irreducible modes of reality": the "system of nature, the intentional order, the existential domain, and the world of objective culture."[52] Many philosophers, he observes, treat human persons as if they were "primarily or even exclusively limited to one of the four orders."[53] Grisez insists that "*within* experience" we can distinguish these four orders, and that we must conclude not that the person is a "quadralism," but that he "somehow" embraces them all.[54] But what is the person who embraces these four "irreducible" modes of reality? In the passage we cited earlier on the personhood of the human embryo, he stated that there is no reason to deny that the embryo is a person; but according to his own fourfold schema, there is certainly no reason to believe that the human embryo embraces the intentional, the existential, or, arguably, the cultural dimension. Unfortunately, he is as vague on this issue as he is on the problem of how the basic, irreducible goods are interrelated. Indeed, his anthropology appears to be a tail-piece to his axiology insofar as we are dealing with intuitive "facts" regarding incommensurables. One should not be surprised, therefore, to discover that Grisez's argument against abortion rests upon his understanding of the good of life rather than on a philosophical notion of what it means to be human.[55] Given his system, abortion can only be wrong because it violates what we find attractive about the good of life rather than the ontological, much less moral, status of the one who lives. This should immediately strike one as the worst possible way to go about making an argument against abortion; yet Grisez firmly believes that he has avoided the problem of subjectivism, because he believes he has made good on his claim that the first principles (i.e., the attractable goods) are objective and indubitable.

Grisez maintains that in the act of choice, and in carrying out choices, a "person constitutes his or her own identity." He goes on to say:

> But choices are needed to resolve the indeterminacy which is present when one might still find various goods fulfilling. Hence, in making choices one brings it about that some possible goods rather than others will be fulfilling for oneself—the self, that is, whom one constitutes by these choices.[56]

This Kierkegaardian-like reference to the self constituting itself is clear enough so long as we remain on the level of moral identity; that is, that one becomes the kind of person one is by the choices one makes. Grisez, however, does *not* want to limit the meaning of personhood to the existential level of choice, even though it is only on that level, he argues, that the category *person* has any unity and hence intelligibility. Without more intricate ontological distinctions (at the very least, a philosophically elaborated distinction between his various uses of the terms *person* and *self*), his theory would seem to be at odds with itself.

Grisez holds that in the act of choice the "self is a unifying principle," but he hastens to add that the "various aspects of the person are unified by the self but not identified with it."[57] If we press the issue by asking how it is possible to envision four irreducible aspects of the person—one of which is the existential order of choice itself—which are not identified with the self that unifies them in the existential act of choice, Grisez appeals to the "mysterious" nature of it all:

> The unity of the person is mysterious and must remain so. This unity is immediately given in human experience, and it cannot be explained discursively, since reason cannot synthesize the distinct orders in a higher positive intelligibility. . . . Thus I conclude that the complex unity of the human person is a fact for which one ought not to expect an explanation.[58]

This passage represents the upshot of Grisez's position. It is quite similar, as we have said, to the position he has held all the way along on the other ontological facets of practical reason regarding the goods: viz., that they are *facts* grasped in experience.

The problem, as it now stands, can be cast in this way. Grisez wants to hold on to what could be called a "realistic" ontology of the four irreducible orders, just as he does with regards to the goods in the area of axiology. In order to maintain their real irreducibility, however, he posits a self whose task is to unify the orders in choice, while not being identified with them. As an account of the self, the theory wants to be a full-blown existentialism, because one of the orders, the existential, is given primacy in terms of being the agent of unity; but so long as the three orders other than the existential are given equal primacy, the theory will be unable to resolve itself.

In summary, we will not find in Grisez's anthropology a coherent explanation of how to speak of a teleological and ontological unity of the human being. There is a teleology for each basic good, to which the moral self is obligated, *but there is no corresponding teleology of the moral self.* Put more sharply, we are dealing with a *homo absconditus,* for we are only given a miscellany of orders which somehow involve a self. This helps to explain the significance of Grisez's shift from emphasizing persons to emphasizing goods, in his value theory as well as in his understanding of moral norms. If one starts with his axiology, one will not reach a philosophical affirmation of persons as preeminent in the domain of values, for these values are irreducible and incommensurable. His understanding of the irreducible facets of the person only reemphasizes the problem. As we have seen, the issue of irreducibility crops up over and over again. We now must move directly to this issue.

In his debate with proportionalists such as Richard McCormick, Grisez concedes that "there are several senses in which goods form a hierarchy."[59] In the first place, there is a hierarchy of values insofar as the basic goods are to be preferred (strictly interpreted, they must be preferred) to the merely instrumental goods. This distinction, of course, depends upon criteria for sorting out these two types of goods.[60] In the second place, moral uprightness is always superior to what is morally bad.[61] This, too, depends upon what we have included or excluded from the list of basic goods, for moral uprightness is the characteristic of a choice that respects the basic goods in accord with the Fpm. In the third place, Grisez maintains that "within the perspective of faith—since faith itself is an act which fulfills human persons by forming their relationship with God—the religious level of the existential domain is most important. Nothing is more important for the Christian than to be in unity with the love of God which comes to us in our Lord Jesus."[62] Obviously, this sense of hierarchy depends entirely, as Grisez says, upon faith in the revelation of Christianity. All three of these senses suggest, but do not ground, how we can intelligently speak of a hierarchy. Grisez has one additional way to regard hierarchy (in terms of a life plan), but we will return to it momentarily, after we outline the senses in which there is not a hierarchy among the goods.

Grisez argues that there is no objective hierarchy among the basic goods because each is "essential." When it comes to making choices, "there is no objective standard by which one can say that any of the human goods immanent in a particular intelligible possibility is definitely a greater good than another."[63] Their irreducibility militates against finding a standard by which to commensurate. In *Beyond the New Morality,* to illustrate his point he gives the example of a person who, on Sunday morning, must face the choice of whether to go to church, play golf, or read the papers. In this case, "all the options possess certain values, and the mere fact that one has not chosen two of them is no reflection on either of them, but simply an indication of the fact that nobody can read the papers, play golf, and go to church simultaneously."[64] The morally upright choice is not determined by any objective or intrinsic differences of rank among the three goods, but rather by the attitude that in choosing to play golf, for instance, one should not disrespect the other two values. One must not choose "exclusivistically."

The problem, however, is that one can remain consistent with this scheme and say that a person who decides to go to church because she thinks that the worship of God has objective priority over playing golf, chooses in a way that is not in accord with the Fpm; whereas a person who decides to read the papers, but who remains vaguely open to the possibility of going to church, makes a morally upright choice. Similarly, a person who chooses to develop his physical health, but who remains "open" to developing his intellect, chooses in a morally upright way that cannot be met by someone who chooses to develop his intellect because this value is grasped as having an intrinsic superiority. Grisez's reasoning certainly places a moral check upon fanaticism, but only at the price of having to identify the person who commits herself to a hierarchical order of value as a virtual fanatic. One perhaps could say that the difference between Sunday worship and a round of golf consists in the fact that worship is a necessary condition for respecting the good of religion, while golf is not a necessary condition for respecting the good of play. Even if this be true, the hierarchical problem remains with regard to the two goods.

To many, if not most, people this position is counterintuitive. Not only in the religious tradition of Christianity, but also in terms of the attitudes and practices which Donagan has characterized as the "common morality," moral goodness is especially identified with a person commited to what are regarded as superior values. As Aristotle himself observed, right reason urges toward what is best. What evidence can be given to alleviate this common prejudice? Grisez states: "The fact that they [the goods] may seem more important to an individual or a group simply reflects the cultural conditioning or psychological leaning of that individual or group."[65] Elsewhere, in the same vein, he says it is simply a "matter of subjective choice and temperament."[66] Indeed, this may be true in fact, but the question is moral—regarding what and how I *ought* to choose. When it comes to this matter of hierarchy, is there any principle under the rug of convention and temperament of which we might avail ourselves?

Both Grisez and Finnis (who holds exactly the same position as Grisez) simply insist once again upon the irreducible nature of each basic good. Grisez states that "each of these eight fundamental purposes is—looked at from its own point of view—the most important."[67] Not to be outdone, Finnis states that each one, "when we focus on it, can be reasonably regarded as the most important."[68] "Hence," he concludes, "there is no objective hierarchy amongst them." For example:

> if one is drowning, or, again, if one is thinking about one's child who died soon after birth, one is inclined to shift one's focus to the value of life simply as such. The life will not be regarded as a mere precondition of anything else; rather, play and knowledge and religion will seem secondary, even rather optional extras.[69]

In the first place, it is interesting that a person who grieves over a departed loved one is described as focusing upon the good of life rather than upon the *person* who is loved. Here we can recall our earlier remarks about the way in which this system tends to focus upon goods rather than persons. There is something curiously, if not ironically, Platonic in this focus upon a general form of a good rather than the concrete good of the person in question.

In the second place—and more importantly—the logic is fallacious. What Grisez and Finnis are proposing is that, because I *can*, in a given experience, regard this or that good as "the most important," it follows that there is no objective order of importance among them. It begs the question, for the first part of the proposition (if it be true) is only a conditional necessity; viz., *if* I happen to be drowning, *then* life seems to be the greatest value. It does not follow that we can straightaway conclude that *therefore* there is no objective difference in rank of value between life, for example, and the integrity of one's own practical rationality, or that it is impossible, prior to choice, to determine that one way of life (a way of life representing a specific organization of the goods) is better than another.

In his response to proportionalists, Grisez admits that "commensuration does occur once one adopts a hierarchy."[70] His point, however, is that no objective grounds exist as a standard for the commensuration prior to choice. To the extent that proportionalism is to be a rational method of judgment prior to choice, it fails. Grisez's argument, however, is a two-edged sword. As we quoted Richard McCormick earlier, the arguments "bite back." By insisting upon the irreducible and incommensurable status of the goods prior to choice, the choice of an *order* of goods (a hierarchy) must remain, as he says, a matter of "subjective choice and temperament."

His objective axiology runs dry right at the point where it pours into the wider problem of choosing an order of goods. This suggests that one of the most important issues in ethics—choosing one kind of life rather than another—is left to the vagaries of subjective temperament and cultural conditioning. Grisez maintains that "one establishes a personal hierarchy of commitments to goods, and this hierarchy shapes an individual life-plan or self-constitution."[71] The Fpm obligates us to pursue integral human flourishing; the lack of objective criteria concerning personal hierarchies, however, means that we cannot judge which orderings of goods (and, correlatively, kinds of lives) are more fit for satisfying the requirement.[72] One could argue that there is not exclusively one hierarchy of goods prior to choice, but many which one might adopt and still satisfy the precepts of morality regarding proper respect for the goods. Nevertheless, if there be plural hierarchies, we still need criteria for assessing whether their merit is grasped prior to choice, and whether one or another of these hierarchies is objectively superior, prior to choice, vis-à-vis the others. Grisez's argument against the proportionalists has been taken too far and represents what we have called a scorched-earth policy. Hasn't he virtually ruled out, at this stage, the possibility that the human relationship to God is a superordinate good that would have to be taken into account, prior to choice, regardless of the range of hierarchies one might consider?

It has been insinuated that Grisez is a subjectivist. He does say things which would provoke such an assessment.[73] In all fairness, it is clear that he is not—so long, that is, as we are dealing with the basic values individually. In choosing a life plan, Grisez would argue that, whatever order of goods happens to suit one's tastes, one ought never to act directly against one of the basic goods. Therefore, the choice of a life plan is at least negatively ordered by moral norms.[74] Nevertheless, there is nothing to be found in the basic goods to justify the superiority of one life plan over another. Provided, of course, that there is no direct violation of a basic good, the adage *de gustibus non est disputadum* would seem to apply.

Grisez's position on the goods and the Fpm is that we should let a thousand flowers bloom, each of which is a categorical in its own right. The arrangement of these categoricals, however, appears to be on an *ad hoc* basis. Questions regarding possible conflicts, and contrasts of importance, among the goods are consigned first to the Fpm, which orders us to let them bloom and enjoy life, and then to the final mode of responsibility, which requires us not to disrespect any of the goods. In the meantime the goods, as categoricals, are in a holding pattern, awaiting some principle by which to further determine and specify orders of importance.

Grisez and Finnis appeal to life plans as a way to introduce an *ordinatio* to the goods. They derive the concept of a life plan from John Rawls, and all three of them refer to Josiah Royce's concept of an "individual self" as defined as "a human life lived according to a plan."[75] The notion of a life plan, as well as analogous concepts like that of "narrative structures," have recently been employed by many philosophers, and ethicians in particular. It is fair to say that whether the concept is taken to be a hermeneutical, regulative, or ontological device, it plays as many roles as there are theorists who employ it within the context of their own ethical theory. Stanley Hauerwas, for example, has used the concept to discuss not only the Aristotelian and Thomistic understanding of moral character, but also the bearing of Anabaptist ecclesiology and Christology upon moral theology.[76] Alasdair MacIntyre introduces the notion of narrative structures in *After Virtue* in order to clarify how one might restore a premodern teleological ethics without relying upon a "metaphysical biology."[77]

Here, it will help to clarify what Grisez is up to if we say a few words about the similarities and differences between himself and Rawls on the matter. The concept of a life plan is employed for the purpose of discussing how various goods are to be ordered, and the question of order is answered somewhat differently depending on whether one starts with a "thin" or a "full" theory of the goods. In *A Theory of Justice,* Rawls first establishes what he calls a "thin" theory of the goods which, in broad categories, are "rights and liberties, opportunities and powers, income and wealth," and, above all, "self respect."[78] Without rehearsing the entire Rawlsian system here, we can say that there are two major reasons why Rawls delimits the goods at the outset of his moral theory. First, in order to arrive at principles of justice, it is necessary to refer to certain primary goods which constitute the issues of justice. In order to secure these goods for further discussion, a "publicly recognized objective measure must be found."[79] But if we build into the list of primary goods all the goods with which persons are concerned, we would never realize a consensus. The moral principles would have to await a resolution to what a "full" meaning of human goods consists in. Second, a "full" theory of the goods requires a principle by which these goods are interrelated. Such a principle will have to take into account many contingent factors. Therefore, a "thin" list of the goods simplifies matters by arriving at certain goods that "a rational man wants whatever else he wants."[80] The method is similar to that of Grisez and Finnis, except that Rawls's is "thin" and theirs is "fat."

Rawls introduces the concept of a life plan only with his move into a "full" theory of the goods. Given the whole range of goods, a reasonable plan will be made up of "sub-plans suitably arranged in a hierarchy, the broad features of the plan allowing for the more permanent aims and interest that complement one another."[81] How do we judge life plans? Rawls answers that a life plan can be critically assessed by showing either "that it violates the principles of rational choice" (already established in the principles of justice) or that "it is not the plan that he would pursue were he to assess his prospects with care in the light of a full knowledge of the situation."[82] Rawls also makes use of what he calls the "Aristotelian Principle," namely, that human beings tend to prefer more inclusive and complex activities.[83] Accordingly, we can judge a life plan in terms of its capacity to comprehend and include other plans and thereby enable one to enjoy activities of a more complex order.

Rawls warns that the notion of a life plan shaped by the Aristotelian principle should not be taken as absolute. He gives a "fanciful case" to illustrate his point. Suppose we find someone whose only pleasure is to count blades of grass in various geometrically shaped areas such as park squares. The individual is quite intelligent and indeed is a math wizard. Rawls says that, however odd such a person might be, and however frivolous the activity, we must conclude that this individual's good is "determined by a plan that gives an especially prominent place to this activity."[84] In short, provided that the principles of justice are met with regard to the "thin" theory, the concept of a rational plan does "not require the truth of the Aristotelian Principle." Whereas Grisez and Finnis would insist that a thousand flowers bloom, Rawls is prepared to live with a considerably thinner garden of categoricals.

There *is* a problem, however, with a life plan lived according to what Rawls calls a "dominant end" theory of the good. He observes, "Loyola holds that the dominant end is serving God, and by this means saving our soul."[85] Furthering the divine intentions is the sole criterion for balancing subordinate aims. Rawls notes that many kinds of theological ethics have employed a dominant end model for resolving the problem of how the goods ought to be subordinated or superordinated. The problem with such a religious ethic is that it solves all of the disputed questions about how one should order the goods by an appeal to revelation.

Although Rawls cautiously admits that there is nothing in his theory that would guarantee that a dominant end model violates the principles of rational choice, it does strike us as "irational, or more likely as mad."[86] It is right on the cusp of a kind of fanaticism that would disfigure the human self by submitting the heterogeneous aims of the self (here we find a similarity between Rawls and the Grisez-Finnis understanding of the self) to a single system. If there is no dominant end that is not truly an inclusive end, then Rawls is certainly correct. How one could possibly account for a concrete dominant end that is also an inclusive end is precisely the sort of question that leads into either metaphysics or religion or both.[87] In the Scholastic tradition, various metaphysics of participation, along with methods of analogous reasoning, were employed to resolve the problem of interrelating dominant and inclusive ends. This is a problem that we shall take up with regard to Grisez and Finnis later.

Apart from the metaphysical and religious dimensions of the problem, Rawls also points out that the dominant end concepts subscribed to by different teleological theories of ethics entail the additional problem of introducing an end that can never be finally achieved, and therefore the "injunction to advance it always applies."[88] This problem, which also crops up in Kant's antinomies of practical reason, stands in sharp contrast to his own system, in which the injunctions of justice always come into play in definite ways. For Grisez and Finnis the "full" theory of the goods certainly entails the injunction continuously to advance the goods, among other reasons because none of the goods are specified in terms of "natures" having proper and determinate completions, either individually or collectively.

There are similarities and differences between Rawls's account and that of Grisez and Finnis. Two points of similarity are these. First, they agree that after the principles governing the basic goods are taken into account, the choice of a particular plan is up to the individual—as Rawls puts it, "without further guidance from principle."[89] Second, they are in agreement about the problem of dominant end concepts. As we said, Grisez rejects the dominant end teleology of Augustine and Aquinas.

One important difference is that Finnis, who follows Grisez in beginning with a "full" theory of the goods, explicitly includes the choice of a life plan among the modes of responsibility (in fact, it is the first mode).[90] The obligation to form a "coherent plan of life" does not mean, for Finnis, that the content is specified—only that one must do so in order to be responsible with regard to the goods. If one begins with an obligation to all of the goods—both individually and in terms of their collateral realization—then it is crucial that some principle of order be introduced. This is even more crucial if one holds that these goods are incommensurable and irreducible, for they bear no inherent order among themselves. Grisez is not as explicit on this as Finnis, but inasmuch as Grisez identifies the self with a life plan, and understands the Fpm as a kind of heuristic concept obligating one to act for the sake of integral fulfillment, one could perhaps infer the requirement.

Against Aquinas's position that one cannot direct one's acts simultaneously to different ultimate ends, Grisez remarks: "But as a matter of fact, people can pursue diverse goods without ordering them to one another and without ordering all of them to anything ulterior." For example, he observes that "a Christian girl of fourteen can sincerely try to live her faith insofar as she is aware of its requirements, yet simultaneously and without reference to her faith (and without serious sin) try to become a cheerleader for the sake of the activity itself and the status it will give her with her schoolmates."[91] Apart from the fact that this is a psychologizing of Aquinas's metaphysical argument, Grisez appears to be at odds with his colleague on this matter. Finnis holds, as we have said, that the choice of a coherent life plan is the first mode of moral responsibility. Strictly applied, Finnis's injunction regarding the adoption of a life plan would appear to render Grisez's adolescent cheerleader either amoral or premoral as an agent, for she has not yet adopted a single world view. Indeed, Finnis's insistence that the adoption of a coherent life plan is the first mode of moral responsibility means that moral agency can only begin when one is able to adopt a life plan or project, or that it changes once one adopts a different life plan. The substitution of the construct of life plans for the older metaphysics of finality strikes us as being more trouble than it is worth—insofar, that is, as it is used as a substitution for the purpose of achieving more or less the same result.[92]

Rawls makes the life plan a requirement not of the principles of justice, but rather of the "full" theory of the goods. To this extent, Rawls avoids the problem in Finnis's position. That is, Finnis is compelled to make the choice of a life plan a fundamental moral obligation even though, on the one hand, it lacks determinate content, and, on the other hand, it deals with interrrelations between the goods about which we have no specific moral norms and about which there are significant disputes among people of good will.[93] No doubt, Rawls would say that this is the price that is paid for trying to begin by wedding together moral norms with a "full" theory of the goods.[94]

Another difference is that Rawls's theory does not

require two things which Grisez is eager to retain. First, Rawls's position is not essentially teleological, for he defines the right independently of the good.[95] Grisez's ethics, while not consequentialist, is teleological; the Fpm and its modal specifications are essentially rules for maximizing human goods, and the right emerges in his system in tandem with the concept of integral human fulfillment. Thus, in a way that Rawls manages to avoid, Grisez must enjoin by the ideality of the Fpm an indefinite injunction to advance the goods. Yet, until this injunction acquires content the system is in suspension; as we pointed out earlier, it will tend to fall back upon rules governing one's choice of this or that good, rather than stipulating in a positive sense how they are to be coordinated. To this extent, the Fpm will lack efficacy for choice. This indicates why Grisez's system is in real need of a way to annul the ideality of the Fpm. It is precisely what he does when he moves into moral theology. The other thing that Grisez must account for is the dominant end motif of religion itself. Unlike Grisez, Rawls makes no claims regarding the fitness of his system for moral theology. How will Grisez deal with the ambition of a Loyola? This will be the subject of our next chapter. Before we conclude this chapter, there are a few things to be said about Grisez's understanding of transcendence.

By *transcendent* we mean that which is other than oneself—whether it be a person, a value, or whatever. Accordingly, by *immanent* we mean that which dwells or remains within oneself—whether it be an experience, a power, or a capacity. In this section, and hereafter, we do not necessarily imply by the distinction between transcendent and immanent the distinction between natural and supernatural. If we are referring to the latter distinction, it will be clearly specified. In this section we are interested in the question of whether practical reason, according to Grisez's system, has a transcendent feature.

Grisez argues that anything sought for its own sake is an

"ultimate end in a given situation of choice."[96] There are as many ultimate ends as there are basic goods and life plans organized around them. "No single complete good," he states, "is naturally available to human persons as their determinate, ultimate end."[97] He explicitly rejects the metaphysic implied in the Augustinian formula of the "restless heart," as well as Aquinas's effort to wed it to a metaphysics of final causality.[98] Without faith, such restlessness only suggests humanity's ordination to the range of human goods in which one can participate more and more. Thus, for Grisez, practical reason is not naturally ordained to an end that transcends (here, in the stronger sense of the term, as that which transcends the range of this-worldly goods) what can be immanently enjoyed in the here and now. As we mentioned earlier, this represents a significant departure from the natural law theory as it has been explicated within the Augustinian-Thomistic nexus.

Furthermore, Grisez argues that the concept of a common good does not add anything over and above the range of human goods and the moral norms for choosing them rightly:

> There is no good which helps to shape morally right action except goods which can be sought for their own sake as a basis for a choice to act. The basic human goods precisely are all the kinds of good which can be sought for their own sake, whether in an individual's or a group's decision to act. Hence, the common good as a principle of moral rectitude cannot be a good other than the basic human goods.[99]

Therefore, for Grisez, there is no way to get a principle of transcendence (significant for choice) from the concept of a common good. Simply put, practical reason is not related (again, in a way significant for choice) to a good that is other than the basic goods which are immanently enjoyed. As we will see later, John Finnis is somewhat diffident about this aspect of the system, for it seems to limit the motivational life of practical reason merely to a concern, or respect, for modes of one's own well-being and fulfillment.

Grisez does hold, however, that his understanding of the Fppr has a "certain transcendence, or at least the possibility of transcendence."[100] The Fppr simply directs human persons to a pursuit of goods, and thereby "provides human fulfillment as the basis for all of the normative demands which reason ever will make upon us."[101] It generates a field of possibilities, and in no way restricts "human good to the goods proportionate to nature."[102] Despite the fact that he repeatedly insists that moral action deals with proportionate human goods, he suggests that the ideality of the Fpm preserves an open-endedness beyond them.[103]

In requiring that one never directly suppress a basic value, the Fpm orients one to maintain a "will to integral human fulfillment," whatever it might prove to be. To "choose immorally," he observes, "is to set up an idol," for it implicitly assumes that a particular good or set of goods absolutely sets the boundary for human fulfillment.[104] A morally upright choice affirms "in an implicit way" the reality of a "more-than-human ground of human possibilities."[105] Whether this is something to which human beings are related in a morally significant way is another—indeed, the most important—question. Grisez is here arguing that the Fppr and the Fpm do not necessarily restrict the possibility that practical reason is related to a good (or goods) which exceeds what is proportionate to human nature. If, however, this good is not proportionate to human nature, then we are speaking of a good that is supernatural, even if that precise term is not explicitly used. The question is this: if there is no self-transcendence by the very nature of practical reason, then how do we acquire an openness to a more-than-human ground of the goods? In other words, is the issue of the self-transcendent capacity of practical reason exclusively reserved for the issue of the relationship between the natural and the supernatural? If so, then we might expect moral theology to play an especially important role in Grisez's account of practical reason.

Grisez further suggests that his ethical theory "might coincide with a religious view" in two ways.[106] First, in requiring that each of the basic goods be "maintained in their irreducible but not absolute positions," the system is geared to prevent a confusion between the basic goods and a more-than-human good.[107] The system, therefore, is consonant with a traditional religious concern that God not be confused with particular human goods. Once again, he is speaking not of a positive meaning of transcendence, but rather of a kind of *via negativa* by which we affirm that none of the goods satisfy or complete the human potentiality for goodness as such. This still leaves us on the threshold of the question. To affirm that no human good is a god is not the same thing as to establish an ethically significant relationship to God—particularly if one means by *God* a person or a value that is in no way proportionate to human cognition and choice.

Second, because there is no objective principle by which the goods are unified, one to another, it leaves open the possibility that they are "diverse participations in a unity beyond all of them"—that is, a participation in a "good which first belongs to God." On this point, Grisez is very tentative: "... if we accept the reference of our conception of goodness to a reality we do not yet understand, our openness to that goodness may count as love of it, although it is not an intelligible objective of any particular action."[108] He is quite clear that this only acquires content, and thus becomes a determinate objective, in the light of faith. His point is that there is nothing in his system that is an obstacle to making such a move. In fact, he states that *"it is only possible for man to love all of the goods properly if he considers each of them a participant in perfect goodness."*[109] We shall explore the meaning of this remark in more detail in the next chapter. Taken at face value, his statement suggests not only that his system is not an obstacle to making an act of faith, but that such an act is necessary in order to achieve, in the order of motivation, all of the requirements of his system.[110]

Grisez remarks in several of his works that without a belief in something transcendent to humanity, one is inexorably compelled to close off the range of goods and thereby fall into a utilitarian quest to maximize what is available here and now.[111] If consequentialism "were meaningful and consistent," he remarks, it "would rule out a religious faith which promises us that this yearning can be fulfilled by the more-than-human love of God and for God."[112] Not only the attention to human inclinations and goods, but also the "inspiration of faith" is "needed to develop an adequate law for human life."[113]

To summarize, Grisez philosophically rejects two of the more traditional natural law doctrines which bear upon the transcendent aspect of practical reason, namely, in the case of human agents, a proper end that transcends participation in finite goods; and in the second place, the principle of a common good that constitutes a value which transcends the individual goods immanently enjoyed by individuals. He argues, however, that his position on the Fppr and the Fpm does not close off the possibility that practical reason is related to a more-than-human ground of the goods, and furthermore, that this possibility is not at odds with a "religious" understanding of God. We raised several questions regarding this notion of transecendence. Our main question is whether or not Grisez's account requires a theological understanding of transcendence in order to secure an ethically significant sense of self-transcendence. This question move us directly into the area of religion and practical reason.

Before moving to the next chapter, it would be helpful to outline briefly certain questions regarding the relationship between religion and the Grisez-Finnis natural law system. First, if religion is counted among the self-evident, basic goods, and is thereby a primary principle of practical reason, then it would seem that all persons are obligated to protect and promote the good of religion. Remember, Grisez does not speak of religion as a right, but as a basic form of human well-being. How is such a moral theory able to handle not only the objections of an atheist, but the inevitable, if not intractable, differences between religious traditions on what constitutes the content of the basic good? At the very least, it will be necessary to distinguish between the good of religion and *a* religion, as well as to offer criteria for assessing whether the latter satisfies the nature of the general good of religion.

Second, if there is no objective hierarchy among the basic goods (which include religion), what are we to make of religion serving as an architectonic for one's life? If it is not ultimate, then what is it? Moreover, isasmuch as individual life plans are determined by different religions, how are we to deal with what appears to be an incommensurability between different religious life plans? Does each one (that of a Muslim and that of a Unitarian) share equally in the same general form of the good of religion? This poses a problem of how Grisez can undertake a consistent transition from his ethical principles to the moral theology of a specific religious tradition.

Third, Grisez defines the good of religion as a harmony between choice and the will of God. He also contends that it is not self-evident that the will of God must be obeyed. Does this not suggest that the self-evident basic good of religion depends upon an act of faith that is not accounted for in his description of the goods?

Fourth, Grisez contends that it is only possible for one to love all of the goods properly if one considers them to be participations in a divine goodness. If this insight depends upon an act of faith, it would seem that no one can fulfill the modes of responsibility without the data of a revealed religion. Would not this lead to a kind of hyper-Augustinianism that Grisez himself rejects?

Fifth, if each of the human goods can be regarded as participations in a divine goodness, and if this can be established by reason, then are we to conclude that an ultimate transcendent good is proportionate in some minimal way to human nature? If so, then it is unclear why Grisez rules out the Augustinian "restless heart" position and Aquinas's argument that God is man's final end by nature, for Aquinas's position explicitly involves a doctrine of participation that enables him to bring metaphysics or natural theology to bear upon practical rationality. If not, then it is unclear why a belief in a metaphysics of participation alluded to by Grisez has any significance for ethics; for a good that is in no way proportionate to man could not be a matter of moral judgment and choice.

Sixth, the Fpm obligates the moral agent to remain continually "open to" an integral human fulfillment. What are the systematic implications of annulling the ideality of the Fpm by an act of faith? Would this not suggest that those who remain under the ideality of the Fpm and those who have annulled it are living in two different moral spheres? We would have a natural law ethics of indeterminate openness on one hand, and on the other hand a theological ethics (purportedly consistent with natural law) that determinately shapes the openness according to a specific and concrete end.

Seventh, to the extent that Grisez's system includes both a respect for goods and a eudaimonistic quest for self-fulfillment, is there any provision in the system to prevent the value of one's relationship to God from being reduced to a mere "good for me"? Simply put, is the "person" of God yet another immanent aspect of my "full-being"? Here, we return to a more basic meaning of *transcendent* as that which is not merely immanent. Grisez's axiology includes at least two basic goods—friendship (which includes justice) and religion—which involve someone other than oneself in the description of the value. Is the disvalue of injustice simply a violation of one's potential to be just? If not, then there is a transcendent pole to the value which cannot adequately be understood by describing the value simply in terms of the immanent modalities of one's own fulfillment. We are asking whether this does not need to be firmly established before moving to the issue of nature and supernature in order to prevent a dichotomy between a naturally closed practical reason and a supernaturally open one.

3

RELIGION, FAITH, AND
PRACTICAL REASON

In one of his early theological essays Hegel chides those who would pity the Greeks for having had a "comfortless" religion. Such sympathy is misplaced, Hegel argues, for among the Greeks "we do not encounter the needs which our practical reason has today when we have learned how to saddle it with plenty of them."[1] Indeed, the transition undertaken by many Enlightenment theorists, from speculative issues in natural theology to an interest in what became known as natural religion, represented a general shift of interest from the speculative to the practical dimensions of theism (which Hegel, of course, lamented).

In his book on *The Emergence of Philosophy of Religion* James Collins proposes that philosophy of religion emerged as a distinct branch of modern philosophy in order to resolve three sorts of problems: (1) speculative problems in natural theology, and especially the issue of what to make of design in nature; (2) practical problems, which include the relationship between religion and morality, as well as the issue of whether it is possible to speak of moral attributes on the part of a deity; and (3) the perennial faith-reason problems, which include not only the issue of how to distinguish between these two domains, but also the issue of how to regard the Christian religion, its biblical texts and sects, and, perhaps most troublesome, its claims about the political order. Having classified these main themes, Collins goes on to point out that the practical one has proved to be the most "radically problematic."[2] The personal and political questions regarding the relationship between religion and morality do not yield easily to speculative debates. In this and in the following chapter, we shall examine why they do not yield easily to debates locked within the discourse of practical reason either.

This subject is, or course, as vast and complex as it is important. It is not our intention here to give a history of the philosophy of religion. There exist several typological schema of religions, sects, and their respective approaches to the political, cultural, and economic orders—from H. Richard Niebuhr's *Christ and Culture* (1951) to the more recent (and quite useful) typology outlined by A. James Reichley in *Religion in American Public Life* (1985).[3] However, it would not be entirely irrelevant to our discussion of the Grisez-Finnis natural law theory to note one particular problem bequeathed by the Enlightenment, namely, the status of the concept *natural religion*.

It was the hope of theorists in the Deist tradition, such as Lord Herbert of Cherbury—and later, many in the Romantic movement, such as Friedrich Schleiermacher—that the category *natural religion* might do justice to the human being as a *homo religiosus,* while on the other hand helping to circumvent the divisive political and ecclesiastical controversies which seem to ensue once *a* religion is invested with determinate historical and dogmatic content. It was believed that if religion were brought under philosophical scrutiny, one could ascertain certain *notitiae communes* which are as universal to humanity in the area of religion as they are in the domain of morality itself. Hence, if religion can be defined in terms of invariable properties (whether ideas or feelings), then the value of religion can reasonably be affirmed.[4] Lord Gifford, who set the requirements for the prestigious Gifford Lectures, summarized the intent of inquiry into natural religion when he stated that the lectures should consist of natural theology "in the widest sense of the term"—including a science of God and of the relationship between him, the world, and human ethics. This should be conducted, he insisted, independently of historical religions or sects, and "without reference to or reliance upon any supposed special exceptional or so-called miraculous revelation."[5]

It is well known that the effort to isolate, and then affirm the value of, natural religion was brought up short by David Hume, Ludwig Feuerbach, Nietzsche, and Freud, to mention a few. Hume and Feuerbach affirmed the premise of natural religion (that it should be studied as a natural phenomenon) but denied the conclusions drawn by the Deists. Feuerbach, of course, argued that religion is a distorted anthropology, and, although "natural," it is nevertheless pathological.[6] More was found under the rug of natural religion than first met the eye. It is generally true to say that the methodological move from doctrines and churches (what in the common morality could be called *a* religion) to the human breast has not proved to be sufficient to demonstrate the practical value of religion. One might recall the debates of the recent past when every-one from the CIA to clinical psychologists tried to deter-mine whether the *delerium tremens* brought about by LSD was a psychosis or a new religious gnosis (what Aldous Huxley referred to as the perceptive "doors" of religion, which no doubt would have interested Lord Gifford).[7]

In *A Common Faith* John Dewey has put his finger on one of the most obvious problems of the effort to evaluate, and especially to affirm, the value of religion. We are forced to acknowledge, he says, that "concretely there is no such thing as religion in the singular"—there is only a "multitude of religions."[8] Indeed, dissatisfaction with the term *religion* runs the gamut of the most diverse thinkers. Dewey him-self wished to distinguish between the adjective *religious* and the noun *religion,* in order to stress that religion is a perspective within the natural frame of things, rather than a peculiar access to a special set of truths.[9] As the title of his book suggests, the effort to speak of religion in general, and to move beyond the restrictions imposed by a specific religion, represents a project of long standing to bring a "common" religion as a mere perspective within the orbit, and as the rightful heir, of what Donagan has called the "common morality" of the West. Pruned of historical and doctrinal specificity, Dewey's "common faith" is in the legacy not only of Schleiermacher but also of the sceptics who regard religion as a perspective that attracts some people and repels others.

Karl Rahner, on the other hand, rejects the possibility of philosophically isolating any religious phenomenon, for such a project, he fears, is bound to "institute a religion which is fundamentally independent of historical events—a religion which all the time can be arrived at equally well from any point in the historical existence of man."[10] Rahner proposes the construction of a metaphysical anthropology which might establish the conditions of the possibility of a relationship between human beings and God. This eternal possibility should receive its specificity from the historical context in which the Word is spoken to human beings. Religion is the possibility of a perspective.

From a completely different quadrant, Karl Barth and neoorthodox theologians in the "Krisis" tradition have contended that whatever is found to belong to religion can only be some potential or need of humanity. Therefore, religion makes human potential the condition of God's revelation and is therefore "sin," because it puts itself in the place of God. As Barth put it in his *Epistle to the Romans,* religion is "the most dangerous enemy a man has on this side of the grave."[11] Barth was acutely aware of the legacy of Schleiermacher, which involves nothing less than *making a religion of the good of religion.* He did not criticize this development as a break with the "common morality" of the West, but he did regard it as a break with the Reformed tradition. For Barth, a recovery of the Reformed tradition requires a radical break with any general notion of *religion,* whether it be one of philosophers or one of theologians. The neoorthodox notion of a religionless Christianity still exerts a considerable influence on Protestant thought.[12]

We have noted these issues only to indicate in a somewhat general fashion that the inclusion of religion on the foundational level of moral theory is fraught with problems, among other reasons because, whether or not there is a "common morality" to be retrieved by philosophical ethicians, there remains the problem of making sense of religion and *a* religion, as well as the problem of which, if either, should be built into the foundation of one's moral theory.[13] Contemporary ethicians like Alan Donagan and Alasdair MacIntyre, for instance, are interested in showing the consonance between moral principles and the sort of everyday religion that has shaped Western culture, including its ethical notions and practices.[14] Neither of them, however, builds religion into his theoretical framework. Along with metaphysics, religion is one of those silent aspects of the tradition of premodern ethics which is to be historically acknowledged but kept at a distance. As we mentioned in the introduction, Elizabeth Anscombe has argued that the Christian heritage represents the silent factor which, once suppressed, inhibits any effort to recover the "common morality."

As we saw in the last chapter, Germain Grisez posits the good of religion as one of the seven *prima principia* of practical reason. This is one of a cluster of problems which we will examine in this chapter. At the outset, it is only fair to say that Grisez's task is not an easy one. He wants to interrelate three things. First, the good of religion, like all of the other basic values in Grisez's scheme, is to be promoted, respected, and never acted against. Second, Grisez argues that it is only by faith in divine revelation that one can have a personal relationship to God. Thus, faith and the good of religion need to be interrelated. Third, Grisez wants to tie together moral principles with a specific credal tradition, and thus set the framework for a moral theology.

In this chapter we shall examine Grisez's effort to inter-relate these three areas. We shall argue that certain anom-alies in his philosophical system make the project difficult to complete. Once again, our analysis and critique will remain philosophical. We intend to enter into neither the substantive content of moral theology nor the hermeneu-tical issues involved in the particular theological tradition that Grisez tries to uphold. Our concern is directed to his natural law system of practical reason and to whether or not it works coherently and consistently once we move into the area of religion.

In the first section of the chapter we will take a brief look at Grisez's philosophical theology. In *Beyond the New Theism* he gives an argument for the existence of God—one that involves a thoroughgoing *via negativa* approach to the problem. We shall outline the argument, but our interest is in the practical and moral implications, particularly in terms of the parameters it sets for speaking about God's moral attributes.

In the next section we shall examine in more detail his definition of the basic good of religion. Following defini-tions given throughout his various writings, we will take a special interest in how Grisez has vacillated in his defini-tion of religion as a value—between an anthropological description of religion that has some affinities to the older rubric of "natural religion" and a description of religion in strictly fideist terms. We will show how the definition has become progressively more determined by the fideist element.

Then we will take up the major cluster of problems per-taining to Grisez's way of interrelating religion, faith, and practical reason. Many of the loose ends of his system, which we discussed in the previous chapters, are brought to light in this problem area. What proves particularly prob-lematic is Grisez's axiology, which is the substratum of his entire system. We shall argue that his axiology requires inconsistent, if not irreconcilable, perspectives on values and moral attitudes. As it turns out, religion is the lightning rod for a problem that systematically includes the other goods as well.

Finally, we will examine John Finnis's treatment of religion and practical reason in order to see whether there is anything in his approach to the issue that would enable us to alleviate the problems which we have located in Grisez's work. Finnis has not moved into moral theology, and for this reason he is perhaps better prepared to reexamine the relationship between religion and the natural law ethic to which he and Grisez subscribe.

3.1 Grisez on Philosophical Theology

Grisez's *Beyond the New Theism* is subtitled, "A Philosophy of Religion." It should be kept in mind that the "new theism," for Grisez, is the so-called process theology or metaphysics.[15] The book contains an argument for the existence of God, a lengthy defense of the argument against other traditions, and finally an apologetic for Christian discourse about God. He states that his philosophical theology is intended to articulate a "view which I think is adequate both for metaphysics and for religion."[16]

His purpose in providing an argument for the existence of God is made clear in the following statement: "An argument is essential to establish the conclusion that God exists; to establish this conclusion is useful, not so much to prove it to persons who do not accept it as to establish a real *referent* for the beliefs of those who do accept it." "At the same time," he concludes, "an argument showing that God exists provides a principle for making *sense* of talk about God."[17] As we will see, Grisez's emphasis upon a *via negativa* is intended not only to establish a "referent," and thereby to counter antitheistic arguments, but also to restrict the range of metaphysical affirmations about God so that the discourse of faith has room to move. The latter is also intended to counter the reduction of the God of Christianity to a process metaphysic.

Grisez points out that his argument does not depend upon an epistemological assumption that we can intuit essences or forms; nor does it assume that the world is composed of substances and accidents.[18] Although his argument has affinities to Aquinas's "real distinction," and indirectly to the *tertia via* sketched in the *Summa theologiae,* it is not derived from a metaphysical analysis of *esse* (which, of course, requires the epistemological and philosophical assumptions regarding composite substances and their causal dependence upon *esse ipsum subsistens*); nor does it employ the logic of analogy derived from the Thomistic method, whereby some attributes can be predicated of God in lieu of quidditative knowledge of the divine being. Rather, the argument begins with the assumption that by propositions one picks out states of affairs which may or may not obtain. If the state of affairs picked out by the proposition does obtain, one is entitled to ask what "extrapropositional" entity or entities makes possible the knowledge of the proposition as true.[19]

His argument leads to the positing of an uncaused cause as a "theoretical entity" sufficient to explain the obtaining of states of affairs which may or may not obtain—in other words, contingent states of affairs picked out by propositions. It is important to bear in mind that Grisez rejects the principle of "sufficient reason."[20] Therefore, he makes no claim to explain the contingency of contingent things. Why one contingent state of affairs obtains rather than others is a question to be answered by the sciences. His argument is geared only to explain why contingent things obtain "despite being contingent."[21]

By a proposition one picks out a contingent state of affairs. By *contingent,* Grisez does not mean "transitory," but only something which might or might not obtain.[22] Once again, one must take care in reading Grisez, for he uses terms which appear to be those of a Thomistic or

Scholastic system. By contingency, Grisez does not assume either the method or the ontology of the older philosophy of nature. For Grisez, the obtaining of a state of affairs does not follow from its being the state of affairs that it is; indeed, for Grisez, the primary evidence for contingency is "that we can know what it would be like for many states of affairs to obtain without knowing whether they obtain."[23] If such a state of affairs obtains, it is reasonable to ask why, and to "expect an answer which would begin to provide an unconditional explanation."[24] Again, it is reasonable to expect an unconditional answer, not to the question of why states of affairs are contingent, but only to the question of why a particular contingent state of affairs obtains at all.

Grisez goes on to reason that it is not satisfactory to answer the question by reference to other contingent states of affairs assumed to exist; again, this question might be amenable to a "scientific" resolution, but it does not bear upon the problem of why any contingent state of affairs should obtain in the first place. Grisez likewise argues that the question cannot be satisfied by positing a necessity identical with some or all contingent states of affairs, for this, he believes, would annul the intelligibility of contingent states of affairs.[25] Nor, he reasons, can we simply say that a contingent state of affairs obtains because it is the state of affairs that it is: "But since a contingent state of affairs is the state of affairs which it is whether it obtains or not, what a contingent state of affairs is cannot explain its obtaining."

Therefore, Grisez concludes that it is necessary to posit an extrapropositional, and theoretical, entity called an "uncaused cause" in order to satisfy the conditions of the problem.[26] This uncaused entity D necessarily obtains, and causes contingent states of affairs to obtain. Thus, three things can be affirmed: it is uncaused; it obtains; and it causes contingent states of affairs to obtain.[27] To say anything else is either to move into scientific inquiries concerning particular states of affairs, or to tread on the thin ice of metaphor about the uncaused cause.

Obviously, there are many issues packed into this argument. We have only outlined what is itself a rather lean approach to the existence of God, and even leaner regarding what perfections might be positively signified of the deity. Our chief interest is in the implications which Grisez derives for the practical issues. Grisez provides a "referent," but the question is whether the referent has moral significance.

Grisez argues that "no predicable of anything in experience can be affirmed of D [the uncaused entity]."[28] Whatever predicable is employed in picking out contingent states of affairs can "only be used to say what D is not."[29] The terms *one, something,* and *true* can be used, because if the uncaused cause exists it is one, something, and true.[30] Any other mode of predication must operate within the parameters of the *via negativa*. Hence, Grisez observes that

> restricting oneself to the results attained by the argument that there is a creator, one finds little reason to admire and love him. The world obviously is beset by many evils. Of course, there are certain goods in it too. If one is not unduly pessimistic, one might feel that the creator is not to be hated, but is to be regarded with a certain wary wonder. Undoubtedly he is great. But is he not also cruel or, at least, lacking in sensitivity? No, this also is excluded by the way of negation.[31]

In the same vein, he denies that the term *holy* can be predicated of the deity, unless it simply means that the uncaused entity is something other than what is found in experience.[32] Grisez likewise rejects the soundness of any argument based upon design or telic order in nature,[33] or any other "way" to God that would enable one to affirm a property of God other than obtains—including the Kantian notion that practical discourse is able to speak philosophically where metaphysics fails.[34] Since the argument is not grounded in an explicit philosophy of being, Grisez has no use for the traditional ways of analogical reasoning—such as the *analogia entis* and the *analogia eminentiae*. He is, however, left with the *via negationis*, which he vigorously employs.

Grisez is quite clear that the theoretical entity posited by his argument *is not*, as such, "an object of religion."[35] Each person, he counsels, "must decide whether D is what he calls God."[36] Where does this leave religious language? In the first place, Grisez believes that the argument establishes a referent that can serve as a foothold for religious language. Simply put, religious discourse about God is not totally without metaphysical foundation. Thus understood, the *via negativa* is a two-edged sword that limits the metaphysical discourse of the believer, but also obstructs the more radical atheistic critique (which says too little) as well as the so-called process natural theology (which says too much).

He is willing to consider the use of analogical models which would permit the believer to make conjectural affirmations about God's personal and moral qualities, especially a model based upon human free choice, which is "somewhat similar" to an uncaused cause.[37] He hastens to add, however, that he does not wish to suggest that the analogy is precise. It does "not warrant the drawing of any firm conclusions."[38] "The way of negation remains," he insists. "The model is suggestive; it indicates a direction that further inquiry concerning D might take. However, considering the model philosophically, one cannot be certain whether the inferences are sound."[39] Grisez has not altered his position in subsequent writings.[40]

In *Christian Moral Principles,* for example, he states that apart from faith we are entitled to think of the Other as "quasipersonal"; that is, "as if it were a free agent, and so as intelligent," for if the uncaused entity created, we might assume that it did so freely.[41] Yet even the characterization of God provided by faith describes him not as he is in himself, but only "insofar as he draws us into personal relationship with himself in the order of salvation."[42] In other words, what one knows about God through faith is based upon God as a *relatum*, namely, the good things he has done for me, not what he is himself. One is reminded of Karl Barth's admonition regarding this very point. Although Barth was in no way a friend of natural theology, he nevertheless insisted that Protestant theology began to stray from its proper course "from the moment when Protestantism itself, and Luther in particular, ceased to be interested in what God is in himself and became emphatically interested in what God is for man."[43] Grisez does not deny the teaching of the two Vatican councils that the existence of God can be known by the natural light of reason; rather, he says it "scarcely provides a basis for knowing whether God is personal," and it is, in any event, "inadequate to establish a relationship of intimacy between him and us."[44] Grisez employs philosophical theology to affirm the existence of a theoretical *D*, but then the inquiry is drawn up short to allow God to emerge as a *relatum* for the individual, according to the glad tidings of revelation.

We see, then, that Grisez's philosophical theology provides little positive guidance to practical reason in terms of the value of religion as grounded in a natural theology. "The invocation of a metaphysics of divine causality and providence," he argues, is of no immediate help to the construction of basic moral principles, "since such a metaphysics consists exclusively of theoretical truths from which reason can derive no practical consequences."[45] This statement suggests that no matter what kind of metaphysical affirmations are made about God, they would have little bearing upon practical reason anyway. As we will see later, Grisez takes a quite different position on the bearing of "facts" derived from faith, which make religion a very attractive "value."

The question, therefore, still remains how we are to reconcile a belief in a God who gives commands with our practical reason. The problem of reconciling divine categorical imperatives with human autonomy, he answers, "is a real question only if one believes traditional Judeo-Christian doctrines." Thus, if one believes by faith that God is personal, and that he issues commands, then one will not take the problem "in abstraction from his whole religious understanding of reality." In what does this "whole understanding" consist? Grisez answers that by faith "God's law should be regarded as a gift rather than as a burden."[46] As we will see later in this chapter, Grisez argues that no divine command can be anything other than a command to act in accord with the Fpm and integral human fulfillment. What is revealed accords precisely with what we wanted all the way along.

We are, nevertheless, thrown back to the problem of how religion can be included among the *prima principia* of practical reason. First, Grisez holds that God can only be conjectured as personal, or as a moral being, but cannot be *known,* without an act of faith in revelation.[47] He states that God cannot be a condition for forming any of the self-evident principles of practical reason "unless those principles happen to be ones that especially concern God."[48] Among these latter ones, Grisez explicitly mentions the principles that "God should be loved above all else," and that "God should be obeyed before all else."[49] These, however, cannot be among the primary principles of the natural law —not, at least, as Grisez interprets it, because they are not self-evident; indeed, as he says, they rely upon faith.[50] Moreover, the superordinate direction of the two precepts concerning God would seem to be at odds with Grisez's understanding of the incommensurable and irreducible status of the goods. Each of the precepts involves a relative judgment concerning the lovability of

God, as well as the priority of obligation in this regard. Clearly there is a problem here. We need to take a closer look at what Grisez means by the basic good of religion.

3.2 The Basic Good of Religion

In this section we will examine various ways that Grisez has defined the good of religion. We will proceed according to the chronological order of his publications in order to give the reader a better sense of how Grisez has wrestled with the definition. Through the course of his career he has vacillated between a general description of religion as a good about which all individuals and cultures are concerned, and the position that religion is constituted by a faith in a special theistic referent. Along with this, we will see that the value of religion oscillates between a concern for human goods, in which case religion is understood principally as a mode of adjusting to the other values within an immanent sphere of self-realization, and on the other hand a concern for one's relationship to a deity, in which case religion is viewed as having a transcendent pole.

In *Contraception and the Natural Law* (1964), Grisez defines the good of religion as "the tendency to try to establish good relationships with unknown higher powers." He states that anthropology can confirm the list of goods, including religion, "precisely because these motives are the principles which collectively define whatever human life might be."[51] One of the problems in this early work is that Grisez is not clear about the meaning of the terms *tendency, inclination, motive, principles,* and several other terms which are used equivocally with the term *good.* Is God an object of our tendency, and if so is it an efficacious tendency?

These questions are not dealt with in the book, which of course is devoted primarily to the problem of contraception. Nevertheless, we can see two elements at work, both of which persist through his subsequent writings on the subject. First, religion is defined as an anthropological constant; that is, it is something that is found among persons everywhere, presumably because everyone finds it attractive. Second, the expression "unknown higher powers" is interesting, for even in this early work Grisez is hesitant to fill the "relationship" with any content prior to faith, except to say that it is "good."

In the book on *Abortion* (1970), he once again mentions that we might find the "categories of human activity found by anthropologists to be useful to interpret the facts of life in any culture." Religion is here defined as "worship and holiness—the reconciliation of mankind to God."[52] The suggestion that religion is a good affirmed by all cultures is still made; but now religion is defined not only in moral terms (holiness), but also in terms which at least insinuate theological content (sin and reconciliation). In this book Grisez maintains that we are conscious of these basic goods experientially, in being "aware of our own inclinations and of what satisfies them."[53] Once again, whether we are self-consciously "inclined" to holiness and reconciliation with God, and whether this is consistent with the assumption that we are somehow not in friendship with God, are not clarified. Rather, we can only say that practices called religious are found to be attractive and experientially satisfying.

In *Beyond the New Morality* (revised edition, 1980) the effort to arrive at a definition of the good of religion becomes more complicated. Grisez writes:

> In this group of reflexive purposes one moves beyond the relationships among people to consider the relationship between human beings and God. It may be objected that we are now entering the realm of theology or that we are attempting to assume the existence of God. That, however, is not our intention. We do not presume either to demonstrate or take for

> granted that God exists. For our purposes, what is significant here is simply the fact that—whether or not God exists—men in all cultures and at all times have been concerned about their relationship with a transcendent Other to whom the name of "God" is usually given. This concern has focused either on the attempt to reestablish a harmonious relationship with the Other (a relationship believed or felt to have been disrupted in some way) or to strengthen and perfect this relationship where it exists.[54]

Elements of previous definitions remain, but what first strikes the reader about this passage is Grisez's insistence that the good of religion can be affirmed quite apart from the issue of whether or not there exists a divine referent.

Similarly, he says elsewhere in this book that "it is entirely possible to recognize a place for the human good of religion in one's life without making that particular good the absolute to which all else must be sacrificed."[55] The human good of religion, he reminds the reader, is "not identical with God." True enough, some distinction ought to be made between religion and God, since Grisez holds that God ought to be distinguished from *everything*; to say, then, that religion is not to be confused with God does not, as such, advance our understanding of the value (as a "concern," "purpose," or "inclination") of religion. Religion is one of the *prima principia* universally spawned by the Fppr, and no distinction is introduced which would permit us to judge what truly satisfies this human good. The division of the natural law method into premoral and moral facets is at work here. There is something attractive about religion, but why one ought to choose, much less promote, it is unclear.

In *Beyond the New Morality* Grisez slides back and forth in trying to nail down the precise nature of the value. For instance, he states that "it is obvious that there is no inevitable connection between religious belief and morally good behavior," and then goes on to put the case even more strongly: "There is no necessary connection between the two things: being good and being religious are separate and distinct."[56] Having distinguished between religion and God, he now distinguishes between religion and morality. On his own theory of the Fpm, however, *all* of the goods are to be distinguished from morality, which concerns the modal principles governing attitudes and choices of the goods. This distinction does not shed light on the value in either its premoral or its moral dimensions.

Again, in the same book, Grisez maintains that a "true religious act" can be "described as 'living a holy life'."[57] This description, however, does not sit well with his previous statement that "being good and being religious are separate and distinct"—unless perhaps being holy and being good are two different things, which may well be true, but needs to be shown.[58] In this regard, it is worth recalling our comments in the previous chapter concerning Grisez's method of defining the good of morality itself in terms of a premoral axiology. A similar problem is at work in his effort to describe the value of religion: that is to say, it is described on the one hand as a value to be affirmed in distinction to, even separate from, either God or morality, and on the other hand it is described as being a state of holiness. As we will discuss in more detail in the next section, the problem is due to something more than terminological anomalies.

Finally, in *Beyond the New Morality,* Grisez treats the subject of religion and hierarchy with regard to life plans. Religion, he suggests, "seems indeed the best choice to receive the emphasis of one's most basic commitments in life."

> To the extent that we identify the transcendent Other with the principle which sustains human goods, even when they are not chosen, making one's religious commitment most fundamental is closely related to—

if not identical with—taking one's stand on the side of
openness to all of the human goods.[59]

In this passage two additional ideas are brought to bear
upon the matter of religion. Religion is a candidate for a
personal hierarchy "to the extent" (1) that the transcendent Other is identified as the principle which sustains all
of the human goods, and (2) that one's commitment to
religion is understood as a commitment to the integral
wholeness of all the human goods.

Regarding the first condition, Grisez's philosophical theology does not establish a deity who is a moral sustainer of
human goods—it only affirms the existence of a transcendent Other. We will see in the next section of this chapter
that this condition will require faith in a historically determinate revelation in order to be available in any significant
way for practical reason. The second condition reveals an
important point about the value of religion. As a condition,
it does not emphasize a specifically theistic referent for the
value. Since there is no objective hierarchy among the basic
values, the personal commitment to religion must be, as we
quoted him above, "identical with" a commitment to all
of the human goods—which would seem to imply that religion is virtually the same as the Fpm. Along these lines,
Grisez argues in another place in the book that "the man
whose basic commitment is to the good of religion has
merely established the emphasis and orientation of his life
according to which he will seek to work out his relationship to all the other goods besides religion."[60]

Grisez certainly does not mean to suggest that the value
of religion is merely instrumental, but it is not explained
why religion should be a good, or even the best, candidate
for a personal hierarchy. Why shouldn't the good of aes-
thetic experience fit the bill? Furthermore, if a religious
commitment is virtually the same as an openness to all of
the goods, what value does one affirm in religion that is
not already being affirmed in any morally upright choice

or attitude?[61] If religion is living a holy life, is holiness to be equated with having a particularly generous attitude regarding one's own fulfillment? Put succinctly, why is religion a distinct value at all?

In *Beyond the New Theism* (1975), Grisez first defines religion in the context of his argument about the existence of a transcendent, uncaused cause:

> The word "god" is used in one sense, at least, to refer to anything which is arrived at by the general pattern of reasoning to something unseen. Not every *invisible* reality is regarded as a god. The whole pattern of reasoning defines the meaning of "god." . . . Corresponding to "god" in this sense is religion in general. In other words, any way of adjusting to the reality of an entity which is a god is religious. An integrated system of such ways of adjusting is a religion.[62]

This definition emphasizes the theistic referent of religion. The reader should note that Grisez is careful to say that the term *god* can only be determined by the "whole pattern of reasoning." The qualification is important, because if religion is identified with *any* way of "adjusting" to any unseen entity, then demonology or perhaps Aztec sacrificial rituals would be included under the basic good of religion. But we need criteria for the "whole pattern of reasoning." Otherwise, we are compelled to say that the premoral facet of natural law would have to include the Aztec rituals, or perhaps Huxley's chemically induced psychedelic "doors," as participations in the "good" of religion. It must be said that Grisez has reserved moral grounds for objecting to such religious practices. For instance, he might argue that these practices violate some other human good, such as life; but this moral judgment does not disqualify the rituals as the good of religion; it only indicates that this particular religious observance violates the good of morality by failing to respect other basic goods. In other words, the Aztecs, according to nature, participate in the good of religion, for they find their religious practices attractive and gratifying; yet the practices, according to natural moral norms, violate the eighth mode of responsibility. Nature appears to speak with a forked tongue.

It *is* consistent with the limits Grisez observes regarding philosophical theology, which can only affirm the existence of an uncaused entity and therefore requires a fuller pattern of reasoning, if the entity affirmed is to be a "god" or, as he says, "an object of religion." As it stands, however, the definition does not prove very helpful in understanding the *value* of religion, for it is clear that the "whole pattern" criterion needs to be determined in order to make any headway beyond a general, anthropological definition. In *Beyond the New Theism* Grisez once again discusses the good of religion in a way that deemphasizes the problems involved in specifying the theistic referent. "Religious fanaticism," he warns, "is a form of idolatry in which the created good of religion is wrongly exalted to the position of divinity."[63] This problem can be alleviated in one of two ways. Either one can specify the precise nature of the divinity to which humanity is related, and thereby set the criteria for what constitutes idolatry (by designating what is not God); or one can take a perspective from within the repertoire of human goods, and argue that their incommensurability and irreducibility stand against making any one of them absolute with regard to the others. Grisez favors the latter approach.

The advantage of the latter approach is that it circumvents the swamp of theoretical problems inherent in any effort to specify the nature of the deity; thus, we can say that whatever the deity turns out to be, and whatever the manner of our relationship to it, the good of the relationship is not absolute. Moreover, however one construes the deity, religious actions cannot violate other basic human goods. The disadvantage of this approach, however, is that the relational object of religion is left unclear. Thus any definition of the value of religion, as a distinct good, is left in suspension until we achieve a clearer understanding of a nonabsolute relation (which is the good of religion) to an absolute being—unless, of course, one is seriously prepared (and, unlike Dewey, Grisez finally is not) to define religion without a special relational object.

Grisez's shift of emphasis from religion as a way of adjusting to some sort of deity, to religion as a manner of adjusting to the range of human goods, is nicely summarized in the following passage:

> Freedom in choosing a good implies its nonabsoluteness, for if one believed that one good included everything of value in another, then it would be impossible to choose the second in preference to the first. Thus the belief that religious commitment is a free choice implied that the religious good is not absolute, that it is only one good among others, that other goods in some respects include aspects of human value which are not present in the religious good itself. Of course, once a person made a religious commitment, he did not see religion as one particular good among others. The religious orientation shaped life as a whole, animating and harmonizing all particular goods. For the devout Jew or Christian a religious concern was the most basic concern of life, yet it was not exclusive of other human concerns. It endorsed other values and sanctified them. An inclusivistic attitude was compatible with traditional theism precisely because God was conceived as a creator who had made all things good, and man was believed to be made in the image of God and appointed ruler of creation.[64]

Here, the theistic referent is invoked not in order to specify a special object of religion, but in order to authorize an inclusivistic attitude toward all of the goods. What is not answered is why the nonabsolute good of religion should be made the basis of a basic commitment in which it is no longer seen as merely one good among others.

If it is particularly fit for serving as an architectonic, then one is making the judgment that it is better, or best, relative to the other values for playing this function. In other words, the issue is not whether we are dealing with an exclusive or an inclusive approach to values, but rather the need to justify this claim concerning the role of religion in establishing an inclusive hierarchy of values. Here, in *Beyond the New Theism,* Grisez's answer is only an adumbration of the answer he will give when he explicitly treats the value of religion in light of faith and revelation. In *Christian Moral Principles* he will argue that the religion of faith plays an architectonic role among the values because it is only by the attitude and revealed data of faith that the Fpm obligation to pursue integral human fulfillment can be met.

In addition to the problem of philosophically justifying a hierarchy, the ambiguity of the "relation" constituted by religion is still problematic. Grisez states that the good of religion is realized in "the relation of harmony or friendship between created persons and God." This harmony or friendship "does not add anything to the creator; he is an uncaused cause." Therefore, "religion is *man's* relation to God."[65] The relational problem is apparent, first of all, in the description of a friendship that has no mutuality. One pole of the relation appears to be inert. This problem pertains to all of Grisez's "goods" to the extent that it is not clear how inclinations, actions, and objects are interrelated to constitute specific goods. How religion is the realization of the good of a "relation," in this respect, is less than clear. This perhaps is why, in the passage above, the "relation" is defined entirely as the realization of immanent human goods *inter alia.* In this case, the theistic referent is quite extrinsic to the precise good being realized; that is to say, religion is envisioned as a mode of harmonizing other human goods, and it is *to* (i.e., for the sake of) these goods that the value is made clear.

To be sure, according to Grisez, such activity is conducted under the auspices of, and in a way compatible with, belief in a God who endorses human goods; but the "relation," or the "adjustment," is devoted to human goods. In other words, he is speaking of religion in two ways, only the latter of which contains the value judgment: (1) religion as harmony between one's will and the will of God; and (2) religion as an efficacious way to harmonize all of the goods. To avoid instrumentalizing the value of religion—not to mention the problem of falling into a Deweyan humanism—the precise nature of the first definition needs to be clarified. What is it in a harmony between one's will and the will of God that is intrinsically valuable, such that we should count it among the incommensurable and irreducible goods?

Moving to the first volume of his theological *summa, Christian Moral Principles* (1983), the good is defined as "religion or holiness, which is harmony with God, found in the agreement of human individual and communal free choices with God's will."[66] Grisez refers the reader to his argument for the existence of God in *Beyond the New Theism.*[67] Now, however, he adds that "the general form of the reasoning by which one comes to know God from experience is simple enough," and it includes: the experience of the "world as incomplete"; the "awareness that we will die," which seems absurd to persons who have an "inherent sense of their own dignity"; the awareness of "solidarity and community with ancestors and descendents," which "suggests another dimension of reality"; and the "poignant sense of evil, especially of our own guilt," which "cries out for salvation and forgiveness."[68] He concludes:

> Nothing within the world of experience nor even the human self grasped in knowing this world is able to

overcome the absurdity of death, unite the community of mankind, overcome evil, and account for the reality of things not real of themselves. And so an Other, apart from the world of experience but required by it, is posited as an invisible and higher reality. This Other almost inevitably is thought of as a person or as something like a person. Virtually every human group seeks ways to live without tension and in harmony with this quasi-personal Other. The ways diverse peoples find and use constitute their religions. Thus, religion of some sort is almost a universal phenomenon.[69]

These remarks concerning the experiential soil of reasoning about God appear at first glance to move well beyond the argument given in *Beyond the New Theism*. If they are read carefully, however, it is clear that Grisez is not attempting to demonstrate the existence of God, but is rather speaking in general of experiences which prompt interest in the good of religion. This can prove confusing, because he mixes together the conclusion of his philosophical argument (that a transcendent Other exists) and general psychological (religion is attractive) and anthropological (everyone does it) observations of the sort we have encountered in his previous works.

Nevertheless, the problems and loose ends noted in the previous books continue in *Christian Moral Principles*. In the first place, Grisez continues to argue that the "starting point for humankind's relationship with God is the reception of his revelation with living faith."[70] He frequently reminds the reader that it is only by faith that God is known as personal, and as a lawgiver. Therefore, the definition of the good of religion, so described, includes a condition that can only be met by faith. As we will discuss in more detail in the next section, the good of religion is inconsistent with Grisez's account of the first principles of practical reason, which are self-evident and universally accessible to the natural light of practical reason. What is attractive about this good as it is viewed first in the light of the premoral natural law theory, and then in the light of faith, has not been shown to be compatible. The anthropological data is, at best, a way of confirming the existence of a value that must be grasped independently of faith, and thus only reiterates one side of the problem.

In the second place, the problem of the relation constituted by religion is not resolved. For instance, Grisez defines *sin* as "moral evil considered precisely insofar as it is contrary to the good of religion—contrary, that is, to the fulfillment of humankind's potential for harmony with God."[71] On the other hand, he maintains: "We tend to think of friendship with God as something too elevated to list alongside other human goods, and of sin as if it were an injury to God rather than a deprivation of human fulfillment."[72] When one acts against the good of religion, is one violating the friend, or the Other (God), or is one violating oneself? One would be tempted to say that the proper answer is *both,* for the value of a relationship requires reciprocity. Grisez, however, does not say this, but rather contends that sin, like immorality in general, is an act or attitude that is not in accord with one's own self-fulfillment. Setting aside the theological issue of whether this understanding of sin is consonant with the theological tradition in which Grisez works, it illuminates the problem of religion's relational object. If the disvalue (sin) is a particular lack of self-fulfillment originating in a free choice, then the value (religion) must consist principally in a particular modality of self-fulfillment. Grisez does not avail himself of the older Thomistic distinction between objective and subjective modes of happiness in the creature's relation to God (or at least some equivalent of the distinction).

Our dissatisfaction with this understanding of values and disvalues perhaps can be seen more clearly if we shift our attention from religion to justice. If one harms another person, is the *reason* for the disvalue simply that one has harmed or obstructed one's own potential to be just, or to realize one's potential to enjoy friends? Is there not also an offense to the other person which must fundamentally enter into a description of the disvalue, and hence into a description of the value as such? Insofar as justice involves other persons, one would not be inclined to define it exclusively in terms of an individual's way of adjusting to other goods. Yet this is what Grisez does with the good of religion. Unless some other principle can be brought to bear upon the situation, Grisez has stumbled into the lair prepared by Feuerbach and others, namely, that religion is a truncated perspective regarding the good that an individual wishes for himself or herself.

To summarize, we have raised at least three different issues concerning Grisez's definition of the good of religion. First, we pointed out that he is somewhat vague in accounting for why religion is a distinct value in the first place. The value, on one hand, is described as harmony with the will of God. This definition raises the problem of requiring an act of faith in revelation in order to grasp the value. On the other hand, religion is described as being a particularly efficacious way to harmonize the other values. Second, the architectonic function of religion is not adequately justified in light of his theory concerning the incommensurability of the basic goods. Third, the transcendent component of the value—namely, the good of the other to whom one is related—is less than clear. This is not simply a problem in the area of religion, but a problem with the axiology, at least insofar as it includes the value of interpersonal relationships. All of these issues will come home to roost in the discussions we shall undertake in the next sections.

3.3 Religion and Revelation

As we said earlier, in his article "Against Consequentialism" Grisez argues against any commensuration of the goods according to a hierarchy. He notes that a Jew or Christian "might object" to this, and say that the good of religion is "infinitely more important than other basic goods." Grisez's answer to this objection is worth quoting in full because it contains in summary the various issues we will treat in this section.

> Some Christians have held that the ethical sphere as a whole must give way to the religious. I think this position arises from a confusion between the created, *immanent good of religion*—which is neither more nor less absolute than other basic goods—and the goodness of God Himself. The good of religion is a finite participation in divine goodness, but so are other basic human goods, and the latter are neither reducible to nor commensurable with the good of religion. However, though there is no objective hierarchy which places religion above other basic human goods, it is reasonable to make one's religious commitment overarch one's whole existence. A commitment to the right sort of religion is an excellent principle by which to integrate one's identity. It gives ground to the highest hopes, yet at the same time allows wide scope to promote and protect other basic human goods. Christians believe that all other basic human goods take on a new meaning from the existential integration of goods with the basic Christian commitment. This commitment is to share in the redemptive work of Christ; the pursuit of other basic goods becomes an effort to build up the Body of Christ. Of course, nonchristians do not see things in this light, nor should they. Moreover, Christians should not confuse the importance religion has for them—because of their God-given, but freely accepted, faith and hope—with the importance which religion has as one basic human good among others. If these are confused, one is on a short road to religious fanaticism.[73]

As the passage indicates, Grisez in the first place wants to distinguish between the "immanent" good of religion and the good that is God, as well as the special gifts, faith and hope, which are given by God. In other words, the value of religion is to be defined apart from supernatural specifications, even though the value (now ascertained in terms of Christ) is grasped only through the mediation of the supernatural gift of faith. In the second place, the relative "importance" of the human good of religion and the supernatural goods should not be confused. In the third place, although there is no objective hierarchy making religion more important than any other human good, Christians believe that a commitment to the good of religion is an excellent principle for one's personal hierarchy—but this only makes sense, he insists, for believers.

What does faith add to the situation, such that a believer comes to view the immanent good of religion in a way that surpasses the obligation of non-Christians with regard to this particular value? As we have already seen, Grisez defines the good of religion in *Christian Moral Principles* in terms of the effort to achieve harmony between human choices and God's will. Immediately, we have the problem of how Grisez can maintain the distinction between the immanent good of religion and the supernatural goods, insofar as the definition now includes two supernatural goods—namely, God as personal, and the gift of faith by which this is known.

Additionally, there is the problem of how to keep ethics and the religious sphere distinct, and yet coherently related. This is further complicated by the question of *which* religion we are intending to interrelate with ethics: the immanent good of religion, or the good of religion once seen in the light of faith. Because, for Grisez, moral norms govern the manner by which goods are chosen, any difference in the formality under which religion is grasped as a good will become crucial. For example, if religion is one good, but is grasped differently depending upon the presence or absence of faith, then we run the risk of saying that there are two different, and morally significant, attitudes toward the same value. If, however, we have two different goods—religion as immanent, and religion as a share in supernatural life—then he must either change his axiology accordingly or run the risk of promoting the same moral attitude toward things which are different in value.

In the following pages we will examine Grisez's effort to resolve these problems. First, we will examine how faith determines the value of religion. Second, we will discuss how the Fpm is shaped by faith. Then, we will discuss certain axiological and moral issues which are generated by Grisez's move into moral theology.

Grisez holds, in *Christian Moral Principles,* that the "starting point for humankind's relationship with God is the reception of his revelation with living faith."[74] He defines faith as a "special relationship" to someone who "is not a human person." Faith "is not an experience of that person," he explains, for "the other's self remains hidden."[75] Rather, by faith one accepts the hidden God and makes a commitment. This includes "both welcoming God's deeds and assenting to the truth of the words by which he gives propositional expression to the mystery contained in the deeds."[76] In short, faith is a submission to divine revelation by way of an assent to revealed truths.

Faith also requires moral obedience, and indeed the very concept of moral obedience to divine law is introduced by the act of faith. As Grisez puts it: "Once God reveals himself as personal and extends his invitation to intimate friendship, humankind *has a moral reason* to cooperate with him."[77] This "mutual commitment" brings into being what Grisez calls "divine positive law": "In making an act of faith, one enters into communion with God by a mutual commitment. At the same time, however, one is aware of one's radical and unique dependence on God. Thus, while the covenant relationship requires our cooperation, only God is in a position to make certain decisions for the life we share with him. These decisions, which determine the requirements of divine positive law, therefore have authority for us.[78]

It is interesting to note that the morally obligatory laws which come into effect *with the faith relationship* include the two rules to love and obey God above all else, as well as the obligation to observe the superordinate status of the good of religion. This is interesting because while the Scholastic Catholic tradition and traditional Protestant thought have ordinarily regarded these either as precepts of the natural law, or at least as intuitions of conscience by which humanity is held accountable (e.g., in Calvin), Grisez now appears to place them exclusively within the category of divine positive law.[79]

Accordingly, in speaking of the old covenant, Grisez states that

> . . . the relationship of the old covenant draws all human life into its context—the context of the relationship with God. Harmony with God, religion, is universally recognized as a human good even outside the covenant relationship, but apart from that relationship it need not be considered the most basic form of harmony. However, the revelation recorded in the Old Testament at once makes it clear that his relationship has primacy. If its perfection is pursued consistently and diligently, every other human good will be served; but if harmony with God is not placed first, nothing else in life will go well. This point is made explicitly in the summary of the law and demand that God be loved above all else.[80]

As we see, faith radically changes the perception of the value of religion, for it not only gives content that religion otherwise lacks, but, more importantly, it introduces obligations which would not otherwise pertain. In short, revelation establishes the precise form which the "harmony" is to take. This strikes one as representing an orthodox Christian position on the matter.

We might recall, however, the example given earlier in *Beyond the New Morality,* in which Grisez argues that the choice between playing golf, going to church, and reading the papers cannot be determined on the basis of any objective difference in rank between the activities. Now, in contrast, consider this passage in *Christian Moral Principles*:

> Common morality enjoins that family members compose differences in religious practice in a way likely to promote the family's solidarity. The norm is nonabsolute, but sound at its level of specification, since apart from revelation religion is not superior to essential social solidarity, and since the good of religion in general does not generate any specific requirement of exclusive worship in one form. Christian revelation, however, is divisive, for it puts the claims of Jesus above those of family solidarity, requires that any form of religious practice incompatible with the gospel be avoided, and even demands a profession of faith when failure to make such a profession would be equivalent to denial by silence. Thus, the specifically Christian norm about religious differences and family solidarity sometimes requires what the nonabsolute norm of common morality would correctly exclude.[81]

When he goes on, in the same work, to say that "there would be no genuine religious community to which any person could belong apart from God's redemptive work,"[82] it is exceedingly difficult to see not only how we are referring to the same value of religion, but how the value can be upheld as a good that satisfies moral requirements in *any* respect without an explicit faith in Christianity.

In the passages quoted above, Grisez stresses the new attitudes and principles governing choice once one comes by faith under divine positive law. Here we find an emphasis upon the traditional biblical injunctions to subordinate one's life to God's will and laws, to give the highest priority to religion, and to be ready to accept the two-edged sword of commitment to God, even if it bring divisiveness. The problem is that, in underscoring what is distinctive about Christian moral obligation, the value of religion is rendered virtually inert prior to faith, and perhaps even a disvalue if it is not conducted within the commands of divine positive law and within the community of faith.

Hence, two incompatible things are being said about the value. On the one hand, as a general form of a basic human good, religion has no intrinsic properties that would obligate one to afford it priority. Indeed, one could not love God above all else, and could play a round of golf rather than going to church, and remain morally upright within the moral scheme outlined prior to faith. On the other hand, with faith it is believed that religion has primacy as a value, and that no genuine religious fellowship exists without the specific revelation of Christianity. In this light, the non-Christian individual who had to choose between playing golf, reading the papers, or going to church might as well have played golf. We are dealing with two different principles determining the moral goodness and badness of our attitudes and choices with regard to religion, depending upon whether we are viewing the matter from a rational position not presupposing faith, or whether a reference to divine positive law is included.

Grisez has to come down one way or another, and either say that we are dealing with two intrinsically different values (one of which is available to, and incumbent upon, choice only for those who believe), or say that we are dealing with one and the same value, but that without faith one cannot act rightly with regard to the value. Either of these options would be more internally consistent, but would lead to undermining the relationship between ethical and theological principles. The first option undercuts the continuity between the value and motivation in the transition from ethics to theological morality; the second option, which in our view is more serious, is tantamount to saying that ordinary morality is inefficacious without faith. The second position is held by many if not most Patristic and Scholastic theologians, but it needs careful treatment, for it entails upholding the natural law norm of human obligations to God even while recognizing the fact of sin, which has existentially (in Grisez's sense of the term) altered the situation. At this point, we need to look at his understanding of the relationship between faith and the Fpm.

Thus far we have seen that the religion of faith brings into effect the command to obey God above all else, the command to love God above all else, and a new appreciation of religion as a particularly important value. All of these are generated by faith in a personal God who reveals himself as a lawgiver. We have underscored the point that none of them are given in Grisez's basic account of practical reason and morality. It is necessary, then, to inquire into the systemic relations between the fideist elements and the overall framework constituted by the Fpm and the modes of responsibility.

Grisez has argued that "as far as experience indicates," integral human fulfillment is "only an ideal."[83] As we interpreted the system earlier, the weight of moral norms is given to the seventh and the eighth modes, which stipulate that no basic human good is to be demoted or directly acted against. One stays in accord with the general dictate of the Fpm insofar as one remains open to—that is, refuses to act directly against—each and every basic human good. The generality of the Fpm is of little help in determining the rectitude of precise kinds of conduct. Now, in the context of moral theology, Grisez argues that "faith teaches us that the ideal is realizable and, indeed is being realized as a part of God's larger plan for his creation."[84]

In *Christian Moral Principles,* the fideist content is brought to bear upon the ideality of the Fpm in this way:

> The first principle of all human morality is: In voluntarily acting for human goods and avoiding what is opposed to them, one ought to choose and otherwise will those and only those possibilities whose willing is compatible with a will toward integral human fulfillment. Such a fulfillment is more than an ideal; it is being accomplished in the fulfillment of all things in Jesus. Thus, Christian love transforms the first principle of morality into a more definite norm: *One ought to will those and only those possibilities which contribute to the integral human fulfillment being realized in the fulfillment of all things in Jesus.*[85]

"Herein," he adds, "lies the ultimate significance of realizing human goods and of the first principle of morality which guides choices toward these goods."[86] What concretely is added or changed by this far-reaching specification of the Fpm? Grisez answers that there is given "a new *incentive* to pursue human goods in a morally upright way."[87]

Although faith "clarifies," or calls "attention to," the basic "principles of natural law," Grisez nonetheless continues to insist that "all of them [the principles] can in principle be known without faith."[88] As we have already pointed out several times, this statement is not consistent with what Grisez says concerning the fideist condition built into his more recent definition of the good of religion (one of the principles of the natural law), not to mention his position on the two commandments which give a superordinate status to obeying and loving God above all else. None of these are included among the *prima principia* of practical reason, nor among the modes of responsibility. We do not wish to belabor this problem any further here, and will take it up in the course of our final assessment. However, it would be worthwhile to take a careful look at what Grisez says about the relationship between faith and morality in order to see whether there is some other level of consistency achieved by his account.

Grisez argues that in moral theology there are no specific norms "other than those required to direct action to the fulfillment of the possibilities proper to human nature as such."[89] Whatever the fideist version of the Fpm accomplishes, it cannot fundamentally alter the fact that moral norms govern choices about human goods. Grisez holds, for example, that even charity "does not dispose to any human fulfillment other than that in basic human goods."[90] The problem, then, is clear enough. How does the transformed version of the Fpm give any material content or direction to choice that is not already available?

If faith is required for the incentive to pursue and choose human goods in a morally upright manner, then it would seem that ordinary morality is quite inefficacious, at least on the existential level. If, on the other hand, faith is only a peculiar viewpoint toward or facet of what practical reason prescribes and does anyway, then no specific norms are introduced by Christianity, except perhaps an admonition to be more sincere and earnest in what one is already supposed to be doing. To paraphrase Karl Barth, moral theology is nothing more than the prerogative to speak about humanity—or in this case, human "goods"—in an especially loud voice.

Grisez's answer to this dilemma is interesting:

> The answer to the question is paradoxical. One begins to resolve the paradox only by recognizing that humankind is fallen and redeemed. Original sin transforms the human situation in many ways, making moral uprightness seem unattractive and the irrationality of immorality seem unimportant. . . . The teachings of faith neither conflict with any of the general principles of morality nor add any new principles to them. Yet faith does generate specific norms

proper to the Christian life. It does this by proposing options both possible for and appealing to fallen men and women—options which either cannot be conceived without faith or would lack sufficient appeal to be considered in deliberation in the absence of Christian hope. Specific moral norms are generated only when proposals are articulated as appealing possibilities for choice. . . . The human race is in a pathological condition. At the same time, it must be in training to accomplish the spectacular feat of reaching integral fulfillment. The facts of the human condition must be taken into account in considering the practical implications of the true, general requirements of human morality. If the facts—which are only fully disclosed by revelation—are ignored, people will behave more or less unrealistically.[91]

If we are interpreting him correctly, Grisez is arguing that the general principles of practical reason and morality are naturally accessible, and are not altered by moral theology. However, human beings are in a "pathological condition," which includes: (1) ignorance of the fact that integral human fulfillment is possible, and that it is actually being achieved by the kingdom of Christ; and (2) a powerful temptation to do evil in order to achieve good, which persists despite our premoral attraction to the basic goods or principles. Although practical reason dictates that each good is to be promoted and respected, the appeal of some goods seems to require a demotion of others. In other words, without faith a consequentialist ethic seems to be justified by the practical limitations and conflicts of our lives.

Christianity, therefore, introduces a new motivational "appeal" to be morally upright, and to reject any course of action that does not promise our integral human fulfillment. It does so both by introducing "facts" and by stipulating norms which help us to keep the moral project in mind. To put it bluntly, Christianity teaches us how to be true eudaimonists without falling into a consequentialist ethic that arbitrarily shortchanges the scope and meaning of integral human fulfillment. This represents Grisez's effort to integrate the pole of respect for goods and the pole of self-fulfillment, the integration of faith and practical reason, as well as the ultimate consonance between what could be called the "prophetic" dimension of the religion of faith (with its theistic referent) and the more mundane pursuit of this-worldly goods. The goods, as categoricals, are no longer in a holding pattern, but are viewed as concrete in the kingdom of Christ. The burden of the law is lightened, for we now have specific and concrete *ordinatio* for the goods which, prior to faith, appear to be a miscellany of categoricals.

Again, in *Christian Moral Principles,* Grisez asks: "How can anyone live in such a world without resorting to the evils necessary to cope with it?" Put in another way, *how* be moral? There is only "one possibility," he argues: "Only in such a new covenant could faithfulness to God and love of all the human goods coincide. . . . members of the new redemptive community must have solid assurance that they will really be fulfilled by being faithful to God and to their own fulfillment.[92] As we mentioned in the previous chapter, it is important to keep in mind how profoundly Grisez's ethics is shaped by his response to consequentialism, or proportionalism. Although he argues that moral logic itself can demonstrate the "meaninglessness" of consequentialism, he nevertheless believes that correcting the motivational pull toward consequentialism requires theological support.[93] The only way to provide this support is to restore the motivational wellsprings of the Fpm by showing that integral fulfillment is something more than a heuristic ideal. The general principles built into the Fpm are left intact by moral theology, and the specific norms introduced by faith are only buttressing the motivation that should be operative in the first place.

In a commitment to Jesus, he argues, we understand that "there is no need to choose between human good and friendship with God." Precisely because it is no longer necessary to envision a conflict between human goods and the choice of a greater good, the either-or ethics of sinful humanity is overcome. This is what grounds the "hope sufficient to motivate Jesus' disciples."[94] Whereas the recipients of revelation in the old covenant obeyed divine revelation, and accordingly subordinated all goods to the good of a religious harmony with God (Grisez frequently suggests that the Jews fell into a mistaken, though sincere, consequentialism in this regard),[95] the new covenant overcomes these "limitations," and shows the "coincidence" of all goods in Jesus. Jesus looks very much like the Kantian postulate of the *summum bonum,* except that the Christian expects a real, not just a regulative, payoff. As Grisez states: "The act of faith, by which Christians give themselves to God, will not be a package without contents, but a package full of human good things."[96]

From the transformed version of the Fpm, Grisez goes on to generate more specific Christian modes of responsibility. Like the previous list of modes, they stand midway between the general norm of willing in accord with integral human fulfillment in Jesus, and even more specific norms.[97] He views these modes as an articulation of the scriptural beatitudes. The modes are summarized as follows:

(1) To expect and accept all good, including the good fruits of one's own work, as God's gift. . . .

(2) To accept one's limited role in the Body of Christ and fulfill it. . . .

(3) To put aside or avoid everything which is not necessary or useful in the fulfillment of one's personal vocation. . . .

(4) To endure fearlessly whatever is necessary or useful for the fulfillment of one's personal vocation. . . .

(5) To be merciful according to the universal and perfect measure of mercy which God has revealed in Jesus. . . .

(6) To strive to conform one's whole self to living faith, and purge anything which does not meet this standard. . . .

(7) To respond to evil with good, not with resistance, much less with destructive action. . . .

(8) To do no evil that good might come of it, but suffer evil together with Jesus in cooperation with God's redeeming love. . . .[98]

These modes could well deserve an essay in their own right. The fifth mode, for instance, introduces the concept of mercy, which is certainly a distinctive moral attitude. The second mode entails a norm of personal vocation, which is not included in his previous list of the modes.[99] The third mode contains the notion of a dominant end that John Rawls raises in connection with Ignatius of Loyola's vow to do everything for the greater glory of God. All of the theological modes are redolent of a language of the virtues and of character that is not so apparent in the previous list. It would take us too far afield, however, to dwell on the modes. We need to retrieve the systematic question of what is added to common principles of morality.

Grisez maintains that only revelation tells us of some norms, for example, "that we are to participate in the liturgy; to protect, live within, and hand on the structure of the Church; to carry on and extend the redemptive work of Jesus to all places and times."[100] Apparently these also include certain attitudes which are inherent to the *imitatio Christi,* such as mercifulness. He does not mention, in this regard, the two superordinate commands concerning obedience and love of God, but one could infer that they are implicit in the theological modes. With the impetus gained from the modal specifications of the Christian life, one might expect Grisez to emphasize the unique motivational and behavioral aspects of Christianity.

He does not do this but, instead, abruptly changes course back to the problem of obedience to God versus the pursuit of human goods, and states: "In most cases we can see, with the help of faith, the wisdom of norms proposed in divine revelation, for they can be reduced to human goods and the modes of responsibility [i.e., the nontheological list]."[101] In other words, when we ask why it is right to obey a specific norm generated by faith in revelation, "we are seeking this norm's basis in human goods and modes of responsibility."[102] We are thrown back to the issue of how it is that revelation issues norms which are virtually the same as those given in the basic system of morality. *Having diluted the efficacy of morality without faith, he now speaks in a way that dilutes the unique features of morality with faith.* A moral attitude (or norm) such as mercy, for instance, is to be reduced back to the motives and norms of the initial framework of morality.

The fact of the matter is that Grisez returns over and over again to the problem of consequentialism, and his moral theology appears to be another (and perhaps the ultimate) way to overcome it. Just as in the previous list of modes of responsibility, Grisez here reemphasizes the importance of the seventh and eighth theological modes. The difference made by specifically Christian norms is the motivation with regard to the goods. As Grisez argues, the nonbelieving person who is inclined to respect the basic principles of morality can enjoy a kind of "fragile rectitude." Such a person, he says, "might consistently respect all the other modes of responsibility, but sooner or later will be tempted to violate the eighth one."[103] He continues by saying, "One either accepts a share in Jesus' self-oblation or separates oneself from him by irreverently violating a human good." This leads Grisez to articulate an unusual sense of *moralia contra mundum*:

> Each society's conventional morality is based upon a limited set of goals, a requirement of fairness necessary for a common life, and the exclusion of certain types of behavior which are unreasonable in view of the common purposes. Conventional moralities represent workable compromises between human aspira-

tions for fulfillment and the hard realities of the fallen human condition. Such moralities are an aspect of culture which defines "the world" over against Jesus. For this reason, the Fathers of the Church were right in regarding the standards of pagan morality as norms of immorality and the pagan virtues as vices.[104]

It is an unusual sense of morality *contra mundum* because, whereas Patristic theorists like Augustine (who delivered the infamous line that the virtues of the pagans, and the Stoics in particular, are only splendid vices) conceived of the difference as between a love of God and a love of self, Grisez holds that the problem with "the world" is that it is too ready to sacrifice one good to another, or to a greater, good.[105]

This reversal of perspective is important, and is crucial to understanding Grisez's thought. For what he is saying is that the chief importance of the Christian faith is that it is necessary for living in conformance with human morality. Although he reverses the axiology of Augustine (the *amor sui* in contrast to the *amor dei*), he ends up affirming a Christian morality that is in many respects more stringent than Augustine's. The "facts" and the "motivation" introduced by faith are absolutely necessary to the moral project, even though the principles are no different from what is stipulated apart from faith. Does this imply that there is no possibility of moral righteousness apart from Christianity, or that the specifically moral facet of natural law requires faith? Grisez maintains that the Church teaches that "somehow those who have not heard the gospel can be united with Jesus by living faith."[106] How this is possible is, of course, a matter of theological doctrine beyond the ken of our inquiry. It is, however, Grisez's answer to the question.

The revised version of the Fpm represents Grisez's way of trying to reconcile the respect for human goods with the quest for self-fulfillment, the immanent and transcen-

dent poles of religion, the domain of moral principles and
the specifics introduced by moral theology, and in general
the integration of faith and practical reason. His theory
takes a decidedly eudaimonistic turn once it moves into
moral theology, for faith in the Kingdom allows one to
envision integral human fulfillment as something more than
an ideal. This makes the human pursuit of morality more
"appealing," because Jesus makes it clear that a "life of
good deeds" is a "guide to one's own true self-interest."[107]

Grisez argues that the dilemma of having to choose between God and human goods—and correlatively, of having
to choose one good over another in order to achieve a
greater net good—is overcome by Christian faith. As we
discussed earlier, the coincidence of integral human fulfillment and commitment to God overcomes the ethical
either-or. In contrast to what Grisez is suggesting, Søren
Kierkegaard argues in *Fear and Trembling* that the motivational core of faith is neither an obedient resignation to
duty nor simply a desire to be happily fulfilled. Rather, it
is a self-donation to another person, in which one believes
that all else will be given besides.[108] Neither duty nor self-
fulfillment are the chief focus of faith, although, by faith,
both are completed and satisfied. We offer this contrast
only to illuminate Grisez's position. For Grisez, faith is
principally marked by the assurance of the concrete possibility of self-fulfillment. It is not a move into a distinct
sphere of values and motives. Faith counsels and assures
one that one can be happy with regard to the goods which
are picked out in the pre-Christian setting.

In addition to this, Grisez also holds that a commitment
to God and a commitment to self-fulfillment cannot vie
with one another because God, as a good, is not a human
good (and therefore is never something to be chosen), and
further that charity is not a human action (but is always
a gift received). To the extent that God is chosen, he
is always chosen as the human good of *our* relationship
to him; that is, under the rubric of the human good of

religion, which is a mode of self-fulfillment. Yet the human good of religion is defined by an act of faith in which one makes a commitment to God. In the following pages we will examine the axiological and motivational problems which ensue from Grisez's position.

In *Christian Moral Principles* Grisez remarks that "an adequate treatise in Christian moral principles" must "explain the dynamic unity of the human and divine aspects of Christian life without mixing the two."[109] Just as the human and divine are "distinct but inseparable in Jesus," the Christian has both a "human nature and an adopted share in divinity."[110] Whatever this might mean in christological theory, it has some interesting implications for Grisez's moral theology.

He states that the divine life that Jesus communicates by the gift of the spirit is "not just one human good among others" and indeed "is beyond all human goods."[111] Furthermore, the achievement of integral human fulfillment can only be realized by God's action. The achievement of the state of integral human fulfillment (the goal of the moral life for ethics and moral theology) is not a human act either. While we can "cooperate with God by a life of faith in Jesus," integral human fulfillment "in relation to human moral effort alone" remains only an "ideal, not a goal toward which we can project lives."[112] This appears to be a case of taking away with one hand what was just given with the other; that is to say, the new Fpm referent that makes possible the new, or efficacious, motivation is not a part of human moral work. It appears to be a contradiction in terms, or at least a paradox of some sort that goes beyond a simple rejection of Pelagianism.

Here it is necessary to keep in mind the context for these remarks. Having emphasized that the Christian version of the Fpm allows one to envision integral human fulfillment as something more than an ideal, Grisez now wants to insure that a religious either-or doesn't emerge from that position. Thus, he argues:

Immoral choices cannot reasonably be understood as opting for human goods over divine goodness. For divine goodness cannot be considered in deliberation as a possible object of choice. Even when one accepts divine adoption by making the act of faith, what one chooses is chosen insofar as it is humanly good—that is, as an instance of the good of religion. Insofar as divine adoption transcends the good of religion, it is not chosen by the Christian, but received entirely as a gift. Since we cannot choose divine goodness, it makes no sense to speak of our choosing something else in preference to it.[113]

Granted that any human choice is a choice to be in relation to something or another, the question is whether it is possible to choose oneself in relation to that which transcends one's own immanent goods. This question can be asked without having to delve into the complex theological problem of whether or not a human person can directly choose grace; rather, regardless of how one gets into the state of grace that transcends, by supernature, specifically human goods, the problem is the status of one's choices, attitudes, and actions once having received it. According to Grisez's theory, all of the basic goods are immanent attractions, and Christianity makes not only religion, but the entire ensemble of the goods, all the more attractive. Given his own position, why shouldn't we say that Christianity makes religion a more attractive option or, to use his word, a better "preference"? Indeed, since this is made possible by a commitment to the divinity of Christ, why not say that there is a hierarchy being introduced? That is to say, prior to choice the goods can be viewed merely as facets of our own fulfillment, or they can be viewed as participations in a divine good; and by faith we see the superiority of the latter (both because of the objective goodness of God, and because it entails a dominant end that is also inclusive).

Without further qualifications, Christian morality turns out to be founded upon a unique relationship which lacks any relational facets significant for human choice and action. The problem is highlighted if we consider the following remarks Grisez makes about charity in *Christian Moral Principles*. He first states that "charity in the Christian life is the first principle of a specifically Christian morality," and, by motivating faith itself, it is the "fundamental option, the basic human act, of the Christian life."[114] Then (on the same page) he notes that, since charity is a participation in the divine nature, "Christian love itself is not a human act, although it is related to human acts." Finally (and again on the same page) Grisez concludes that "charity is a disposition toward fulfillment in divine life. As such, it is not something one is asked to do but something one is asked to remain in. Love of God is not a human action, and is presupposed rather than directly commanded." The statements contradict one another.

In the first statement he contends that charity is the "basic human act" of Christian morality; in the second, he states that it is "not a human act," but it is "related to human acts"; in the third, he argues that the love of God is not a human action, but is something we are asked to "remain in." How one can remain in an attitude (or be disposed, in the sense of a virtue), without thereby choosing to act in such a way, is quite mysterious. It is tantamount to saying—in a context that would not be altogether different—that one should love one's spouse, but that such love is not one's action, and indeed is not a matter of choice at all. Certainly, in a theological vein, even if the virtue of charity is received or infused as a gift, it is not something that remains extrinsic to the person's choice and actions.[115] To say simply that charity is "related to" human actions is either to have a rather vague concept of the term *relation,* or to suggest that "related to" is in no way similar to what is ordinarily meant by a relationship (meaning at the very least mutual actions constituting a common good of one form or another). In other words, the fact that we are dealing with a difference between natural and supernatural goods does not obviate the need to account for the moral significance of reciprocity, and the significance, for choice, of the other person to whom one is related.

To make matters more complicated, Grisez says elsewhere in *Christian Moral Principles* that "divine goodness and human fulfillment are not direct alternatives. The love of God includes and transforms all the natural forms of simple volition. Hence, out of love of God, Christians act both for the human fulfillment to which they are naturally disposed by simple volition and also for fulfillment in divine goodness. The morally significant acts of Christian life are always inspired both by love of God and by love of some human good."[116] This indicates that we now have two completely different theories to explain why there cannot be a morally significant choice between a transcendent good (in this case, supernatural) and the immanent human goods. The first theory, given in the passages cited in the previous paragraphs, explains that we cannot choose between the two (or prefer one to the other) because the transcendent, supernatural good cannot be chosen at all. This theory reduces moral choice to the immanent goods. While it avoids any kind of fanaticism, it renders the specifically Christian norms of morality completely irrelevant— for the conditions specifying the Christian life are not human goods, and are not human acts. How, according to Grisez's axiological principles, something can be called a good or a value without practical reason's consideration of it as a possibility for choice and action is not explained.

The second theory, outlined in the passage immediately above, states that one cannot choose between the immanent and the transcendent because the choice of one, properly understood, includes the other. This theory is capable of retaining a sense of continuity between moral principles and Christian norms because there is a morally significant motivation at work in both spheres. It emphasizes the transformative aspects of Christian faith and charity, while retaining the place of human choice and action. Further-more, it reflects the traditional biblical notion that in choosing God all else will be given besides. To the extent that one wishes to establish continuity between moral prin-ciples and moral theology, the second theory is preferable. However, the second theory, if it is to make sense, entails that there can be a morally significant choice between the transcendent and immanent poles of the goods (that one can choose a relationship to the Other for its own sake, and love it above all else), as well as a morally significant choice for the sake of a supernatural mode of fulfillment.

Grisez holds to both theories and does not reconcile them. One theory eliminates a decisional either-or by mak-ing the terms of the decision reside in completely different orders, and therefore there is no relational intelligibility to such a choice. The other theory envisions the terms of the decision as part and parcel of the same immanent good of religion, and therefore there cannot be a relational dis-tinction significant for choice The first moves by an abso-lute separation, the latter by a reduction.

In our estimation, this explains a number of anomalies in his system once he moves into moral theology. These anomalies have to do with what could be called the *ordo amoris* (the order of love). For example, consider the three following remarks made on the same page of *Christian Moral Principles*:

> In making an act of living faith (that is, faith motivated by the love of God), one makes a free choice to accept God's personal communication. The choice is made *for the sake of the human goods of truth and religion.* By the commitment of faith, one causes one-self to share in the human goods of the Christian community. The act of faith also contributes intrin-sically to constituting, from the believer's side, the intimate relationship with God.
>
> Now, in the act of living faith, one's acceptance of God's proposal is transformed by being made *out of*

love of him. This transformation occurs by God's gift, the love poured forth in our hearts through the Holy Spirit, and not by a self-creative act of our own.

To understand the role of human goods in the act of faith it is necessary to bear in mind that any human choice whatsoever is directed to some basic human good. . . . Such an act of reasonable submission, which is not suspended when the gift of faith is received, is *directed to the human goods of truth and religion.*[117]

Two things should be noticed in these passages. In the first place, Grisez states in the first of the passages that the *act* of faith constitutes, at least in part, a relationship with God. In fact, he states that "one causes oneself to share" in this good. In the second and third passages, he argues that supernaturality of faith is not a self-creative act of our own, and that it is something received. Although one would think that it is now necessary to explain how both facets—the act of the self and the reception of a gift—are interrelated, Grisez does not do so.

In the second place, one should take note of the difference in the motivational referent. In the first and third passages he states that the act is "for the sake of" or "directed to" the immanent goods of truth and religion, while in the second he maintains that it is done out of love of God. The latter, of course, calls attention to a value response to a good that is transcendent in the technical sense of the term: viz., to something that is not merely immanent. Perhaps Grisez wants to say that we can only act for a human good—in this case the good of religion. By his own theory, however, not only is God not a human good, but the condition of grasping God as a good involves the mediation of supernatural gifts which are not human goods. Once again, we find ourselves in the dilemma of either (1) separating the two orders of value, in which case when we consent to the good of religion we cannot be consenting to both orders as integrally the same value; or

(2) reducing, for the purpose of choice, one value to the other, in which case the essential difference between them cannot be maintained—but it is precisely such a difference that justifies Grisez's argument that the value of God and the value of human goods cannot, in principle, be alternatives for choice. Without further distinctions, it is difficult to understand what is being loved for what reason.

Using the life of Jesus as a model for what he is speaking about, Grisez argues that Jesus chose to live according to a religious commitment, for a "commitment to doing God's will is a commitment to the good of religion, that is, to that human fulfillment which consists in harmony between humankind and God."[118] He adds that this is "also a commitment to the persons involved: to humankind and God." Thus, he interprets the scriptural story of Jesus' fast in the desert in this way: "The choice here is between satisfying a natural appetite, hunger, and carrying out the fast which had been chosen for religious motives. There is nothing inherently wrong in eating, but it would be wrong to break one's fast out of mere hunger once one committed oneself to it in one's effort to do God's will."[119] The point that Grisez wishes to make is that Jesus did not choose between human goods and a divine good, for he chose the human good of religion (harmony with God) which he had made the basis of his own personal hierarchy or life plan. Nevertheless, he also states that Jesus' commitment was to the person of God, who is not simply an immanent human good.

What moral lesson are we to learn from the story? Grisez has already made it clear that basic human goods—such as life or health—are not to be equated with the good of satisfying an urge. We might conclude, then, that Jesus chose to participate in a *basic* human good rather than in a merely instrumental one. However, if Jesus chose the human good of religion rather than health (which appears to be the meaning of Grisez's interpretation), then we want to know why he chose this value. To say that he chose religion

because he had already made a commitment to this particular value as a way of organizing his life plan simply does
not answer the question. The story would work equally
well (although the moral point would change dramatically)
if he had gone into the desert to play the harp, and thereby
participate in the basic good of play—in which case the
devil might tempt him with the good of religion. Is it unreasonable to want to understand problematic contrasts
and comparisons between goods in order to appreciate
why Jesus made the choice that he did, and what reasons
and motives were involved?

In this regard, if the story is to be read as a moral lesson
in subordinating goods to one's relationship to God, then
there is not only a hierarchy involved, but also a range of
morally relevant choices: i.e., there are not only individual
goods one can rightly choose, but also complex relations
between goods which can profoundly alter the terms of
moral choice. The relations are complex because the moral
self has the freedom to relate problematically not only to
immanent goods *inter alia,* but also to a supernatural
person who is in no wise immanent. Thus, there is the
possibility of risk, of morally relevant decisions, and of
interesting either-or situations for moral agency. At least
theoretically, none of this necessitates a consequentialist
ethic of suppressing a value for the sake of another.

As we have pointed out before, Grisez's axiology is one-
dimensional, and this influences his understanding of moral
choice. For Grisez there are two types of values which
either cannot be chosen or ought not to be chosen; namely,
divine goods which we cannot directly choose, and merely
instrumental goods which ought not to be chosen as ends
in themselves. The type of good relevant to moral choice is
a "basic value." Accordingly, the only type of morally
relevant choice is whether one will be a consequentialist
or will remain open to participation in all of the basic
goods without restricting or shortchanging one's fulfillment.
Grisez's axiology wanders in the shadowland of Kant's

antinomies of practical reason and is in need of postulates to harmonize the goods.

This, in our judgment, is why his move into moral theology becomes ultimately disappointing. Rather than introducing new levels of opportunity and complexity with respect to value and choice, the religion of faith plunges us back into the sphere of immanence by giving us added incentive, even an obligation, to remain there—just as Kant's postulates keep the moral project afloat once he reaches the antinomies of practical reason. This stems, in part, from Grisez's method of absorbing ethics into revealed religion in order to reposit ethics in its "natural" state. Lest our criticism be taken wrongly, it is important to say that we are not suggesting that moral theology should not be in continuity with, or supportive of, the moral project of practical reason. For Grisez, however, faith makes up for a certain deficiency in the motivation that ought to be at work without faith. As we put it earlier, the results are these: on the one hand, the integrity of practical reason prior to faith is radically called into question, for inefficacy of motive is a worm that spoils the moral apple. On the other hand, once faith is introduced, the efficacy of the eudaimonistic motive is restored, but little if anything is added in terms of unique content or motivation.

Moreover, although much of Grisez's concern is focused on the problem of consequentialism, one is led to wonder whether his ethics, at this point, only avoids consequentialism *per accidens*. Consider, for example, a moral agent who wants to be fulfilled, but who lacks the "facts" of the religion of faith, as well as the gift of charity. On the basis of experience, he judges that human fulfillment requires him to act for the greatest net good in any situation of choice. Given the finite and problematic nature of the world, this requires that some fulfillments be abandoned and others pursued. Consider, on the other hand, a moral agent who enjoys the wherewithal of the religion of faith. She, too, wants to be fulfilled, but she believes that her fulfillment is guaranteed so long as she "remains in" charity and refuses to shortchange any of the goods by a consequentialist calculus. Although we might expect these two agents to act differently with regard to the goods (especially once divine or ecclesiastical positive laws are introduced), it is difficult to see how their motivation is different; for each allows himself to be determined by the prospect of fulfillment, and they differ only according to the "facts" which respectively inform the nature of that prospect. Grisez, of course, would point out that the consequentialist stands prepared to act against (in Grisez's sense of the term) any human good for the sake of some aggregate good, and so long as he has this intent, his motive is significantly different from that of an agent whose choices remain inclusivistic.

Our example, however, is pointing out that, in lieu of evidence to show that human flourishing requires an inclusivist, integral state of completion, it is not so clear that an agent must abandon *some* fulfillments in order to respect absolutely each and every instance of a basic good. To argue otherwise is tantamount to arguing for a noneudaimonistic standard of moral motivation (the duty to keep each of the goods in a holding pattern, even though one does not know whether there is any teleological point to the miscellany). If the first agent were to be informed of the credal "facts," he would be expected to change his behavior but not his motivation, for the "appealing" facts of the gospel, according to Grisez, presuppose and give added incentive to precisely that motivation in the first place. In other words, the only thing distinguishing the believer and the consequentialist is the seemingly incidental factor that the believer has certain information (through no agency of her own) that permits her to play the stakes of human fulfillment somewhat differently, as well as a gift of charity (again, through no agency of her own) which imparts efficacy to the eudaimonistic motive.

A careful reading of *Christian Moral Principles* indicates

that Grisez *sometimes* suggests a transcendent pole for some of the values and, along with that, a respect or concern for values which go beyond a mere interest in self-fulfillment. For instance, he contends that "no one can live with two ultimate orientations."[120] Here, despite having argued to the opposite effect against Scholastic moral theory, he criticizes the proponents of "liberalized" Christianity who "generally ignore heaven."[121] Furthermore, despite his argument, which we considered in the previous chapter, that the concept of the common good adds nothing to moral principles, Grisez now states: "Plainly, the whole universe is the greatest good, because it is the fullest created expression of God's goodness. Human fulfillment is only a part of this whole and, as such, not ultimate. . . . We are called to live for God's glory, not merely for our own happiness."[122]

While we had quoted him earlier to say that human beings cannot be ordered as a part to a whole, he is willing to say in this theological context that the concept of the body of Christ is important for Christian moral behavior, because "the welfare and fulfillment of every part of the body is bound up with the welfare of the whole."[123] The notion of a hierarchy prior to, and pertinent to, choice is introduced, along with a different emphasis on the level of motives. Whether this is a matter of Grisez's merely including theological doctrines by way of exposition, or whether he believes that theology renders them pertinent to the moral life in a way that ordinary ethics does not, is difficult, if not impossible, to determine. Unfortunately, he does not comment upon this apparent reversal of perspective concerning the common good, nor on the implications it might hold for the rest of his system. In the next section, we will point out that Finnis is more explicit about the problem.

Moreover, in *Christian Moral Principles,* one finds Grisez in some passages suggesting that moral growth in the Christian life (i.e., holiness) requires one to break out of the ordinary motivation with regard to immanent goods. For example, he writes: "As St. John of the Cross explains, the good shared by God and the soul is common to both. Moreover, one who adheres to God with living faith is not seeking eternal life with God for the sake of something—a merely human good—other and less than God, but for the sake of the divine goodness by which one hopes to be fulfilled with God."[124] Although the quest or "hope" of self-fulfillment is still prominent in this passage, and although the context is strictly theological, there is a strong implication that the motive is not operating solely within the ambit of self-fulfillment. A "personal loyalty" to God, he argues, is an "aspect of the moral motivation of Christian life [that] is essential to its growth toward perfection."[125] Here he reinforces his point by citing the passage from Paul: "But whatever gain I had, I counted it as loss for the sake of Christ" (Phil. 3:7).

These comments, of course, imply a more complex understanding of values and motivation. The fact that they are few and far between in his writings does not mean that they should not be taken seriously. Indeed, as Grisez completes the subsequent volumes in his *summa* of moral theology, it will be interesting to see whether the transcendent pole of values, and the corresponding difference it makes for motivation, is given more weight. At this point, we have to conclude that Grisez's remarks about the transcendent pole either contradict what he says elsewhere or, more seriously, are out of step with the main thrust of his systematic understanding of practical reason, moral principles, and the relation between values and motivation. We shall now turn to John Finnis's treatment of the subject.

3.4 Finnis's Treatment of Practical Reason and Religion

John Finnis's writings provide us with a unique opportunity to reflect further upon Grisez's work. Grisez and

Finnis hold the same view on the substantive and method-ological issues concerning the nature of human values, the role of the Fpm and the modes of responsibility, and the critique of consequentialism. Thus we have two different minds working with the same philosophical premises. Finnis's work, however, affords an interesting counterpoint to Grisez's on the issue of practical reason and religion because he does not explicitly advance the system into the domain of moral theology; and, as we will see, he has some reservations about the definition and meaning of the good of religion. A brief examination of Finnis's position will help us to explore whether there is any way within the sys-tem to alleviate, clarify, or otherwise advance beyond some of the problems we have dealt with heretofore.

In the chapter of *Natural Law and Natural Rights* in which Finnis deals with the basic goods, he says that "there is the value of what, since Cicero, we summarily call 'reli-gion'."[126] He notes: "I follow Grisez in using this label, but am aware that 'religion is not an analytical concept of anything, but a topical response to certain problems in the roman subsection of an ecumenic-imperial society'."[127] He goes on to admit: "Misgivings may be aroused by the notion that one of the basic human values is the establish-ment and maintenance of the proper relationships between oneself (and the orders one can create and maintain) and the divine."[128]

At the very outset Finnis observes that those who deny that there is a "universal order of things" that transcends what is known by the natural sciences will have reason to doubt the value of religion, for the practical thrust of the value consists in things which can and ought to be done with regard to this "order of things"[129] (i.e., to establish and maintain a relationship). This presupposes not only the possibility of the existence of such an order, but also that is has significance for human agency. The problem is cast in Kantian terms. Lacking metaphysical, empirical, or historical evidence to demonstrate the existence of a trancendent order, much less a personal God, one is indeed faced with the problem of affirming the good of religion.

Before he defers the problem to another chapter in the book, Finnis has two things to say. In the first place, he asks whether it is "reasonable to deny that it is, at any rate, peculiarly important to have thought reasonably and (where possible) correctly about these questions of the origins of cosmic order and of human freedom and reason —whatever the answer to those questions turns out to be, and even if the answers have to be agnostic or negative?" Here practical reason can at least affirm the good of the inquiry. If nothing else, this would come under the good of knowledge. In the second place, he asks whether "one's own sense of 'responsibility,' in choosing what one is to be and do, amounts to a concern that is not reducible to the concern to live, play, procreate, relate to others, and be intelligent?"[130]

The first question does not adequately differentiate the good of religion from Finnis's description of the basic good of knowledge. Although the good of thinking about the problem of religion might be construed as an entry point into philosophy of religion, the practical value of religion, much less of a religion, is still unclear. The second question, however, strikes closer to the practical thrust of the value, for it is a "concern" about the scope and meaning of one's conduct. At this juncture, the reader has a sense that some interesting things will be said about the problem of religion and practical reason. Finnis asks: "Without wishing to beg any question, may we not for convenience call that concern, which is concern for a good consisting in an irreducibly distinct form of order, religious?" In this regard Finnis's definition of the value of religion as a concern for an irreducible and distinct form of "order" contains at least the possibility of avoiding problems we discussed with Grisez's definition, namely, the reduction of the value of religion back to a concern for the other goods. Finnis suggests that the good of religion may be a good quite unlike the others. Noting that "the present remarks are no more than placeholders," he defers the discussion to the final chapter of his book.[131]

The final chapter of *Natural Law and Natural Rights* is entitled, "Nature, Reason, God."[132] Finnis begins his reflections by observing that individual and communal participation in human goods is "even at best, extremely limited."[133] This is evident not only in terms of the fragility of substantive goods such as health, but perhaps even more poignantly in the "succession of human persons" in which individuals become separated by time and death. The question arises whether "my good (and the well-being of my communities) has any *further* point, i.e., whether it relates to any more comprehensive human participation in good."[134]

Finnis explains that this is "an extension of, or analogous to" certain unsettled questions regarding the good of friendship. For example:

> An aspect of my well-being is the well-being of my friend; if he or she is ruined or destroyed, I am worse off. What then is to be made of (and done in) situations in which his or her well-being can be secured only by my ruin or destruction? What is the good of it? This question does not question the good of my friend's good, either as his or hers or as an aspect of mine; but it asks whether *further* sense can be made of the whole situation, in which the limitation of one's participation in human good arises not from time and decay but from a kind of conflict of opportunities.[135]

Finnis continues by pointing out that it is necessary to inquire whether there is any further way to understand why it is reasonable to sacrifice oneself to a friend or a community which will pass away sooner or later anyway.

Given the system to which both he and Grisez subscribe, these questions are significant for at least three reasons. Their axiology of incommensurable and irreducible goods displaces the concept of a common good that is something more than the goods as a miscellany. But while Grisez simply posits a theological concept of a common good without ever reconciling it to his philosophical system, Finnis acknowledges the problem on philosophical grounds. The second point is that the question must be faced by any eudaimonistic ethics, for an ethics of self-fulfillment needs to account for the limitations and for the dystelic features which appear to be inherent to the world as it is.[136] Furthermore, as we mentioned in connection with Grisez, a eudaimonism that remains on the immanent level of goods flirts precipitously with an understanding of any good as a mere *bonum mihi*. Why this or that should be a good for someone else, and why I am morally obligated to promote that good for the other person, require answers which are not easily extracted from the Grisez-Finnis system. At least indirectly, Finnis recognizes this problem too.

What, then, are we to make of a value that necessarily includes a respect for the other—a value that we earlier described as having a transcendent, although not necessarily a supernatural, structure? In the passage quoted above, Finnis describes friendship as an "aspect of my well-being," and goes on to note a certain "conflict of opportunities" that emerges once we have to make sense of an action that is not immediately (or perhaps in no way) fulfilling for the agent: viz., when one sacrifices oneself for the other. What good does one participate in when one sacrifices oneself for a friend? A eudaimonistic ethics that lacks a notion of the common good, or which does not give a prominent place to what could be called other-regarding virtues, will find itself entangled on this question.[137]

Finnis elaborates upon the issue by arguing that the two problems which come to the fore are relativism and self-love. He gives an unusual, though important, twist to the problem of relativism. "In the absence of any answers to such questions, the basic human values will seem, to any thoughtful person, to be weakened, in their attractiveness

to reasonableness, by a certain relativity or subjectivity—
not so much the 'subjectivity' of arbitrary opining, but
rather the 'subjectivity' of the *merely* relative to us' (where
'us' has an uncertain but restricted reference)."[138]

In his *Fundamentals of Ethics* he refers in a similar vein
to a "debilitating subjectivity," by which the individual
pursuit of the goods, though reasonable in a piecemeal
fashion for the individual, simply lacks a coherent meaning
as an overall project.[139] Although he does not explicitly
state it in these terms, Finnis is here very close to putting
his finger on the problem engendered by the Grisez-Finnis
conception of the Fpm. By the stated intent of the system,
relativism is avoided if each of the goods is attractive in
such a way that cannot be gainsaid. Yet until the Fpm
acquires teeth, the overall point of the moral life can seem
either meaningless or simply relative to a particular agent.

A piecemeal eudaimonism does not satisfactorily answer
the question, as Aristotle put it, of an entire life that is
something more than the sum of episodes. Without a larger
construct, such a eudaimonism will either have to remain
dissatisfied with the lack of an answer concerning the overall meaning of the project or, as we said earlier, revert to a
noneudaimonist principle of duty; namely, to a norm that
stipulates that whether or not integral fulfillment is possible
one must respect each and every fulfilling good.[140] As we
have seen, Grisez's way of handling this issue is to make
the modes of responsibility a kind of holding pattern until
the ideality of the Fpm is annulled by the religion of faith,
at which point the thoroughgoing eudaimonism is fully
reinstated by the ultimate theological meaning.

Finnis argues that a concept like friendship with God is
necessary not merely to give meaning to moral eudaimonism, but in order to "relativize our self-love and [to]
dispel the anxiety that most insidiously undermines any
and every ethics, the anxiety that concern to be practically
reasonable (virtuous, upright . . .) is ultimately no more
than a refined form of self-cultivation."[141] He puts the

same point in another way by asking: "Is the point of being reasonable simply to be better off, myself—to be flourishing in one more aspect (even if that aspect be rather strategic of the architectonic)?"[142] Like Grisez, Finnis makes no bones about the fact that eudaimonism is the architectonic of the system. But unlike Grisez, Finnis has a reflective grasp of the problem. This is especially apparent in their respective treatments of religion. Grisez moves into revealed religion in order finally to secure, and to extend, the eudaimonistic project. Finnis, however, identifies the religious question with the problem of properly qualifying the eudaimonism, and of bringing it under some other level of morally significant principles.

Finnis is prepared to make the religious problem work to a different end than Grisez. We say "prepared" because once Finnis formulates the questions he does not go on to resolve them. Perhaps one reason for Finnis's failure to follow through is the fact that he accepts Grisez's philosophical theology. In the final chapter of *Natural Law and Natural Rights* he gives an abbreviated version of Grisez's method of reasoning to an uncaused entity.[143] Like Grisez, Finnis conjectures that one might be able speculatively to postulate "something like" personal life on the part of the uncaused entity.[144] In other words, Finnis runs into the same problems with the *via negativa,* which is inadequate, without other modes of analogous predication, to establish reasonable grounds for affirming the moral properties of God, much less morally significant grounds for human agency in relation to God. To put it as simply as possible, Finnis does no better than Grisez in giving grounds for a theistic object of religion. To his credit, he does not leap to a sheerly fideistic solution either. Rather, he vacillates, and then stops (which is probably the best thing to do, all things considered).

Nevertheless, Finnis concludes that the "assumptions" concerning a personal God would, "if verified," entitle us to "remove the question mark with which I originally introduced the basic human value of religion."[145] He explains what difference all of this would make for practical reason:

> This would not entail that we no longer loved the common good for its own sake, nor that we no longer loved our friends for their own sakes. Rather, it would mean that 'for their own sakes' would gain a further (and explanatory) dimension of meaning. For then other persons (and ourselves!) could be regarded not simply as persons whose good we happen to favour, rather inexplicably (in view of their inevitable imperfections), but as persons whose good is favoured also by the one whose own goodness is unrestricted and whose love is in no way blind but rather is given knowing fully the true worth and all-explaining point of everything, of the existence of every person, and of the history of every community. And this would not only explain, in principle, how self-sacrifice in friendship can make sense; it also would account for our obligation to favour the common good.[146]

By his own admission, Finnis's problem is that the value of religion, friendship, and the common good are held in suspension (or, at least, are under a "question mark") until he can find some way to verify this perspective. The obligation to "favour" the common good remains troublesome; friendship remains a mere *bonum mihi*; and a life plan commitment to any of the goods continues to be something that inexplicably "happens" for merely personal or cultural reasons (like the drowning man who finds the value of life most important).

Moreover, the transcendent principle about which Finnis speculates is not exactly the same thing as the self-transcendence of a moral agent. Even if his postulates were verified, we would still need to account for the capacity of the moral agent to transcend merely immanent goods constituting self-fulfillment; otherwise, the existence of a transcendent, and personal, God would have little or no bearing for practical reason until a supernatural dimension could be brought into the picture. Yet, as we have pointed out several times in previous sections of our investigation, a supernatural capacity (as a "gift") without a corresponding natural capacity of self-transcendence inexorably leads to the problem of simply making rather than also perfecting the human ordination to a dominant and inclusive End.

We conclude that Finnis does not move us beyond the problems in Grisez, but he does clarify somewhat the terms of the problems. In any event, he does not burn any bridges behind himself through a fideistic solution. His recognition of the problem of the basic human good of religion, as well as the problem of eudaimonism, could provide a constructive way to begin a reconsideration of the system. Our view is that the axiological and motivational problems should not be left for the context of the religious issues alone, certainly not for theology. The issues of self-love, the common good, and friendship are so central to practical reason that religion should not be reserved for an inconclusive treatment at the end of one's system. This seems particularly prudent so long as Grisez and Finnis hold on exclusively to the method of a *via negativa* in philosophical theology, for this method practically guarantees that the quadrant of speculative rationality will have little definitive to say about the theistic referent of religion and the moral significance of God. As we have pointed out, their natural law method curiously leads to the Kantian problem of generating postulates in order to make complete sense of practical rationality, its motivational springs, and its ability to execute action toward a system of ends.

4

ON FOUNDATIONAL AND
IMPLICATIONAL APPROACHES TO
RELIGION AND PRACTICAL REASON

In the previous chapter we introduced a distinction between foundational and implicational approaches to the problem of systematically interrelating religion and practical reason. The distinction was drawn from James Collins's work *The Emergence of Philosophy of Religion,* in which he argues that one of Kant's chief contributions to modern philosophy of religion is his methodical distinction between the foundations of practical reason as rooted in the free and autonomous moral subject, and further implications which arise once the moral project is consented to on the foundational level. Collins explains that

> . .. the question of the foundation of morality does not comprise the whole of Kant's ethics and does not even, by itself alone, give us full access to his interpretation of moral life. What the philosopher of religion must learn to do is to distinguish firmly between *foundational* and *implicational* issues, and then to establish the proper order between them. His task is not to determine a theological foundation for moral judgments, but to determine the implications concerning God and religion which must be drawn from our basic moral judgments and principles themselves. We cannot infer from the autonomy of the basic moral principles that man's moral life is so sealed up in the realm of pure practical reason that it permits

155

no further references of moral activity to be made. There are implications of man's moral situation which have to be followed out, as they point toward religious belief and action. Thereby, we gain a critical basis for ascertaining the religious attitude which is proportioned to the human moral condition.[1]

Collins points out that the use of this distinction between religious implications and moral foundations permitted Kant constructively to move beyond Hume's scepticism regarding the place of religion in the moral life.

Hume, in effect, argued that if religion is built into the foundational level of morality, any successful critique of natural theology will prove to be a critique of moral judgment itself. Hence, as Collins observes, Hume adopted a "separatist" approach in order to protect the foundational level of moral judgment. Seen in this light, Kant's distinction is geared to protect the foundational level, while keeping open the possibility of understanding how there might be morally significant religious action in the implicational sphere. The key point is that whatever arises implicationally can be reflectively ascertained in terms of whether it is proportionate to foundational principles. The implicational phase of the method, therefore, is not a place simply to deposit all of the quodlibetal issues which are left over from the foundational account; it is a way to extend the intelligibility of the foundation.

The distinction between foundational and implicational approaches has merit even apart from the particular textual and historical issues in the classical modern philosophies of religion. Our use of the distinction is meant to highlight a methodological problem that has only been indirectly alluded to in the foregoing chapters; namely, whether religion and the cluster of issues related to it are to be assigned to the foundational level of an account of practical reason, or whether they are best reserved for implicational issues which arise after the foundation has been determined.

At the outset, however, it is important to bear in mind that this distinction does not necessarily imply that an account of the place of religion in practical reason must exclusively be either foundational or implicational. The critical question—which is, at once, one of method and of system—concerns *which* specific principles and issues are reserved for the foundation and which are reserved for implicational concerns of practical reason. As we have seen, Germain Grisez builds religion, as a *prima principia* of practical reason, into the foundation of his system. It is one of the universal forms of the good and therefore enters into the fundamental principles of moral judgment. Prior to choice, we have a categorical obligation to respect and promote, and, at the very least, never to act against, religion as a basic form of human flourishing. Although Grisez does not regard religion as an absolute good (at least not relative to the other basic goods), it is, even prior to the religion of faith, attractive and categorically binding.

It is reintroduced by Grisez, as revealed religion, in a way that might suggest an implicational phase. That is, the specific revelation of Christianity, assented to by faith, discloses the ultimate meaning of the Fpm. Moral theology, he argues, adds no new foundational principles but rather introduces norms specific to the Christian way of life. These norms establish a harmony between action and the specifically Christian Fpm. However, as we have shown in considerable detail in the previous chapter, the religion of faith does in fact enter into the foundation, and does so in three respects.[2] First, it is only by faith in a specific revelation that the good of religion acquires sufficient content and intelligibility to function as a *prima principia* of practical reason in the foundation. Second, the revelation brings into effect the obligations to love and obey God above all else. Both are superordinate obligations, and neither is justified in, or by, the foundation explicated prior to faith. Third, and perhaps more important, it is only with the *credenda* of Christianity that the eudaimonistic motive of practical reason acquires sufficient reason to overcome a consequentialist adjustment to the world as it is, or at least as it appears to be prior to faith.[3] Grisez holds that faith simply renders the attractiveness of the foundational goods more attractive, and therefore revelation does not substitute for the foundation but amplifies and extends it. Yet, so long as the Fpm direction to act in accord with integral human fulfillment has no intelligibility other than heuristic, a question mark is left over the attractiveness of the goods as an ensemble. We are left with a retail teleology of individual goods and a wholesale deontology that urges us to respect them in lieu of a concrete possibility of their integral coordination and fulfillment. Insofar as revelation allows the agent to pursue integral fulfillment as something more than conjectural, one has not extended the original foundational principle of the Fpm (in the manner of filling it in, as it were); but a new Fpm has been generated which, from a methodological standpoint, is foundational. For all intents and purposes, the revealed Fpm establishes a substantially different ethic, since the deontological requirement of respecting the goods in a holding pattern simply evaporates—except for those who lack the faith.

Any methodological confusion between the foundational and implicational aspects will lead precisely to the kinds of problems we have found in Grisez's system—the problem of fideism in particular. By *fideism* we do not mean that the act or data of faith are given a place in one's account of practical reason, but rather we are referring to an account of practical reason that requires it in the foundation; in this case, faith supplies evidence for the basic principles and norms of what is called a natural law method of morality. To the extent that faith is built into the foundation, either in whole or in part, then to that extent it suffers from fideism. Intuitionism does not necessarily imply any theistic or supernatural content; but, once again, to the extent that it supplies the foundational evidence for principles and norms, intuitionism differs from fideism only by denomination. Fideism can be defined as the intuition of revealed or supernatural data which are purported to be foundational.

In this chapter we shall argue that fideism can be avoided in either of two ways. On one hand, it would be necessary to show, by something more than data posited by intuition, that practical rationality as such requires a morally significant theistic referent for its activity, and that certain attitudes and actions are required in order to satisfy one's relationship to this good. Thus, the introduction of the data of faith concerning this referent will be at least minimally proportionate to the principles and norms given in the foundational account. In short, a theological treatment of the referent would not exclusively establish the basal principles regulating practical reason's relationship to such a deity. Such a position would fall within the Thomistic paradigm, in which ethics, philosophy of nature, and metaphysics are conjointly employed to treat the so-called *praeambula fidei*. On the other hand, it would be necessary to show by some other route that the basal principles of practical rationality can be explicated without a theistic referent or religious practices, but that the foundational account leaves open the possibility of morally significant action in the sphere of faith. Such a position would resemble the Kantian paradigm. Here, too, the proportionality between faith and the foundational framework is kept intact, for whatever is revealed by faith, or discovered about the peculiar perspective called religion, cannot, in principle, abrogate the principles and meaning of human subjectivity which are laid in the foundation. The first approach represents a foundational treatment of religion and practical reason, while the second one represents an implicational approach. From the standpoint of consistency, either of these is preferable to Grisez's system as it presently stands.

*4.1 A Summary Assessment
of the New Natural Law Method*

Here we should make a brief summary assessment of the Grisez-Finnis natural law position as it presently stands. The problem of how Grisez relates religion to practical reason first needs to be viewed against the background of his natural law theory. He distinguishes his own theory of natural law from scholastic or conventional theories, and, although he claims to have rescued the main kernel of Aquinas's natural law ethic, both he and Finnis diverge sharply from Aquinas's understanding of how the "natural" and the "preceptive" facets constitute a distinctively natural law method. Nevertheless, Grisez's system includes many of the same components as that of a traditional natural law theory. Before we go on to discuss specific problems in his account, let us first note the major components which constitute his natural law approach.

In the first place, Grisez's understanding of practical reason begins with reason's relationship to goods. These goods are sometimes called "possibilities," "objectives" or "purposes," but what should not be lost sight of is the fact that they represent content derived from inclinations. The Fppr, the *prima principia,* and the Fpm all take their meaning from the foundational relationship between practical reason and human goods. The goods are "natural" in the sense that they are constitutive of whatever a human agent might find attractive—so pervasively attractive, indeed, that it is possible to establish a list of basic goods similar in function to what the conventional natural law theory called the primary precepts.

In the second place, the basic goods are regarded not only as *prima principia* of practical reason, but as ends or finalities. Each one, Finnis explains, is a *bonum honestum.* In *Christian Moral Principles* Grisez explicitly criticizes John Dewey for having rejected the objective nature of these goods as finalities, and for failing to recognize an objective ontology of means and ends.[4] For Grisez, we recall, the difference between goods which are ends, and goods which are means, is a difference in principle independent of choice and independent of situational contexts in which the goods might be chosen. Therefore, prior to choice, one is obligated to respect and promote these goods, for the goods *are* the principles of practical rationality. Grisez's use of terms can prove misleading if we take his language of goods (as objectives or possibilities) apart from his language of precepts. Despite the fact that the method proceeds at each step as though there is a difference between the premoral and moral, the two are firmly wedded together in Grisez's understanding of natural law. They are so intimately related, in fact, that we suggested earlier, in examining his position on contraception, that one can move from the *prima principia* to a moral judgment without explicitly having to take into account the Fpm directive to act in accord with integral human fulfillment. The distinction between the premoral and moral facets of natural law can be interpreted to be a distinction without a difference. The basic goods, as objective principles, are irreducible, precisely because they are the primary principles of natural law. Accordingly, Grisez insists that it is no more rational to subordinate one basic good to another than it is to subordinate one primary principle to another.

In the third place, this account of the goods is meant (in contrast to Kant and Rawls) to be a full theory of human flourishing, and therefore of the good of humanity as such.[5] Although he provides no specific telos for man *qua* man, the basic goods are exhaustive, not implicationally, but foundationally. They are exhaustive on the foundational level for two reasons: (1) together, they ontologically constitute the essential goods of humanity; and (2) in principle, no one of them can be left out, or suppressed, without distorting practical rationality itself. Therefore, each one of these goods is intended to be not a mere *bonum mihi*, but a universal form of the good, which is universally binding upon practical reason.

If we prescind for a moment from various theorists and texts in the history of the natural law tradition, as well as from the ancillary issues in epistemology and metaphysics, these three components of Grisez's natural law system represent the essential framework of a natural law theory: the content of the goods is derived from inclination; the goods are regarded as principles themselves; the difference between goods as means and as ends is objective, prior to choice and situational context; and the goods are principles which are universally binding. Not surprisingly, the system, for the most part, arrives at the same conclusions as the older natural law tradition regarding various issues in moral conduct—particularly, issues like abortion and contraception, in which the foundational unity between nature and precepts is decisive.

Grisez understands his system as departing from conventional natural law theory in one important respect. He argues that his theory does not require a speculative doctrine of nature in order to establish the foundational principles. The nature and proper ends of human inclinations, for instance, are not the objects of theoretical reason, but are objectives of practical evaluation. The *ratio* of the goods does not require an *ordinatio* derived from the philosophy of nature at work in the older natural law systems. In establishing their practical axioms, neither Grisez nor Finnis proceeds *ex conditione finis*, nor perforce *ex suppositione naturae*, where nature is understood to constitute the wider setting in which the *convenientia* (to use Finnis's term) between human agents and nature is presupposed.[6] Moreover, in contrast to earlier Scholastic theory, Grisez explains that his system does not require a natural theology to mediate between a natural teleology of inclinations and the moral command to obey nature. For this reason, both

Grisez and Finnis regard their theory as being a constructive breakthrough in the history of natural law reasoning. In effect, they have claimed to generate what could be called "natural categoricals" in such a way as to overcome the limitations of the conventional natural law theory (which stressed the "natural"), the utilitarian tradition (which stressed the goods, but which shortchanged them), and the deontological tradition (which had the categoricals, but an insufficient appreciation of the goods). The project is ambitious, and is especially interesting inasmuch as they call it a natural law method.

In the foregoing chapters, however, we have given several reasons to doubt whether this system represents a constructive advance beyond conventional natural law theory. Prior to our examination of the problem of religion, one of the first problems we encountered was Grisez's treatment of the issue of contraception. As we saw, he argues that his position does not require the perverted faculty argument; that is to say, contraception is wrong not because it involves the perversion of a biological function, but because it violates a practical valuation of the function. This practical judgment determines the status of the power of procreation as a good, and thereby as one of the *prima principia* of practical reason. Hence, Grisez concludes that a deliberate suppression of the procreative good entails "volitional absurdity," which is to say that the act is practically irrational because practical reason violates itself.

As we pointed out in our earlier discussion of the issue, Grisez's distinction between biological functions and practical objectives is suggestive, but he is compelled nevertheless to appeal to theoretical data in order to show that the procreative power is a basic good. His arguments concerning the value of human organicity do not constitute a merely indirect confirmation of the original practical insight (or, as Finnis puts it, a mere "assemblage of reminders"), but rather determine the practical insight itself. We are urged to proceed *ex suppositione naturae,* where nature is not merely a fact, intuition, or mere attraction, but where nature specifies the structure and meaning of the procreative power, and thus sets the context for what qualifies as appropriate behavior. In other words, in order to secure the preceptive facet of natural law, Grisez finds himself having to move back to justify the premoral "natural" facet, even though his method rules out the necessity of such a move. Is Grisez confused about his own method?

We can get at the nerve of this problem by characterizing Grisez's system as a natural law theory that substitutes intuitions for a philosophy of nature. Insofar as the method begins with axiological data posited by intuition, Grisez does satisfy his criterion that ethical reflection must acknowledge the thoroughly "practical" point of departure. But the status and meaning of the data, as well as the mode of derivation, are locked within the intuitive orbit.

Thus, if it is asked why we are morally bound to respect and promote, and, at the least, not to act against, the procreative power, Grisez is forced to grab one or the other horn of a dilemma: either simply to reposit the intuitional data, or, as he in fact does, to appeal to some other foundation for judgment (in this case, a theoretical account of a natural power). The method rules out any need for making the latter type of move. Grisez and Finnis want the results of a natural law theory but are unwilling to defend and deploy the theoretical apparatus necessary to sustain it. It is a case of wanting to have one's cake and eat it too. Having on one hand departed so drastically from the older natural law theory, it is difficult to understand why they would want to brand their theory with the rubric of such a maligned term as *natural law*—except that the term continues to carry some credibility in Catholic ethics. On the other hand, since Grisez has to bring justifications, *ex suppositione naturae,* in through the back door, and since Finnis readily acknowledges that the speculative issues concerning nature place a question mark over the project, it is difficult to understand why neither is willing to make some provision for the employment of speculative rationality.

The foundation of the system is flawed, and this is manifest in the fact that Grisez himself cannot remain consistently within the intuitional approach that undergirds the Fppr, the *prima principia,* and the Fpm. If our interpretation is correct, it helps to explain the source of problems which emerge once Grisez moves into the area of religion and practical reason. For instance, the first problem we encountered in the relationship between religion and practical reason was exactly the same problem that we uncovered in the issue of contraception. Religion, like the good of procreation, is one of the first principles of practical reason. It is a good that should be evident to any rational agent, for it is, quite literally, one of the foundational principles of practical rationality. But why should it be foundational? Indeed, what is it in the first place?

In the previous chapter we examined various efforts by Grisez to reach a satisfactory definition of religion that would help us to understand its status as a basic good. Some of his earliest efforts at a definition stress what could be called "natural religion," whereby the good of religion is definied primarily according to anthropological or cultural traits rather than by precise philosophical doctrines concerning the theistic referent—for example, he states that all cultures have recognized the need to establish good relations with "unknown higher powers." In *Beyond the New Morality,* he proposes that the good of religion is intelligible, even if we prescind altogether from the problem of a theistic referent. Here, presumably, he means that there is an inclination toward, or a need for, something which can be called religion; therefore, the practical valuation of that need suffices to include it among the first principles of practical reason. Once again, the problem is that the principle, along with the content, is posited by intuition. Despite an agnosticism regarding the bearing of a philosophy of nature or a metaphysics upon practical rationality, a conciliatory gesture is made toward the empirical sciences which, Grisez and Finnis reason, ought to be able to come up with some "parallel" list or evidence for the goods.

Grisez's own method dictates that the anthropological data—such as they are—cannot be foundational evidence. At best, the data might prove to be an indirect confirmation of the basal intuition. Grisez fails to provide a philosophical justifiction for moving from these rather casually posited anthropological findings to the practical judgments concerning the value of religion, much less to the matter of moral obligation. Furthermore, his philosophical theology does not provide either a speculative or a practical basis for a morally significant theistic referent. Even if Grisez's method were to permit some ground of judgment other than intuition concerning the nature of the good of religion, he contends that it is not needed. In the case of contraception, he outright employs a theoretical argument regarding the meaning of human organicity; in the case of religion, there is nothing but the intuition and an ancillary argument from a philosophical theology that seeks to demonstrate by a *via negativa* that God exists—an argument that does not demonstrate any morally significant properties on the part of the deity. Not only is there no basis for obligations with respect to the deity, there is no basis for understanding why there should be any sense whatsoever to religious practices. Atheists and agnostics, as well as theists, are bound by a universal form of the good that is defined simply as a need to establish good relations with unknown higher powers.

In *Christian Moral Principles* the problem becomes more acute, for here religion is defined as the good of harmony between the human will and the will of God. From a definitional standpoint, it is a clearer statement than what we find in previous works. However, both the descriptive and normative aspects of the issue now require the introduction of the data of faith. Grisez repeatedly insists that it cannot be known that God is personal, that he gives commands, or that he has any morally significant properties, except by an act of faith in revelation. What began as a problem of merely intuitional evidence for a foundational principle of practical reason now becomes a problem of fideism. Because one of the *prima principia* requires the mediation of faith for its intelligibility, at least part of the foundation rests on fideistic grounds. As we proceeded in our analysis, it turned out, however, that arguably the whole of the foundation requires faith in Christian revelation, for Grisez argues that it is only by faith that we have sufficient data to establish the rationality of the eudaimonistic motive, and thus of the first principle of morality (as Grisez understands it). We therefore concluded not only that religion is a particular instance of a problem with Grisez's axiology and natural law method, but that it becomes a bellwether for problems with the system as such.

The fideism is closely related to the original commitment to retain (at least functionally) a natural law system of goods which are universally binding, while jettisoning an antecedent philosophy of nature in favor of the data of intuitions. As we stated above, in the case of contraception Grisez finds it necessary to abandon the intuitional standpoint in favor of a theory of nature, whereas in the case of religion he finds it necessary to make a direct move to the data of faith. In either case, we must conclude that the foundational account of practical reason has not been adequately established. The move into moral theology requires Grisez to make a number of moves to compensate for that insufficiency. For his part, Finnis is aware of the difficulty, but is genuinely diffident about what to do. He sees, however dimly, that religion must be a good quite unlike the others in the repertoire, and that at some point or another theoretical reason will have to be brought to bear upon the problem of the self, its goods, and a theistic referent. To follow through on these problems would entail major remedial work within the system. As it is, the system stands on the precipice of, if it has not already crossed the boundary into, what could be called an ethico-religious positivism.[7]

4.2 Foundational Problems

In this section we shall address issues which need to be considered if religion is to be kept on the foundational level of an account of practical reason. Our task here is not to reconstitute Grisez's system; nor do we purport to work out some other systematic way to justify the inclusion of religion on the foundational level. Rather, we shall raise certain key issues as a preliminary to any resolution of the problem. Our use of other theorists in the history of philosophy is meant simply to illustrate the philosophical and methodological points under discussion. Operating today, under the shadow of Derrida and Rorty, it is not evident to many philosophers that a foundation can be given for anything, much less in this particular area of religion and ethics. Let us, nevertheless, suppose that the problem of foundations is still compelling, especially for a method that would call itself a natural law method of ethics.

A foundational approach to the relationship between religion and practical reason will include one or more of the following elements. First, it must show that the basic principle or principles of practical reason require propositions concerning the religious nature of humanity, or the human relationship to God, or both. Second, in order to show why these enter into the foundational account, there must be evidence to indicate that the omission or suppression of religion distorts, either in whole or in part, the fundamental rationality of practical reason. Third, it must be shown that there is a duty to obey divine commands, or at least to participate in certain religious practices. If these three criteria can be met, one has a strong case for a foundational approach to the subject.[8]

In the history of philosophy there have been any number of different foundational approaches. Aquinas, and certainly Augustine, were thoroughgoing foundationalists (Grisez's observation that Aquinas wedded Augustine's formula of the restless heart to an Aristotelian theory of final causality seems accurate enough), as have been most theorists in the natural law tradition. As James Collins has pointed out, the main lines of modern philosophy of religion have been either separatist in emphasis (such as Hume, and certainly Sartre) or implicationalist (such as Kant). Nevertheless, in the work of a theorist like John Locke, one finds the basic recipe for a foundational approach. In *The Second Treatise of Government,* for instance, Locke invokes divine commands in order to establish the principle of equality in the state of nature, as well as the so-called spoilage principle governing proper use of property.[9] Not surprisingly, Locke's appeal to God for foundational principles dovetails with those places where he relies upon a more traditional natural law account of moral obligation, and in particular where he uses Richard Hooker's natural law theory.[10] Locke's account is foundational only in part. On the other end of the spectrum, a theorist like Spinoza proposes a radically foundationalist approach. In his *Ethics* and his *Theologico-Political Treatise,* he dissolves not only practical reason, but religion itself, into the speculative *amor dei.*[11]

For his part, Grisez wishes to defend a natural law account of the good of religion as a first principle of practical reason. In *Christian Moral Principles,* he states that "the natural law disposes toward friendship with God as one form of humanly fulfilling harmony; living faith superabundantly satisfies this natural disposition."[12] In terms of the intent of the system, Grisez is following the general structure of the Thomistic approach. Religion is a basic good, as well as a good that is to be completed supernaturally. A natural law account of the foundation of practical reason reveals that religion is one of the basic inclinations or goods. Presumably, this can be established without having to introduce data drawn from an act of faith in supernatural revelation. Hence, theology can play what is essentially an implicational role. It is first assigned the task of showing why the supernatural "superabundantly" completes the foundational principles, even while preserving a principle of proportionality; and in the second place, it has the task of introducing positive laws which more finely determine moral conduct in religion.

Before we turn to why Grisez does not achieve this systematic intention, it would be helpful to say a few words about the way Aquinas handles the problem of religion on the foundational level, for Grisez views his own system as being derived, at least in part, from Aquinas. Of course, we cannot rehearse the entire structure of his method here, but we can outline the main discussion of religion in the *Summa theologiae*. In Question 81 of the *secunda-secundae*, Aquinas discusses the natural "virtue of religion" in terms of principles of justice.[13] He argues that the virtue of religion is a species of justice, and principally entails giving to God what is his due, namely, reverence and obedience.

The reason for this, Aquinas maintains, is threefold: first, because God is the "first principle of the creation and government of things," a debt is owed to the author of one's being; second, honor is due "under the aspect of excellence," as God surpasses all things in this regard—it is thus a proper response of the created will to this kind of being; third, religion is a good because the human soul is ordered to God as end, and in this regard Aquinas goes on to argue that religion "commands all other virtues."[14] From here, Aquinas goes on to discuss various kinds of actions which are either commanded by this virtue or appropriate to it (such as the giving of sacrifice, which for Aquinas is not just a divine positive law, but a law of reason).[15] So, for Aquinas, religion is not only one of the foundational goods but also a superordinate good—the summit of justice itself.[16]

It is important, however, to note that Aquinas explicitly distinguishes between religion (with its attendant obligations and practices) and the good of a supernatural relationship to God.[17] The latter, he explains, involves the relationship to God not just as an end, but as a personal communion. This requires theological explication, for it involves not only faith, but other supernatural virtues as well. In *Christian Moral Principles* Grisez cites this distinction by Aquinas and correctly concludes that the basic good (or, in Aquinas's terms, the virtue) of religion ought not to be confused with the good of God himself.[18] Grisez, however, uses the Thomistic distinction to reinforce his own position that the basic goods, including religion, are incommensurable, and that there does not exist, prior to choice, a hierarchy amongst them. What he overlooks is the theoretical apparatus that Aquinas employs in order to justify the so-called natural good of religion and its place in the natural law system. Not only is it presupposed that certain aspects of God's being are demonstrable (such as excellence of being, governance of the world, and his status as final cause of human nature), but Aquinas's discussion of religion likewise presupposes a philosophy of human nature—in particular, a hierarchical and teleological account of the intellect and the will's relation to objects and ends. Indeed, Aquinas argues that the virtue of religion is superior to the other natural virtues precisely because it governs man more immediately with regard to his final end. It is not one categorical among others, but an architectonic virtue.

When, in the *Summa*, Aquinas finally concludes that "all the other powers become inordinate" if the will is not properly oriented to God, the judgment proceeds from the foundational work that has already been set in place.[19] Regarding practical rationality, Aquinas recognizes that God turned each individual over into the hands of the individual's own counsel [*Deus reliquit hominem in manu consilii sui*], but he is quick to add, "not that he may do as he wills" [*non quia liceat ei facere omne quod vellit*].[20] He agrees with the Augustinian judgment regarding the soul, which is made such that it cannot find satisfaction in turning to either itself or anything else other than the one who made it [*nec ipsa sibi, nec ei quidquam sufficit recedenti ab illo qui solus sufficit*].[21] For Aquinas, these principles hold *secundum naturam,* and the system stands or falls according to whether he can make good on these claims. There is no good reason to water down Aquinas to make his account more palatable, or to render some of his principles more easily extractable from the system.

Grisez argues that Aquinas has an "overly definite" notion of the human *summum bonum,* yet for Aquinas the subject of final causality is not an implicational issue; it is one of the main ingredients in the foundation. To say, then, that practical reason's relationship to God as *summum bonum* is mistaken is to imply that Aquinas's foundational point of departure is flawed, which is precisely what Grisez does not want to concede (since he argues that he has captured the essence of the Thomistic natural law ethic). For Aquinas, the human relationship to goods is not open-ended, for the individual and the goods pursued have proper natural completions which are "given." Indeed, Aquinas argues that the first exercise of the will is not an act of freedom but a necessary inclination to beatitude (viz., God).[22] The first five questions of the *prima-secundae* do not constitute a mere conjecture that God is man's end but clearly represent an effort to demonstrate that no created good, but only God, can satisfy human nature. The intent of traditional natural law theory is sufficiently clear in this regard.[23] As Henry Veatch has observed in his recent book *Human Rights: Fact or Fancy*:

> For how can one suppose, much less maintain, that as human beings we must recognize there to be a single goal, or standard of perfection toward which our lives

are oriented and which, if we do not achieve it or attain, our lives can be said to have fallen short or perhaps even to have been downright failures? Indeed, if we cannot make good on this notion of a natural end in human life, then we certainly cannot make good on any notion of an ethics of natural law.[24]

The Thomistic system does not traffic in what we have called a kind of retail teleology of individual goods with a wholesale deontology. The position, as Veatch says, stands or falls on making good on the claim that there is a natural end.

Nor is God, for Aquinas, invoked (as in Suarezian thought) in order to establish an extrinsic, preceptive dimension for natural inclinations, but rather in order to make sense of rational appetite itself. In other words, there are not two foundations (nature and morals) which need to be joined by the "middle" of a divine command. For Aquinas, each and every act of the will involves a specification of the original relationship to God in the order of finality, and this is why the two superordinate commands regarding love and obedience do not rest merely upon divine positive law. The "*convenientia*," as Finnis puts it, between God, nature, and the self is settled foundationally in the Thomistic system well before the Fppr or the virtues are treated.[25]

We need not enter into a detailed account of Aquinas's philosophy of nature in order simply to point out that the good of religion is not posited by an intuition regarding the value of an inclination. Whatever else one may find unsatisfactory in Aquinas, he does not fail philosophically to explicate the foundational principles at work in his treatment of various moral subjects. Indeed, it may be objected that the foundation is too highly determined—so highly determined, in fact, that the implicational status of theology becomes a mere extension of the science worked out in the foundation regarding the *praeambula fidei*.[26]

Our main point is not simply that Grisez overlooks something in the text of Aquinas, but that he misses the systematic issue that holds philosophical implications in its own right. Grisez himself should be alert to the problem; after all, his critique of conventional natural law focuses upon the problem of having to invoke God as a "middle," linking together natural teleology and the obligation to obey these telic structures. This is the problem that Aquinas tries to overcome—of course, on a basis other than a sheerly extrinsic divine command. His treatment of the good of religion presupposes that this project has been successfully accomplished. If Grisez does not believe, in principle, that such a project can be successful, or that it is immediately pertinent to the foundational account of practical reason, then he ought either to reconsider his own natural law approach to the good of religion or to explore some other way philosophically to justify its inclusion on the foundational level.[27] Unless some adjustment is made, religion as a first principle of practical reason will rest entirely upon a divine positive law, and this is exactly the same systematic deficiency that prompted Grisez's critique of scholastic natural law theory.

Once again, it is our judgment that the effort to retain a natural law foundation for practical reason by substituting intuitions for the evidence derived from a philosophy of nature does not work. It either presupposes or postpones a philosophical explication of the interrelation between inclinations, goods, and precepts, which in turn presupposes the intricate groundwork laid in philosophy of nature and in natural theology. As John Wipple has observed in *Metaphysical Themes in Thomas Aquinas,* Aquinas "came to take Moses Maimonides' restrictive position concerning the divine names very seriously. It is within the context of his refutation of Maimonides both in the *De potentia* and then in the *Summa theologiae* that Thomas counters by defending the possibility of substantial predication of certain divine names."[28]

Wipple does not explore the implications this holds for practical reason, but they are clear enough once one sees how Grisez's "proof" for the existence of God leads to a dead end without something more than a merely conjectural way to predicate certain perfections of God. For Aquinas, God can be an object of religion not only because the existence of a deity is proved, but because certain things can reasonably be said of this deity in order to elicit and justify a distinctively religious response and obligations. Only in this way, or in a way very similar to it, is it possible to affirm on the one hand the good of religion, while on the other hand retaining criteria which would allow one to ascertain whether *a* particular religion and its practices satisfy the formality of that good. Given Grisez's system, it is impossible to disqualify *per se* a religion or its practices as participations in the good of religion; he can only say that this or that religious practice bears unfavorably on some other good. In lieu of adequate foundational work, religion will inevitably find itself described according to the absentee landlord "natural religion" of the deists, or consigned exclusively to faith or to some humanist "totalizing" concept. As Garrigou-Lagrange pointed out some years ago, the issue of God's attributes, as well as his status as man's final end, is something that can prompt one to "prove too much or not enough."[29] Our point is that there is no cheap way around the problem if one wishes to hold a natural law position on religion and practical reason. Grisez's description of the good of religion as a basic attraction says too little, which in turn prompts him to say too much once he moves into revealed religion.

Perhaps it is true, as Alan Donagan has said, that "traditional morality has been able to find a place in secular academic philosophy only in the form of intuitionism."[30] To call an intuitional defense of traditional morality "natural law" strikes us as misleading, for one of the main reasons that a defense of traditional moral precepts has gravitated to intuitionism is the fact that a natural law defense of those precepts has been proved wanting (or, as J. L. Mackie puts it, "queer") by the main lines of modern and contemporary philosophy.[31]

4.3 Implicational Issues

As we have seen, Grisez does not adequately account for the inclusion of religion as one of the *prima principia* of practical reason. Faith in revelation is invoked in order to make intelligible a principle to which we are morally bound on the foundational level. We suggested that one way to handle the problem would be to abandon the intuitional approach, and to justify on other grounds the reason for our fundamental obligation to respect and promote the good of religion. If this cannot be accomplished on the foundational level, then at least we know where we stand: either we must affirm this good on the basis of a philosophically unmediated faith, or we might take what can be called an implicational approach to the problem.

An implicational approach would retain a place for faith, but it would be mediated by principles which have already been worked out in the foundation. In this scheme, the questions which emerge *for* faith are drawn from the foundation, and therefore whatever answers, or even new questions, are given *by* faith retain some rational proportionality to the originating framework. As we have suggested already, John Finnis takes a position that is very close to what we are calling an implicational approach.

As a model, the implicational approach will not view the human relationship to God, or certain religious practices, in terms of basic principles of practical reason and moral obligation. The foundational nexus of inclinations, principles, and obligations will shift in favor of the implicational nexus of questions and concerns—or, in the Kantian system, the matter of hope. Accordingly, the main issue is not an inclination to God, but rather the implications of the openness of the human subject to such a value. For Kant, of course, this involves the problem of how to make further sense of moral activity beyond the limitations posed by the account of pure practical reason. Similarly, for a theorist like Josiah Royce this involves a belief in "the latent union of morality and religion," which becomes problematic only when the basic purposes of the moral life are set into action.[32] Kierkegaard could be called an implicationalist to the extent that religion not only represents the problem of advancing the moral project beyond strict issues of duty to those concerning happiness (termed "Religion A"), but also entails a move into a distinctly transethical sphere of action (termed "Religion B"); the latter requires a shift of attention toward theology proper in order to grasp how religion is a good in itself, beyond its role in completing the moral project.[33] For an implicational approach, it is not immediately critical whether the implicational issues are theoretical or practical, or whether they are philosophical or theological. The decisive point is how the issues are raised relative to the foundational framework of the nature of practical reason.

There are aspects of Grisez's thought which would lend themselves to the implicational approach. In addition to his basic claim that the Fppr can be detached from a speculative theory of nature in which reason's relationship to God constitutes a systematic point of departure (this alone should move Grisez toward an implicational rather than a foundational approach to religion), another important area is suggested by his belief that the moral life is very difficult, if not impossible, to live with integrity unless one adopts a religious perspective concerning the possibility of an integral self-realization. What Grisez appears to be saying is that the world as it is does not necessarily fit the duties to which one is obligated on the foundational level—especially the duty to act in conformance with integral human fulfillment. Thus, the consequentialist perspective on the eudaimonistic thrust of practical reason will appear to be more reasonable, for in the absence of a nonarbitrary standard by which to conceive of an obligation to pursue integral human fulfillment, consequentialism recommends strategies for accomplishing *some* fulfillments, by sacrificing one good to another in a particular situation.

The problem, thus formulated, strongly suggests the need for an implicational approach to the problem of religion in practical reason. A life lived strictly in accord with each of the goods as separate values, without an overarching value or point to such a life, strikes us, as apparently it does Finnis too, as being a rather grim prospect. It is not unlike being handcuffed to a string of goods, and being obligated to go along for the ride. Finnis characterizes it as a "self-athleticism" that verges on Stoicism. The problem of Stoicism is indeed pertinent. It is not only built into the Kantian paradigm (whether there is an overarching convergence between the goods, and whether the world allows practical reason effectively to execute this larger purpose), but it is also built into the Grisez-Finnis account of the goods. In his recent book on *The Philosophy of History*, John William Miller characterizes Stoicism as an "alliance with the universe, but no local and actual alliance with persons or institutions."[34] While this would seem to be the precise opposite of the Grisez-Finnis position, the dilemma is similar. Grisez and Finnis would have us strike an alliance with the goods, even though there is no good reason to believe that either the goods or humanity itself enjoys an overarching telos. We simply have a duty to respect them. Without some other principle that can be brought to bear upon the situation, it may turn out that there is no further point than the respect enjoined by practical reason. A so-called full theory of the goods, therefore, does not escape, but rather precipitates, the problem of Stoicism.

At least since Kant, the implicational approach is geared fully to humanize the project of the moral life in light of the aforementioned problem. A theory of religion perhaps could now be developed in order to understand why and how religion supports, gives further meaning to, and opens up a new horizon within, the basic project of the moral life. The move could employ a philosophy of religion, a theological investigation, or both. However, as Grisez's system presently stands, the implicational approach is frustrated not only by the fact that religion is one of the first principles in the foundation, and therefore ought to make sense on the level at which it is introduced, but also by the fact that the theological superstructure has to be invoked to make sense of the foundation itself. In the former, we are morally bound to a good that has no intelligibility without faith, while in the latter we need faith in order to secure the point of departure for the system. An implicational treatment cannot be expected to overcome systematic flaws in the foundation.

The late Ernst Bloch, for example, is a thoroughgoing implicationalist, for he builds his philosophy of rights upon what he calls the *"logos spermatikos"* of the ideal of an unalienated society.[35] Yet even Bloch concedes that the logic of this hope must be rooted in a foundational theory of nature (which, in Bloch's case, is Marxist) in order to generate and orient the implicational questions. Consider the following passage from the conclusion of his three-volume work *The Principle of Hope*: value meanings, he insists,

> are solely ciphers of a content which is as yet real-utopian; they are not ontically pre-ordered realities to which subjectivity is assigned merely as receptive participation instead of a common awakening call. For the world, even with regard to its objective value-material, is no museum and as yet no cathedral; it is a process. Precisely the existing gradation of values, referring to the goal-value of the highest good, is not a climax in the sense of an ultimately Thomistic hierarchy of being but solely the climax of a temporal-processive *goal-perspective*.[36]

Other than the fact that Bloch's remarks strike one as
rather similar to what Grisez and Finnis have to say about
values and the Fpm prior to faith, the passage is cited here
only to indicate what is entailed in an implicationalist
approach. In Bloch's case, the foundation is established in
terms of a temporal-processive ontology of nature and
human nature. If Bloch can make good on the foundational
claims (he takes over thirteen hundred pages to set them
forth), then he is prepared to introduce religion as an implicational issue. In other words, a coherent implicational
approach cannot avoid very complex foundational considerations. It should be recalled that it took Kant three
critiques before he was prepared to unfurl the implicational
sails with regard to religion and morality.

Another aspect of both Grisez's and Finnis's thought
that would lend itself to an implicational perspective is the
subject of life plans. Along with Rawls, they borrow the
concept from Josiah Royce. For Royce, the concept of a
life plan is both ontological and implicational in nature.
In the first place, it is employed as a way to understand
the unity of the self. In the second place, however, it is
used as a model for understanding the pursuit of a good or
value that transcends the individual's "seeking of his own
delight."[37] Given the various purposes of the moral life,
Royce asks how the different loyalties can be linked
together to achieve a focal purpose or loyalty. For Royce,
then, the philosophy of loyalty begins implicationally—
precisely when the scheme of duties and delights suggests
the need for another horizon. Religion, he maintains, is "at
least a latent belief in the superhuman reality of the cause
[or loyalty]."[38]

Rawls comes closer than either Grisez or Finnis to
Royce's concept of a life plan, because Rawls introduces it
only with the move into a full theory of the goods. It is
reserved, in other words, for what we have been calling the
implicational phase of the method. We pointed out in an
earlier chapter why Rawls insists upon the need to work

out the requirements of the theory of justice prior to a consideration of the full theory of human goods. Simply put, a full theory of the goods would require a nonarbitrary principle for coordinating the goods; and given the numerous contingent matters which would have to be considered and agreed upon, the foundational principles will be difficult, if not impossible, to establish. If it is placed in the foundation, we cannot help suspecting that morality is subject to merely ad hoc arrangements. Yet Finnis regards the consent to a life plan as one of the basic modes of responsibility. This makes sense if one begins with a full theory of the goods (one of which is religion). But this particular obligation is virtually empty, and Finnis simply decides not to treat the contingent matters which, as Rawls warns, need to be addressed if one is to begin with a full theory of the goods. The Grisez-Finnis position on life plans leaves us with the suspicion of merely ad hoc arrangements. Distinctions of importance among the goods, and the development of hierarchies implicated in life plans, are introduced by habit and convenience, or by divine command.

For his part, Grisez frequently insists that religion is the best candidate for organizing a life plan. Once again, the problem is that religion is one of the basic goods, and therefore one of the principles, in the foundation. Lacking sufficient content and specificity prior to faith, there is no evident reason why religion should be the best candidate for organizing a life plan. Furthermore, religion, like all of the basic goods, is irreducible and incommensurable with regard to the other values—hence there is no ground for making religion a master, or superordinate, good for organizing the remaining values. The strict linkage between goods as irreducible values and goods as principles of obligation resists any constructive move into an implicational phase. Implicationalists of the stripe of Kant or Royce are careful to keep religion out of, or merely latent in, the foundation precisely so that it can emerge implicationally, and so that one is not forced to reckon with two notions of religion.

In the final chapter of *Natural Law and Natural Rights,* Finnis provides a more highly nuanced consideration of the good of religion. He explicitly recognizes the problem of why it should be included among the basic goods. The crux of the issue is whether there are other grounds for understanding the value of religion; that is to say, if religion should not prove to be one of the *prima principia,* it means not necessarily that there is no intelligibility or value to religion, but only that this "concern" should be assigned to some other place in the system. Unfortunately, Finnis is diffident about the matter; he vacillates right where the systematic question emerges, decides to keep religion as one of the basic principles (as a "placeholder"), and then defers the discussion to the final chapter.

Once he goes on to treat the problem of religion and practical reason, Finnis develops a cluster of themes which suggest the rationality of pursuing questions which can be regarded as religious. First, there is the problem (both theoretical and practical) of participation in various kinds of communal goods despite the evident fact that the "succession of human individuals" separates not only individuals, but also communities of individuals, in terms of time and death. Finnis asks whether "further sense can be made of the whole situation." One cannot help noticing that this is quite similar to the way Kant raises the same issue in his *Idea for a Universal History with a Cosmopolitan Intent,* and in his other writings on the problem of history and the *summum bonum.*[39] In other words, a theodicy is not brought into the foundation in order to justify the basic integrity of practical reason, but emerges along with the implicational issue concerning the ultimate meaning of morality in human history. Although, in Finnis's case, the theodicy involves speculative questions, they develop (in a way similar to Kant and Royce) from an antecedent practical framework.

Second, Finnis raises the problem of whether morality is finally a matter simply of "self-athleticism," or merely a "refined form of self-cultivation," that would lead to a "debilitating subjectivity" regarding the overarching meaning, or point, of morality. Here Finnis tackles a problem that escapes Grisez's attention, namely, whether it is possible to move beyond a pursuit of goods in which these goods are viewed primarily as forms of self-love or merely as forms of self-realization. This prompts Finnis to raise the larger metaphysical issue of how we might conceive of the interrelation between nature, reason, and God. As he explains in the final chapter of his book:

> The fact that human beings have a certain range of urges, drives, or inclinations; and the fact that these have a certain correspondence, parallelism, or "fit" with the states of affairs that anyone intelligent would consider constitute human flourishing . . . [and] the remarkable fact that there is an order of nature which, like the orders of human artefacts, actions, and thoughts, is amenable to human understanding calls for some explanation.[40]

Finnis argues that the *"convenientia,"* or apparent fitness, between these different orders suggests the existence of a distinct form of order that is practically interesting. The questions and concerns regarding this form of order can be called religion.

These are intelligent, perhaps even "religious," questions, but the problem under consideration here is whether the foundational account requires that they be satisfactorily answered in order to secure the foundation itself, or whether they should be reserved for the implicational phase. Although Finnis does not explicitly resolve the problem, the manner in which he develops the order of topics in *Natural Law and Natural Rights* implies that the question should be not merely deferred, but systematically assigned to the implicational phase. It is revealing that, at one point in the final chapter, Finnis speaks of "the rather unhappy term 'natural law'."[41] Since his treatment of the relationship between God, nature, and reason is given after the foundational work, perhaps he ought to drop the term *natural law* in order to indicate more clearly the difference between resolving questions concerning the relationship of practical reason to nature in the foundation and doing so in the implicational phase.

If this is a reasonable interpretation of his method, then Finnis also ought to follow his original hunch and remove religion from the list of primary principles, treating it in tandem with the problem of how to understand the *convenientia* between nature, God, and human rationality. This move would likewise solve the problem of having two different goods of religion in the system. Grisez's effort to add supernatural content to the basic good of religion results, unfortunately, only in an effort to clarify *obscurum per obscurius.* Setting aside the other anomalies in his account, the problem of two different goods of religion has to be solved if the system is to speak with any coherence about practical reason and religion.

If, however, Finnis finds something at the end of his investigation that indicates that the foundation itself has not been properly laid—that what was treated implicationally proves to be needed in the foundation—then he has a much larger problem on his hands. It would suggest that the originating level of his account of practical reason requires an explicit and antecedent metaphysics; it would mean, in short, that the problem of the *convenientia* between nature, reason, and God is methodologically foundational. The lack of reflective control over this systematic issue leads Grisez, in our view, to reintroduce foundational principles via theology. This only further complicates the matter. Since Finnis does not deal with theology, he perhaps is better prepared to reexamine just what needs to be adjusted to make the account consistent with itself. In *Natural Law and Natural Rights,* his hesitance in the face of the question of whether religion should be treated in the beginning, or systematically deferred until the end, summarizes the larger systematic question we have raised in this chapter.

Given the limitations of our investigation, we cannot reconstruct Grisez's or Finnis's system to render it consistent with either a foundational or an implicational approach to the relationship between religion and practical reason. Our task has been to uncover interpretively the systematic issues, and to explain what they mean. Yet, if an implicational route is to be considered, it would first be important to reconsider carefully their methodological shift from persons to goods. Alan Donagan is correct in noting how decisively this shapes Grisez's system (which separates Aquinas's Fppr from the antecedent philosophy of human nature), and of course Finnis's as well (who is interested in separating Kant's second categorical imperative from the antecedent philosophy of the noumenal self). This difference of focus is related to what we earlier proposed as the distinction between an inclination and an openness to religious values. What is sorely underdeveloped in the philosophy of both Grisez and Finnis is an account of the self that would permit us to understand how it is open to God. At the very least, we need a theory of the moral subject, and its capacity for self-transcendence, as a propaedeutic to the problem of religion and to the problem of supernaturality.

Throughout our study we raised the question of whether the human subject is something more than the sum of the parts of the goods which are pursued. In this respect, Grisez's account of the structure of human subjectivity strikes us as a tailpiece of his axiological theory. Thus, we find the human person consisting of four irreducible orders, but it is less than clear how or why the self is, or has, a principle of unity—much less whether it is distinct from what he calls the person. (Whether either of these is distinct from the human body is yet another question.) The self is bound to certain goods before we have an adequate idea of what the self is, in terms of its structure, meaning, and value. It is not surprising, therefore, that the puzzles we encountered regarding the irreducibility and incommensurability of the goods are the same puzzles involved in the relationship between the self and the person. Grisez argues that his account of practical reason begins with a thoroughly practical point of departure, but the dimension of human subjectivity is immediately bound to the axiological dimension in order to generate a system of obligations. We never get a glimpse of the inside, as it were, of the human subject. As we put it earlier, the topic of moral motivation and values receives a one-dimensional treatment: all agents pursue fulfillments, and all of the basic goods are modes of fulfillment to which we are morally bound.

This will not do for an implicational approach to the problem of religion because, among other reasons, the self-transcendence, or openness, of the human subject is left in the lurch. Practical reason is morally bound to the good of religion, not only before it is established that a morally significant divine referent exists, but more importantly before it is established that the subject is open to anything more than the immanent sphere of inclinations. Unless the latter is worked out, the former cannot emerge implicationally. Indeed, in Grisez's system as it presently stands, the value of a relationship to the person of God is simply posited by faith and, once posited, has no proportionality to the human subject. To put it bluntly, it cannot be the implication of anything. For this reason, Grisez is forced to redefine the value of the relationship posited by faith as an instance of the immanent good of religion—which, as we have shown in considerable detail, is not itself adequately founded.

By refocusing attention on persons, the dimension of self-transcendence could emerge in a way that allows us to treat it in its own right—at least in distinction to the issue of moral obligation to certain goods. Methodologically, these two issues (self and moral agent) have to be distinguished, even in order to reunite them. We have pointed out that religion is not the only instance of the problem. The treatment of the values of justice and friendship likewise lacks an account of interpersonality that would enable us to understand how we are related to other persons in such a way that the value does not solely consist in realizing an immanent inclination within ourselves.

Finnis is on the right track in this regard by seeing that further questions of order and meaning arise for the value of friendship, but the basal openness of the subject to other persons is not established. We are instructed by Grisez and Finnis on the meaning and value of goods, but it is not so clear in what the meaning and value of persons consists. While religion may prove to be an important implicational issue for friendship, the openness of the human subject to other rational subjects cannot await the implicational phase; nor can it be exclusively left for a theological treatment of the supernatural. Otherwise, the self-transcendent structure of human subjectivity will have to be posited by divine revelation. This virtually insures an ethico-religious positivism in which the principles governing our relationship not only to the person of God, but to all other persons, are drawn from outside the sphere of practical rationality.

The problem might also be alleviated by affording more attention to the role of the virtues. The goods constituted by Grisez's axiology are curiously Platonic-like forms. He vigorously admonishes Scholastic natural law theory for rendering practical reason a mere footnote to the speculative sciences, but Grisez's own understanding of the goods is rather Euclidian. The virtues, on the other hand, are not so readily abstracted from the unity of the self and the unity of the moral project. The point of the virtues cannot be grasped in piecemeal fashion, and therefore an ethics of virtue is forced to deal forthrightly with the issue of selfhood.[42] Moreover, as both MacIntyre and Hauerwas have shown, the virtues are in large part determined and organized in terms of one's society and the practices which are deemed worthwhile. They are not grasped *more geometrico*. For Grisez, however, the virtues are embodiments of moral propositions. This may be true in one respect, but not if it requires one to grasp one or another axiom and then embody it without already enjoying the virtuous disposition by which the proposition is embodied. Here is another instance of how his method proceeds well into the moral life before the questions about selfhood can come to the fore.

Nevertheless, a shift from goods to virtues would still have to meet the systematic criteria which we have outlined concerning the distinction between foundational and implicational approaches, as well as the need to explicate philosophically the value of persons as something more than realizations of immanent inclinations. Can the virtues, for instance, be envisioned as necessitating a move to implicational questions which are identifiably religious? If so, can this be explicated without having to build the foundation according to the metaphysical scaffolding of the older natural law theory?

These are important questions which cannot be settled here. Alasdair MacIntyre's recent effort to deal constructively with these questions has not, by his own admission, proved entirely successful. His stated ambition has been to recover a premodern ethics of virtue without the traditional speculative scaffolding. As he has admitted, however, his account presupposes "a systematic, although here unstated, account of rationality."[43] In this respect, MacIntyre is caught in a problem that is not altogether different from Grisez's effort to recover a natural law ethics of morally binding goods without either the older scaffolding or a theory of practical rationality sufficient to do the job according to an implicational approach. One might applaud the move toward an ethics of virtue, but there remains the suspicion that making sense of the virtues requires something more than making sense of conventions in which the virtues are, at least in part, intelligible. Quite apart from the problem of religion, one can entertain the sneaking suspicion that an ethics of virtue is but a halfway house that is stranded between a full-fledged natural law theory in the grand tradition and a thoroughly modern rejection of nature as having any constructive bearing upon ethics. It is a conventionalism that has premodern credentials.

CONCLUSION

At the outset we set at least two goals for this investigation. First, we wanted to understand in a systematic fashion the Grisez-Finnis natural law account of practical reason as it pertains both to the domain of values and to moral principles. Given the fact that, heretofore, this task had not yet been done to our satisfaction, it was necessary to investigate for ourselves how the various parts of this system fit together, especially the division of natural law method into premoral and moral parts. It was also necessary to our second goal, which was to give a critical analysis of how practical reason is related to religion in the light of a strictly philosophical account of the subject prior to faith, as well as in terms of the relationship between practical reason and the religion of faith. In the last chapter, we brought together the major problems and themes in order to understand them further according to a systematic distinction between foundational and implicational approaches to the relationship between religion and practical reason.

Although we have been critical of several aspects of the Grisez-Finnis method, we are not unsympathetic to the stated objectives of the system. Taking it in terms of its broadest aspirations, the project is important. It is no secret that the "common morality" referred to by Donagan was, for centuries, philosophically explicated by one or another natural law theory. Likewise, it is no secret that natural law, since the waning days of the Enlightenment, has been, as Henry Veatch observes, the "stone which the builders rejected."[1] Within the context of Roman Catholic moral discourse, it is dubious that natural law reasoning will be jettisoned altogether, for it is intertwined with centuries

190

of work in philosophy, morality, and theology—not to mention dogmatic pronouncements. Therefore, anyone who develops a natural law theory serviceable for use within Catholic moral discourse will have considerable impact. Something more than a merely textual recovery of natural law would indeed be an impressive achievement. Hence, we made every effort to downplay Grisez and Finnis's interpretation and use of texts in the history of natural law theory in order to examine the system on its own terms (except in a few cases where their interpretation of the tradition has an immediate and striking bearing upon the substantive issues). Grisez and Finnis wish to rehabilitate a traditional view of the moral life by weeding out problems inherent to the older natural law theory and by incorporating a more contemporary view of practical reason, without, of course, the problems inherent to the utilitarian or the deontological approaches.

If we broaden the lens to include issues beyond the specialized concerns in Catholic ethics, we can see that Grisez and Finnis are trying to do something similar to what Alasdair MacIntyre and Alan Donagan have proposed. All three wish to recapture the essence of a nonutilitarian, traditional ethics without becoming entangled in the problems which are bound to arise once one tackles those areas in which philosophy of nature touches upon practical reason. While MacIntyre wants to emphasize the role of the virtues, and Donagan the autonomy of persons, Grisez and Finnis are particularly interested in defending a "full" theory of the goods in a natural law context. Grisez has extended the method to include moral theology proper. They are not about the business of recovering one or another isolated strand of a premodern ethics. This is certainly what sets them apart from the other recoverists. As we said earlier, one cannot but sit up and take notice of what they are doing.

Yet, if our exposition and interpretation of their natural law system is correct, it has serious deficiencies. We focused upon the place of religion in their natural law system because it summarizes a number of problems which, for the most part, stem from their retrieval of the Thomistic Fppr, stripped of the philosophy of nature which sets the presuppositions for making sense of Aquinas's account of practical reason. The point is not merely historical and textual, but substantive. A natural law theory must show how nature is normative with regard to practical rationality. This has not been accomplished by the Grisez-Finnis method. The failure, however, can shed light on the wider problem of retrieving a premodern ethic.

As Alan Donagan puts it in *The Theory of Morality,* the problem with the so-called common morality and philosophy is that "academic moral philosophy has become dominated by a theory alien to the habitual morality that has survived, not only in society at large, but in academic philosophers themselves."[2] Donagan is more sanguine about the presence of this "habitual morality" than are MacIntyre and Hauerwas, who view the older moral discourse and practices as being but shards or pockets within a social situation that has mostly crumbled. Here, we would like to underscore Donagan's observation that moral philosophy has become dominated by a theory or theories "alien" to the habitual morality. Although it is certainly necessary to distinguish between practical reason as a human work distinct from speculative reason, and a *science* of morality, the key issue is the latter. To put it more sharply, the issue is the very possibility of the latter.

It is interesting that most everyone has a theory of what constitutes practical reason, but with the exception of a few Marxists, Thomists, and process philosophers, most ethicians remain agnostics about the prospect of practicing theoretical reason, and of employing it in some constructive way in ethics. Of course, it is entirely possible on the everyday level of experience to act and to hold certain moral convictions without having to use the compass of speculative rationality. For nearly two centuries there has been a general agnosticism regarding metaphysics, and yet people continue to act, learn by example, and have their characters shaped to some degree by various communities and friends. But what strains credibility is that one could purport to have a coherent theory of practical rationality, even while disclaiming to know (in the strong sense of the term *to know*) what it is to be human, whether human beings have ends, and how the overall setting of nature either orients or disorients human action. Credibility is further strained by one who would insist that the latter type of knowledge is unnecessary, even if one should have it. Such a notion would not be tolerated in the community of scientists, in which whether something is known or is merely conjectural has a direct bearing upon practice.

Alasdair MacIntyre has made the important point that one's prior notion of what is good or excellent will lead to a hierarchy of the virtues, and that rival notions of the good will lead to rival tables of the virtues.[3] MacIntyre is particularly interested in the way social narratives shape the individual's prior notion of excellence. Where there occur narrative revisions and conflicts, one can expect significant changes and confusion in ethics. Having said this, MacIntyre nevertheless wishes to retrieve a workable notion of the virtues without Aristotle's "metaphysical biology" —a term that is taken to mean Aristotle's philosophy of nature. The problem for MacIntyre converges upon the problem we examined, and perhaps belabored, with regard to the Grisez-Finnis method. From a normative standpoint, by what criteria do we determine this notion of the good from which flows relevant hierarchies and the *ordinatio* of the goods or virtues, if not by recourse to a philosophy of nature? Certainly the employment of a philosophy of nature represents Aristotle's method when, in the first book of the *Ethics*, he provides an inventory of human powers and their objects and thereby arrives at what constitutes the most excellent life.[4] He does not justify his philosophy of nature there, but he straightforwardly applies it. So, too, does Aquinas in the *prima-secundae,* where, in the first five questions, he attempts to demonstrate that no created good can serve as the ultimate end for human beings. The difference, for instance, between Aristotelian and Thomistic ethics is decisively determined by their different conceptions of a philosophy of nature, particularly by their respective conceptions of the scope in which such a philosophy can be applied.[5]

Similarly, a society that holds a Deweyan or Marxist philosophy of nature—or, indeed, a society that holds that no coherent philosophy of nature is at all possible—will have an ethics more or less in accord with those beliefs. MacIntyre's own historical method ought to show that Aristotelian ethics was jettisoned not simply because it was out of accord with religious and cultural changes at work in the Reformation and early Enlightenment, but because it was viewed as deficient as a science. It would seem vain to rescue Aristotelian ethics, either in whole or in part, without directly addressing the precise reasons why it was dismissed in the first place. The same holds for the grand tradition of natural law theory.

So, then, are not we stumbling over the same issue time and time again? We should admit the truth: it is not advisable to suppress the issues in a philosophy of nature and then, as it were, to take the ethics and run. We need to determine whether it is possible to provide a coherent philosophy of nature, and, if there be competing systems, which one is true. If, indeed, it is not possible to provide one, or to adjudge the best among competing systems, then we know where we stand; namely, that what MacIntyre has called the "interminability" of moral discourse is due to our inability to provide a foundation that would relieve our suspicion that ethics is based solely on strands of convention.

Or, to put it in another way, we can conclude that we live in a society avowing a philosophy of nature which chokes what Donagan has called the "common morality."

One suspects that among the retrievists the symptoms are made to fit the diagnosis. Recently Walker Percy wrote a very favorably received book entitled *Lost in the Cosmos,* in which he proposes that although we fancy ourselves as knowing quite a lot about astrophysics and the positive sciences, there has been a loss of selfhood.[6] Percy provides some interesting and ironic diagnoses about the problem. What we are proposing, however, is that prior to questions regarding a retrieval of selfhood, we should ask why it is that the cosmos is envisaged as something in which one could get lost in the first place. If selfhood were to be retrieved without resolving the coimplicate problem of nature, then one has only retrieved something resembling the Sartrean wayfarer who enjoys "authenticity" while being quite thoroughly lost. The questions posed by Finnis at the end of his *Natural Law and Natural Rights* concerning the alignment between the self, nature, and God are crucial and ought to be foundational.

If it is true that the common morality, or what is left of it, is being choked from the quadrant of "alien theories," then we need to address the theories—in particular, the belief that a coherent philosophy of nature cannot constructively be brought to bear upon ethical reasoning. Should it turn out that the regnant theories of nature since Kant merit our intellectual assent (that one or another of them is true), then it is reasonable to ask why we should fret over the demise of the common morality; for it would then be clear that the common morality was fundamentally mistaken about itself and indeed lacked foundations. Any effort to extract a part of the ethic in the absence of its proper foundations, or to assign that part to some other foundation, is tantamount to constructing a materially different ethic. If there is anything to be learned from the failure of the Grisez-Finnis system it is this. Hence, to retreat from this problem by attempting to locate some strand or pocket of moral discourse represents a loss of nerve in the face of the question. Rather than being a way of recovery, it is a symptom of the problem. If there are no "natures," and no proper telic completions to humanity and the goods sought, then I see no compelling reason to opt for Aristotelian virtue rather than Nietzsche.

In the meantime, it would seem that Stanley Hauerwas has articulated a position on the matter of practical reason and religion that is somewhat reasonable within its own terms. Hauerwas incorporates many strands which have interested the other retrievists—the importance of virtue and character, for example, and the manner in which narratives display fundamental commitments. He concedes that there are aspects of our moral experience which converge with specifically Christian convictions. Yet he is set against having Christian ethics create a metaphysics, an anthropology, or a morality when one is missing. One is reminded of Karl Barth's admonition that the God of Christianity is not to be viewed merely as a means for bailing out our antinomies. "Christian ethics," Hauerwas argues, "must insist upon the qualifier 'Christian' " and is not to be confounded with the ambition to construct a universal ethic amid the "fragments" of other ethical systems.[7] Hauerwas's ethic represents a very astute recovery of Protestant neoorthodoxy, and, as recoveries go, his would seem to be the most successful. He is not under the burden of having to account for religion in the common morality as well as its relationship to a particular religious tradition determined by a specific historical revelation. Simply put, a natural theology is not required. At the beginning of Christian moral reflection, one first allows one's life to be transformed by Christ, rather than first establishing what is normative and then trying to determine how Christianity "fits" the norms. It is a distinct alternative to classical natural law theory, which Ernst Bloch has aptly characterized as setting up the *facultas agendi* of finite unalienated man in the *norma agendi* of finite unalienated society.[8] This quite obviously will not do for Christianity, which must consider the difference made by sin and salvation.

However, Bloch has also correctly noted that medieval and, in particular, Thomistic, natural law theory is rather different than the classical theories. He calls it "relative natural law," because it recognizes the "no-longer-just-Adam," even while retaining a normative theory of nature. Likewise, Bloch is no doubt correct when he goes on to remark that the "harmony" of Saint Thomas "is tenable only in a relative natural law."[9]

On the matter of the relationship between practical reason and religion, if there is to be a constructive debate between the kind of Christian ethic advocated by Hauerwas and the Christian natural law tradition, it will of necessity focus upon the status of what Bloch has termed "relative natural law," and whether it can meet Hauerwas's requirement that the specificity of Christianity not be watered down.[10] However, as it stands, Hauerwas's position exacts a price; for the more specific his "qualified ethic" becomes, the larger the problem of different Christian traditions looms. Given fundamental differences between churches, the "qualified ethic" must be invoked with regard to Christian ethics as well, and some further principle needs to be invoked to prevent the specificity of a Christian ethic from becoming self-devouring. Otherwise, it will be as problematic to speak of Christian ethics as it is to speak of the so-called common morality. The long tradition of Western ethics has held that there is something more fundamental than conventions, whether social, civil, or ecclesial. Hauerwas states that the something else is Jesus, but he also argues that the story of Jesus is conveyed and enacted within specific ecclesial communities. While Hauerwas's position does not involve the intricate mess which we encountered in Grisez's moral theology, he is subject to the criticism of falling into an ethico-religious positivism—or conventionalism, as the case may be.

Perhaps Hauerwas is correct in saying that the effort to reconstruct a universal ethic amid the fragments of the common morality is misbegotten. Not only is it dubious to what extent the common morality continues to exist—even in contrast to the "alien" theories of academic ethicians—but the issue is, once again, whether it is possible to provide a philosophical account of ethics that is not just another trope on conventions. Viewed in this way, the failure of the Grisez-Finnis system is disturbing and enlightening. The missing ingredient in their system is conspicuously absent in the work of other retrievists. MacIntyre is correct in *After Virtue* when he concludes that we are not "waiting for Godot." What we are awaiting is a retrieval of natural law, or something very much like it. Having reached the end of this investigation, we are sorry to report that despite the ambition of the Grisez-Finnis project, we are still waiting. What is clear is that there is no way to recover natural law theory by way of shortcuts.

ABBREVIATIONS

This table includes abbreviations of terms frequently used in the text, as well as of books and articles frequently cited in the notes. Full bibliographical information is available in the bibliography.

Fppr   the first principle of practical reason
Fpm   the first principle of morality

AB   Grisez, *Abortion: The Myths, the Realities, and Arguments*
AC   Grisez, "Against Consequentialism"
BNM   Grisez, *Beyond the New Morality*
BNT   Grisez, *Beyond the New Theism*
CMP   Grisez, *Christian Moral Principles*
CNL   Grisez, *Contraception and the Natural Law*
FE   Finnis, *Fundamentals of Ethics*
FPPR   Grisez, "The First Principle of Practical Reason"
NLNR   Finnis, *Natural Law and Natural Rights*
MEI   Grisez, "Methods of Ethical Inquiry"
RRM   Grisez, "The Basic Principles of Natural Law: A Reply to Ralph McInerny"

NOTES

INTRODUCTION

1. Alan Donagan, *The Theory of Morality* (Chicago: University of Chicago Press, 1977), p. 26.

2. Alan Donagan, "Teleology and Consistency in Theories of Morality as Natural Law," in *The Georgetown Symposium on Ethics* (hereafter, *Georgetown Symposium*), ed. Rocco Porreco (Lanham, Md.: University Press of America, 1984), p. 93.

3. Elizabeth Anscombe, "Modern Moral Philosophy," in *The Collected Philosophical Papers*, vol. 3, *Ethics, Religion, and Politics* (Minneapolis: University of Minnesota Press, 1981), p. 30.

4. See Stanley Hauerwas, *The Peaceable Kingdom* (Notre Dame, Ind.: University of Notre Dame Press, 1983), chap. 1, "Christian Ethics in a Fragmented and Violent World," pp. 1–16.

5. Ernst Bloch, *Natural Law and Human Dignity*, trans. Dennis J. Schmidt (Cambridge, Mass.: MIT Press, 1986), p. xi.

6. Ernst Bloch, *The Principle of Hope*, 3 vols., trans. Neville Plaice, Stephen Plaice, and Paul Knight (Cambridge, Mass.: MIT Press, 1986).

7. Henry B. Veatch, *Human Rights: Fact or Fancy?* (Baton Rouge, La.: Louisiana State University Press, 1985), p. 96.

8. NLNR, p. vii; and the Preface of FE.

9. RRM, p. 21.

1. THE GRISEZ–FINNIS ACCOUNT OF PRACTICAL REASON AND HUMAN VALUES

1. CMP, p. 105.
2. CNL, p. 48.
3. Ibid., p. 60.
4. CMP, p. 183.
5. Ibid., pp. 3–39.
6. Ibid., pp. 12f.

7. Ibid., p. 103.

8. Ibid., p. 36, note 17. See CNL, p. 14.

9. Ibid., pp. 103f. See FPPR, p. 103.

10. Ibid., p. 12.

11. FPPR, p. 193. Suarez *De Legibus* 2. 7.

12. CMP, p. 104.

13. CNL, pp. 47–50.

14. CMP, p. 13.

15. Ibid., p. 25.

16. Ibid., p. 26, note 29.

17. Ibid., p. 17.

18. AC, p. 32; CNL, pp. 60f.

19. CMP, pp. 105f.

20. Ibid., p. 107.

21. CNL, p. 20.

22. Ibid., pp. 27f.

23. Ibid., p. 51.

24. Ibid., p. 28.

25. CMP, p. 105.

26. For a more recent summary, see Germain Grisez, "Christian Moral Theology and Consequentialism," in *Principles of Catholic Moral Life*, ed. William E. May (Chicago: Franciscan Herald Press, 1980), pp. 293-327.

27. See Finnis's account of the various terms used for the utilitarian tradition, in FE, pp. 80-86.

28. CMP, p. 145.

29. Ibid., p. 166, note 16.

30. Ibid., p. 173.

31. Ibid., p. 152.

32. Ibid., p. 153. See AC, p. 48.

33. AC, p. 41.

34. Ibid., pp. 27-31. See CMP, p. 151.

35. CMP, p. 157.

36. Richard A. McCormick, *Notes on Moral Theology; 1981-1984* (Lanham, Md.: University Press of America, 1985), p. 136.

37. CMP, p. 156.

38. Ibid., p. 155.

39. Ibid., p. 145.

40. AC, pp. 70f.

41. CMP, p. 108.

42. AB, p. 314.

43. See Finnis's remarks on Rawls's "thin" theory of the goods, in NLNR, pp. 105f.

44. FE, pp. 228f.

45. Alan Donagan, *The Theory of Morality*, pp. 64f.

46. An abridged version of the article has been printed in *Aquinas: A Collection of Critical Essays*, ed. Anthony Kenny. (London, 1970; rpt. Notre Dame, Ind.: University of Notre Dame Press, 1976), pp. 340–82. It is, however, an abridgement that Grisez does not regard as an accurate representation of his original article—see RRM, p. 21, note 2. On Donagan's acceptance of the interpretation, see his *Theory of Morality*, pp. xv, 61–63. See Finnis's remarks in NLNR, p. vii.

47. FPPR, p. 175.

48. CMP, p. 179

49. FPPR, pp. 180f.

50. CMP, p. 180.

51. CNL. pp. 61f.

52. CMP, p. 180.

53. CNL, p. 67.

54. Aquinas *Summa theologiae* 1.2, q. 94, a.2.

55. FPPR, p. 173. See NLNR, pp. 33f.

56. Ibid.

57. CNL, p. 65.

58. NLNR, p. 34.

59. FE, p. 51.

60. CMP, p. 179.

61. See, for example, Vernon Bourke, "The Synderesis Rule and Right Reason," *The Monist* 66 (January 1983): 70–82, where he gives a historical treatment of the formula *declina a malo et fac bonum* which emphasizes the good as the opposite of evil, and hence the good as a specifically moral good. Ralph McInerny makes much the same point against Grisez and Finnis in *Ethica Thomistica* (Washington, D.C.: Catholic University of America Press, 1982), pp. 43–53. See Henry Veatch's criticism in *Human Rights*, pp. 95–104. For a brief but revealing critique of Finnis, see Ernest L. Fortin, "The New Rights Theory and the Natural Law," *Review of Politics* 44 (October 1982): 590–612. Grisez and Finnis's interpretation of the Fppr, and perforce their division of natural law method into moral and premoral facets, has not been well received by Thomistic scholars.

62. FPPR, p. 187.

63. CNL, p. 62.

64. Ibid., p. 66.

65. Ralph McInerny's critique originally appeared under the title "The Principles of Natural Law," in *American Journal of Jurisprudence* 25 (1980): 1–15. Later this material was incorporated into his *Ethica Thomistica*.

66. McInerny, *Ethica Thomistica*, p. 44.

67. Ernest Bloch, *Natural Law and Human Dignity*, p. xiii.

68. RRM, p. 27.

69. CMP, p. 179 (emphasis added). Elsewhere he states that the Fppr governs all "*coherent* practical thinking" (CMP, p. 70); and that it entails an "*adequate* understanding" of intelligible goods (FPPR, p. 173)—emphases added. Finnis says it is a grasp of "opportunities rather than dead ends" (FE, p. 51). The emphases here underscore the notion that the intuitions are fallible, for there can be a lack of adequation or coherence. When Grisez examines the nature of an immoral act, he describes it as "partly irrational insofar as it is inadequately responsive to some principle of practical thinking" (CMP, p. 198). If, however, we must factor in the fallibility of the original insight with regard to the *prima principia*, then it would be impossible to find an agent's behavior blameworthy insofar as his or her premoral intuition or insight was awry.

70. FE, pp. 22, 30.

71. CMP, p. 115.

72. In CNL: "goods" (p. 65); "possibilities" (p. 65); "values" (p. 69); "sources of motivation" (p. 65); "tendencies" (pp. 64f.); "basic inclinations" (p. 64); "primary practical principles" (p. 66); "essential goods" (p. 67); "ideals" (p. 70). In AB, they are called "basic human needs" (pp. 313f); and in BNM, "purposes" (p. 69).

73. NLNR, pp. 76, 61.

74. CMP, pp. 122, 393.

75. Ibid; FE, p. 124.

76. CMP, p. 125.

77. See CNL, p. 64; AB, pp. 312f.; BNM, pp. 69f.

78. CMP, p. 124.

79. Ibid.

80. Ibid.

81. NLNR, pp. 86–90.

82. Ibid., p. 92.

83. BNM, p. 74.

84. NLNR, pp. 33f.

85. Grisez and Finnis have responded to Thomist critics by saying that their use of Aquinas "prescinds from the question of whether it is *ad mentem Divi Thomae* (RRM, p. 21). See, however, Vernon Bourke's essay "The Background of Aquinas's Synderesis Principle," in *Graceful Reason: Essays in Ancient and Medieval Philosophy Presented to Joseph Owens*, ed. Loyd P. Gerson (Toronto: Institute of Mediaeval Studies, 1983), pp. 345–60; and his review of Finnis's NLNR in *American Journal of Jurisprudence* 24 (1981): 243–47.

Bourke contends that there is a confusion in Grisez's theory between *prudentia* and a *philosophia moralis*. The former, he observes, is somewhat private and intuitive, while the latter is concerned with a universal form of practical discourse (i.e., what might be placed in the first premise of a practical syllogism). Bourke goes on to note that if these two aspects of practical reason are confused, one is liable to fall into a thoroughgoing intuitionist ethics. If attention is diverted to the matter of interpreting Aquinas, it is easy to lose sight of the substantive point. Our study will make it amply clear that the Grisez-Finnis position is severely crippled by intuitionism. Unfortunately, Grisez and Finnis tend to brush their Thomist critics off by saying that the criticism involves "a neoscholastic commingling of historical interpretation and philosophical construction" (RRM, p. 31).

86. AB, pp. 313f.

87. CMP, p. 195.

88. CNL, p. 64.

89. Ibid., p. 63.

90. AB, p. 312.

91. NLNR, p. 136. The expression "an assemblage of reminders" is somewhat evasive in terms of what role is envisaged for the social sciences. In their reply to McInerny's criticism, Grisez and Finnis contend: "We have never said that one cannot pass from metaphysical and/or factual truths *together with principles of practical reason* to normative conclusions" (RRM, p. 24). The "together with" is the crucial term, which is nowhere explained in their writings. Finnis states that although Aquinas does list the goods in what might appear to be a hierarchical and teleological order, Aquinas's remarks in question 94, a.2, are a "speculative appendage added by way of metaphysical reflection, *not* a counter with which to advance either to or from the practical *prima principia per se nota*" (NLNR, p. 36). For other texts, indicating Grisez and Finnis's dismissal of the role of speculative reason, see FPPR, p. 196; FE, pp. 15f., 70f.; NLNR, p. 52.

92. Thomas Russman, "Foundations, Objective and Objections: Adler and Finnis on Objective Goods and Replies to Four Objections," in *Georgetown Symposium*, p. 115.

93. CMP, p. 133; BNT, p. 171.

94. See Joseph M. Boyle, Jr., Germain Grisez, and Olaf Tollefsen, *Free Choice: A Self-Referential Argument* (Notre Dame, Ind.: University of Notre Dame Press, 1976). Grisez is more cautious than Finnis on the use of the self-referential method. See BNT, pp. 155f., 174f.

95. FE, p. 58.

96. NLNR, p. 65.

97. Ibid., pp. 74f.

98. Ibid., pp. 29f.

2. NATURAL LAW, MORAL PRINCIPLES, AND ENDS

1. AB, p. 315.
2. CMP, p. 184. "Good acts," he adds, "will harmonize with—not necessarily realize—the true good of humankind."
3. NLNR, p. 103.
4. CMP, p. 185.
5. CNL, p. 69.
6. CMP, p. 197.
7. CNL, p. 69.
8. CMP, p. 186.
9. Ibid., p. 185.
10. Ibid.
11. Ibid., p. 186.
12. Ibid., p. 185.
13. Ibid., p. 186.
14. Ibid., p. 185.
15. CMP, p. 185; RRM, p. 28.
16. Ibid., p. 575.
17. In this regard, see my article on Aquinas's use of the distinction between *amor concupiscentiae* and *amor amiticitiae*: "When It Is More Excellent to Love than to Know: The Other Side of Thomistic 'Realism'," in *Proceedings of the American Catholic Philosophical Association* 57, ed. Daniel O. Dahlstrom (1983), pp. 171–79. On the question of values and fulfillments, see Dietrich von Hildebrand's *Ethics* (Chicago: Franciscan Herald Press, 1953), pp. 97ff. Von Hildebrand discusses the problems in saying that a value, such as evidence of a truth, is nothing but the capacity of the object to satisfy one's needs. See Grisez's description of the good of knowledge in BNM, where it is characterized as "knowledge sought to satisfy curiosity" (p. 67).
18. CMP, p. 189.
19. Ibid.
20. Ibid., pp. 189–92; 205–22.
21. Ibid., pp. 205–22.
22. Ibid., p. 192.
23. Finnis's list, NLNR, pp. 103–26. See Ernest L. Fortin, "The New Rights Theory and the Natural Law," for a critique of their theory of virtue. For the Grisez-Finnis response, see RRM, p. 28, note 33.
24. CMP, p. 267.
25. Ibid., p. 124.
26. CNL, p. 83.
27. Ibid., p. 98.

28. Ibid., p. 92.

29. Ibid.

30. Ibid., p. 93.

31. Ibid., p. 79.

32. Ibid., p. 81.

33. Ibid.

34. Ibid., pp. 110f.

35. Here it is worth recalling Vernon Bourke's remarks about intuitionism in note 83 of the previous chapter. The basal "insight" is prodigious indeed, for it manages to swallow every part of the older natural law theory.

36. CNL, p. 71.

37. Ibid., pp. 1f.

38. AB, p. 306.

39. CNL, p. 63.

40. BNT, pp. 347, 12, 387, note 7.

41. Ibid., p. 346.

42. For a useful study of Thomas's emendation of Aristotelian hylemorphism, see Anton Pegis, *At the Origins of the Thomistic Notion of Man* (New York: Macmillan, 1963).

43. AC, p. 31.

44. FE, p. 17, 121f.

45. Ibid., p. 124.

46. CNL, p. 33.

47. Ibid., p. 41.

48. Aquinas *Ethics* 1, lectio 1.9.

49. Ibid.

50. For the omission, see CMP, p. 42; BNT, pp. 230–35, 347ff.

51. NLNR, p. 136.

52. CMP, p. 42.

53. BNT, p. 47.

54. Ibid.

55. AB, p. 321.

56. CMP. p. 55.

57. BNT, p. 351.

58. Ibid., p. 352.

59. CMP, p. 156.

60. Grisez argues that the so-called existential goods are inter-related such that no one of them can be achieved without the others. See BNM, pp. 76f. This is not the case with the substantive goods, nor, apparently, with the interrelation between existential and substantive goods. The problem of axiological atomism is not alleviated.

61. CMP, p. 156.

62. Ibid.

63. Ibid.

64. BNM, pp. 94f. See also CMP, p. 156.

65. Ibid., p. 73.

66. Ibid., pp. 74f.

67. Ibid.

68. NLNR, p. 92.

69. Ibid., p. 93. Grisez uses the same example in BNM, p. 65.

70. CMP, p. 157.

71. AC, p. 23.

72. For a discussion of this problem, see Fortin, "New Rights Theory," pp. 602f., where Fortin asks whether there is any principle by which to judge the relative merit of life plans fit for a "statesman" and for a "ski bum."

73. For example: the effect of practical reason is to "invent the possibility of all human goods" (CNL, p. 66); "human action is soul-making" (CMP, p. 155); and, of course, he frequently remarks on the lack of objective criteria for a life plan. See the Grisez-Finnis response to McInerny, in RRM, p. 25.

74. As an interesting counterpoint to Finnis's contention that the Aristotelian unique *ergon* concept is the erratic boulder tumbling through the history of Western ethics, see George Allan, *The Importances of the Past* (Albany: SUNY, 1986), pp. 21ff. Allan argues that the Cartesian method of treating ideas as equally dubitable spilled over into the domain of values, which can be regarded as equally valuable or valueless. In this "desert island of egalitarian significance," distinctions of importance or irrelevance have to be introduced by habit and convenience. Grisez and Finnis lock on to a list of *per se nota* basic values, but they are egalitarian, subject only to habit and convenience once one tries to establish a gradation. Neither Grisez nor Finnis realizes how this value egalitarianism flirts precipitously with certain assumptions of the utilitarian tradition.

75. For Grisez, see AC, p. 23, note 2. For Finnis, see NLNR, p. 129. For Rawls, see John Rawls, *A Theory of Justice* (Cambridge, Mass.: Belknap Press, 1971), p. 408, note 10. Royce's theory is found in Josiah Royce, *The Basic Writings of Josiah Royce*, vol. 2, *The Philosophy of Loyalty*, ed. J. J. McDermott (Chicago: University of Chicago Press, 1969), p. 921. Royce uses the concept of a life plan in order to find an object of loyalty that interrelates all of the other purposes of selfhood and society. It is envisaged not as a convenient grocery list of loyalties but as an architectonic that affirms gradations of importance. One suspects that Royce's concept has been poached upon for purposes quite different from what Royce himself

had in mind. For a quite different use of Royce's concept (one that adheres closely to his original intent), see Gabriel Marcel, *Homo Viator,* trans. Emma Craufurd (Chicago: Regnery, 1951), p. 155.

76. See Stanley Hauerwas, "From System to Story," in *Truthfulness and Tragedy* (Notre Dame, Ind.: University of Notre Dame Press, 1977), pp. 15–39; and *The Peaceable Kingdom.*

77. Alasdair MacIntyre, *After Virtue,* 2d ed. (Notre Dame, Ind.: University of Notre Dame Press, 1984), pp. 156, 203–25.

78. Rawls, *Theory of Justice,* p. 433.

79. Ibid., p. 95.

80. Ibid., p. 92.

81. Ibid., p. 411.

82. Ibid., p. 409.

83. Ibid., p. 414.

84. Ibid., p. 432.

85. Ibid., p. 553.

86. Ibid., p. 554.

87. See Joseph Owens, *Human Destiny* (Washington, D.C.: Catholic University of America Press, 1985), p. 77. Owens argues that if the perennial philosophy is to move constructively into the contemporary mode of philosophy of religion, its chief contribution would be to point out the possibility of envisaging such an end in contemplation, which he admits "is not an easy task in the contemporary world."

88. Rawls, *Theory of Justice,* pp. 565f.

89. Ibid., p. 551.

90. NLNR, p. 103.

91. CMP, p. 393.

92. We emphasize here "as a substitution" because the concept of life plans can reveal quite a lot about human psychology, moral rhetoric, and the sociological dimension of moral systems. What we have found in the Grisez-Finnis system is that the concept presupposes a notion of finality which is not fully brought to light so long as one continues to refer to life plans. In this regard, the problems with the Grisez-Finnis position should carefully be considered by others who employ the life plan construct. We shall have a few words to say about it in the conclusion.

93. The incommensurability between different individual or societal life plans (or narratives) is a real problem for anyone who would want this construct to serve systematic ends. This is why Rawls keeps it at bay until he enters the final stage of his account of justice —where the life plan bears only tangentially upon fundamental norms of morality. His system, then, seems to be immune to the epistemological and ontological problems inherent in the area of

life plans. Finnis, however, makes the choice of a life plan a matter of moral obligation, though we lack any positive criteria for judging whether the norm is being met in any particular case. In linking together the rationality of moral virtues with societal narratives, Alasdair MacIntyre has admitted that his theory has not yet sufficiently answered the problem of historicism. See the Postscript to *After Virtue*, pp. 272–78.

94. For Finnis's critique of Rawls, see NLNR, pp. 105f.

95. Rawls, *Theory of Justice*, p. 24.

96. CMP, p. 393.

97. Ibid., p. 809.

98. Ibid.

99. CMP, p. 270.

100. FPPR, p. 200.

101. CMP, p. 179.

102. FPPR, p. 200.

103. For passages in which he states that the goods must be proportionate to human choice, see CNL, p. 72; BNT, p. 311; BNM, pp. 30f.

104. CMP, p. 188.

105. Ibid.

106. AB, pp. 316f.

107. CNL, p. 71.

108. AB, p. 316.

109. CNL, p. 71. Emphasis added.

110. One is struck by the similarity between Grisez's understanding of the open-endedness of the Fpm prior to faith and Descartes' argument in Meditation IV that since only God can regard all of his creations together, "it does not appear to me that I can without temerity seek to investigate the [inscrutable] ends of God." See Rene Descartes, *The Philosophical Works of Descartes*, vol. 1, *Meditations on First Philosophy*, trans. E. S. Haldane and G. R. T. Ross (Cambridge: Cambridge University Press, 1931), pp. 173f. Descartes holds that it is reasonable to believe that there exists a providential purpose for all things, but this exceeds the method of philosophy, and therefore finality can be dismissed from his method. Such a move, however, requires an antecedent argument or assumption that there is no distinction between finality and providence. Descartes glides over the problem. In the absence of a distinction between finality and providence, the issue of "purposes" will have to either (1) await theological resolution, or (2) be resolved in terms of what appears useful or convenient. In the next chapter we will indicate how Grisez solves the problem in terms of a peculiar combination of both of the alternatives just outlined.

111. See CMP, p. 184; MEI, p. 168; FPPR, p. 201; AC, pp. 40f.
112. AC, p. 72.
113. FPPR, p. 201.

3. RELIGION, FAITH, AND PRACTICAL REASON

1. G. W. F. Hegel, *The Positivity of the Christian Religion*, in *Early Theological Writings*, trans. T. M. Knox (Philadelphia: University of Pennsylvania Press, 1977), p. 152. On the lamentations which followed Kant's "saddle" of practical reason, see Heinrich Heine, *Religion and Philosophy in Germany* (first published in 1834), trans. John Snodgrass (Albany: SUNY, 1986), pp. 119ff. Heine complained that when Kant extinguished the positive role of speculative reason, "he acted almost as sagely as a Westphalian friend of mine, who smashed all the lanterns in the Grohnder Street in Gottingen, and then proceeded to deliver to us in the dark a long lecture of the practical necessity of lanterns, which he had theoretically broken in order to show how, without them, we could see nothing."

2. James Collins, *The Emergence of Philosophy of Religion* (New Haven: Yale University Press, 1967), pp. 18-28. Collins finds three dominant paradigms of the Enlightenment on the relation between religion and practical reason: (1) the "separatist" approach, advocated by Hume, which isolates religion from morality in order to preserve moral judgments; (2) the "completional" approach of Kant, which attempts to ground moral judgment prior to religion, but which allows religion to emerge as a way of sustaining hope in the moral project; and (3) the "organic modalizing" approach of Hegel, which envisions morals and religion as distinct modes of a spiritual totality. Obviously, historical investigation could cull out other models. Grisez and Finnis have certain affinities to the "completional" paradigm of Kant. These will be discussed in due course, particularly in the following chapter.

3. H. R. Niebuhr's typology is well known. See A. James Reichley's typology and comments in *Religion in American Public Life* (Washington, D.C.: Brookings Institution, 1985), especially chap. 2, "Religion, Politics, and Human Values," pp. 9-52.

4. Friedrich Schleiermacher argued, for instance, that "fundamental feelings" are the "middle point of all religions." See his *On Religion: Speeches to Its Cultured Despisers*, John Oman (New York: Ungar, 1955), p. 142.

5. See Karl Barth, *The Knowledge of God and the Service of God*, The Gifford Lectures of 1937-38, trans. J. L. M. Haire and Ian Henderson (1939; reprint ed., New York: AMS Press, 1979), pp. 3ff.

The lectures are a commentary on the *Confessio Scotica* of 1650, and represent perhaps the clearest statement Barth made on the notion of "natural religion."

6. See Ludwig Feuerbach, *Lectures on the Essence of Religion*, trans. Ralph Manheim (New York: Harper & Row, 1967).

7. As odd as it might seem, the psychedelia of the recent past is one of the most interesting chapters in the history of this effort to locate a distinctively "religious" experience accessible to anyone—in this case, anyone who has the biochemical prerequisites. To date, the most comprehensive scholarly treatment of the subject is Martin A. Lee and Bruce Shlain, *Acid Dreams* (New York: Grove Press, 1985).

8. John Dewey, *A Common Faith* (New Haven, Conn.: Yale University Press, 1934), p. 7.

9. Ibid., pp. 24-33.

10. Karl Rahner, *Hearers of the Word*, trans. Michael Richards (New York: Herder & Herder, 1969), p. 13.

11. Karl Barth, *Epistle to the Romans*, trans. Edwyn C. Hoskyns (Oxford: Oxford University Press, 1933), p. 268. That Barth was prepared to side with Feuerbach against Schleiermacher on the issue of religion is important for anyone who wants to understand the development of modern Protestant theology. See Barth's chapters on the two in Karl Barth, *Protestant Theology in the Nineteenth Century*, trans. Brian Cozens (London: SCM Press, 1972).

12. For an overview, see W. C. Smith, *The Meaning and End of Religion* (New York: Macmillan, 1963).

13. I have taken this distinction between foundational and implicational issues from Collins, *Emergence of Philosophy of Religion*, p. 144. It shall be employed throughout the next chapter.

14. The constructive premises of Alasdair MacIntyre, *After Virtue*, do not include religion—though the last sentence of the book is suggestive. Alan Donagan admits in *The Theory of Morality* to having been much affected by Elizabeth Anscombe's argument concerning the missing religious premises as the key to the paralysis of modern moral philosophy. He writes: "Had I not become persuaded that she was mistaken, as a result of reading Kant's ethical writings . . . I could not have embarked on the present study" (p. xv). His own foundations are based upon "that part of the common morality according to the Hebrew-Christian tradition that does not depend on any theistic belief" (p. 29).

15. BNT, pp. 3f., 314ff.

16. Ibid., p. 4.

17. Ibid.

18. Ibid., pp. 51f.

19. Ibid., p. 50.

20. Ibid., pp. 70ff.
21. Ibid., p. 72.
22. Ibid., p. 23.
23. Ibid.
24. Ibid., p. 82.
25. Ibid., p. 83.
26. Ibid.
27. Ibid., p. 230.
28. Ibid., p. 233.
29. Ibid., p. 244.
30. Ibid., pp. 253f., 266.
31. Ibid., p. 297.
32. Ibid., p. 249.
33. Ibid., p. 301; see also p. 12.
34. Ibid., pp. 246, 151.
35. Ibid., p. 89.
36. Ibid., p. 85.
37. Ibid., p. 269.
38. Ibid., p. 270.
39. Ibid., p. 271.
40. CMP, pp. 65f., 480.
41. Ibid., p. 66.
42. Ibid., pp. 480, 477.
43. Karl Barth, *Protestant Theology in the Nineteenth Century*, p. 356.
44. CMP, p. 478.
45. FPPR, p. 196.
46. BNT, pp. 284ff., 299, 303. See also CMP, p. 115. Here it is worth recalling the remarks made in note 103 of the previous chapter.
47. CMP, 477f.
48. FPPR, pp. 192f.
49. Ibid., p. 172.
50. Ibid. Grisez goes on to state: "Man can be ignorant of these precepts because God does not fall within our grasp so that the grounds of his lovability and authority are evident to everybody." Finnis makes the same point in NLNR, p. 32. Of course, although Aquinas admits the difficulty of demonstrating the existence of God, and the inaccessibility of quidditative knowledge of God in this life, he nevertheless contends that the existence of God can be demonstrated. Moreover, in *Summa theologiae* 1 q. 60, a. 5, he argues that it is by nature that God should be loved above all else. In *Summa theologiae* 2. 2 q. 81, a. 6, he makes this norm of nature more explicit when he argues, in the section on the natural virtue of

religion, that right reason requires obedience and service of God. Grisez and Finnis generally take a minimalist view of what can be said philosophically about the existence of God, and the bearing it has on practical reason. They likewise take a minimalist view of what other theorists, like Aquinas, say about the matter. In either case, if we have no knowledge whatsoever of why God should be lovable, or demand obedience and service, then it is difficult to understand why we should "know" that the so-called good of religion is attractive and obligatory.

51. CNL, p. 64.
52. AB, p. 313.
53. Ibid.
54. BNM, p. 72.
55. Ibid., p. 206.
56. Ibid., p. 199.
57. Ibid., pp. 201f.
58. Kant, of course, distinguishes between the holiness of God and the moral goodness of human persons in Immanuel Kant, *Critique of Practical Reason*, trans. Lewis W. Beck (Indianapolis: Bobbs-Merrill, 1956), pp. 33, 86. See also Immanuel Kant, *Religion within the Limits of Reason Alone*, trans. Theodore M. Greene and Hoyt H. Hudson (New York: Harper & Row, 1960), p. 60. Kant makes the distinction because the *potestas non peccandi* in the case of God makes the moral "ought" meaningless, and hence is a transmoral category. It is not easy to determine why Grisez makes the distinction, except perhaps to note that holiness is characteristic of charity and the inner life of God. If this is what he has in mind, then he has taken things too far, for holiness would seem to be the preeminent instance of what it means to be good (morally or otherwise). Moreover, it would be necessary to soften the term *separate*, if for no other reason than to allow for the possibility that human creatures can share in the distinctive kind of divine goodness called holiness.

59. BNM, pp. 216f.
60. Ibid., pp. 202f.
61. Ibid., pp. 208f.
62. BNT, pp. 87f.
63. Ibid., p. 309.
64. Ibid., p. 308.
65. Ibid. Emphasis added.
66. CMP, p. 124.
67. Ibid., pp. 65f.
68. Ibid.
69. Ibid.

70. Ibid., p. 706.
71. Ibid., p. 314.
72. Ibid., p. 136.
73. AC, pp. 60f. Emphasis added.
74. CMP, p. 706.
75. BNT, p. 361.
76. CMP, p. 482.
77. Ibid., p. 278. Emphasis added.
78. Iibd.
79. For Aquinas, see note 50 above. In *The Knowledge of God and the Service of God*, p. 8, Karl Barth grudgingly concedes that the Reformers made a "guarded" and an "unguarded" use of natural theology to secure these superordinate laws. Whether guarded or not, see John Calvin, *Institutes of the Christian Religion*, trans. Ford Lewis Battles (Philadelphia: Westminster Press, 1960), pp. 43–44. See also John Calvin, *Catechism of the Church of Geneva*, trans. J. K. S. Reid, *Library of Christian Classics*, vol. 22 (Philadelphia: Westminster Press, 1954), pp. 107ff.
80. CMP, p. 511.
81. Ibid., p. 666.
82. Ibid., p. 349.
83. Ibid., p. 459.
84. Ibid.
85. Ibid., p. 605. Emphasis added.
86. Ibid., p. 459.
87. Ibid., p. 606.
88. Ibid.
89. Ibid., p. 607.
90. Ibid.
91. Ibid.
92. Ibid., p. 514.
93. Peter Geach takes a similar approach. "The knowledge of God is thus *not* prerequisite to our having *any* moral knowledge. I shall argue however that we do need it in order to see that we must not do evil that good may come, and that this principle actually follows from a certain conception of God." See Peter Geach, "The Moral Law and God," in *God and the Soul* (New York: Schocken Books, 1969), p. 120. Geach, like his wife and colleague Elizabeth Anscombe, argues that without a religious concept of God as a lawgiver, human beings will usually stop short of admitting that whole classes of actions are absolutely, and without exception, forbidden. Geach contends that the concept of a sovereign, providential God undermines the practical rationality of doing evil to achieve good because, were such a God to exist, any calculus justifying good consequences

by evil deeds would come to naught anyway (p. 129). What is interesting about Grisez and Geach is that while they argue against the philosophical logic of consequentialism, they are quite prepared on the other hand to say that its practical appeal cannot be countered unless God is factored into the picture: in the case of Geach, a God who will ultimately thwart the consequences; in the case of Grisez, a God who reveals that one can enjoy the entirety of good consequences anyway, and hence there is no need to shortchange one's choices. The upshot is that the motivational sinews of consequentialism are left intact, and are qualified only extrinsically.

94. CMP, p. 514.

95. Ibid., pp. 513, 219, 279.

96. Ibid., p. 603.

97. Ibid., p. 638.

98. Ibid., pp. 654ff.

99. As we have pointed out, Finnis includes a pretheological equivalent of this norm regarding vocation as his first mode of moral responsibility, in NLNR, pp. 103ff.

100. CMP, p. 278.

101. Ibid.

102. Ibid.

103. Ibid., p. 652.

104. Ibid., p. 655.

105. For this oft-quoted remark, see Augustine, *City of God* (trans. Dods) 19.25. It is important to remember that Augustine's remark is set in the context of his critique of the Stoics, who refused to admit that the natural virtues are telically ordered to an end beyond themselves.

106. CMP, p. 655.

107. Ibid., p. 493.

108. This theme is explored particularly in Soren Kierkegaard, *Kierkegaard's Writings*, vol. 6, *Fear and Trembling*, trans. H. V. Hong and E. H. Hong (Princeton, N.J.: Princeton University Press, 1983), "Eulogy on Abraham" and "Problema 2," pp. 15–21, 68–81.

109. CMP, p. 18.

110. Ibid., p. 22.

111. Ibid., p. 220.

112. Ibid., p. 222.

113. Ibid., p. 588.

114. Ibid., p. 599.

115. Grisez himself describes prayer as a human act of charity in CMP, p. 600.

116. CMP, pp. 600f.

117. Ibid., p. 485. Emphases added.

118. Ibid., p. 530.

119. Ibid., p. 531. See his discussion of martyrdom on p. 588.

120. Ibid., p. 814.

121. Ibid. See also pp. 765, 810.

122. Ibid., p. 460.

123. Ibid., p. 562. Yet elsewhere he says that persons "cannot be ordered to a good as any part to a whole" (AC, p. 31). Thus, in CMP Grisez has reversed, and perhaps contradicted, himself on the question of the common good. It is unsettling, because if, according to nature, human beings cannot be ordered to a good as a part to a whole, it implies that grace acts against nature. It is likewise important to note that in CMP, p. 198, Grisez contends that "the moral teaching of *Humanae Vitae* is not based on any concept of natural law or any philosophical argument at all. It is received teaching in the Church, and it originated (probably before Christ) before there was any natural-law theory to articulate and defend it. *Natural law theories are theology;* the Church's moral teaching is part of the Judeo-Christian heritage" [emphasis added]. This, too, represents a significant departure from his previous arguments on the subject of contraception and the natural law. In context, one could interpret the remark as involving an equivocation between the philosophical and historical meanings of natural law. Yet he directly states that "natural law theories are theology." Grisez's own work lends credence to the claim.

124. Ibid., p. 585.

125. Ibid., p. 577.

126. NLNR, p. 89.

127. Ibid., p. 98.

128. Ibid., p. 90.

129. Ibid., p. 89.

130. Ibid.

131. Ibid., p. 91.

132. The parallel chapter in FE is entitled "Ethics and Our Destiny."

133. NLNR, p. 372.

134. Ibid.

135. Ibid.

136. Aristotle raises but does not answer this problem in the *Nicomachean Ethics*, 1.10 (1100a–1101a). For an insightful discussion comparing Aristotle and Kant on the problem of novelty and fortune in the moral life, see William A. Galston, *Kant and the Problem of History* (Chicago: University of Chicago Press, 1975), pp. 37ff., 66ff.

137. In this regard, a thoroughgoing individualism at least escapes

the presumption that another agent is simply an "aspect" of my good. See, for instance, John Stuart Mill, *On Liberty* (Indianapolis: Hacker Publishing, 1978). In chapter 3 he argues that it is necessary to conceive of a common (albeit historical and prospective) good, since the free experiments of individuals are justifiable because they increase the well-being and progress of humanity. This prospective of heuristic common good may be rather thin, but Mill recognizes that it is necessary to ground the virtue of tolerance (i.e., why I should allow others the freedom I wish for myself).

138. NLNR, p. 373.
139. FE, p. 145.
140. This is precisely the Stoic response to the tension between happiness and duty. Finnis has some very insightful things to say about Stoicism in FE, p. 149, and on Augustine's critique of the Stoics in NLNR, p. 378. One is not so certain that he has adequately enough applied these insights to his own theory.
141. FE, p. 48.
142. NLNR, p. 378.
143. Ibid., pp. 382ff.
144. Ibid., p. 406.
145. Ibid., p. 410.
146. Ibid., p. 406.

4. ON FOUNDATIONAL AND IMPLICATIONAL APPROACHES TO RELIGION AND PRACTICAL REASON

1. James Collins, *The Emergence of Philosophy of Religion*, p. 144.
2. See Grisez's recent article on the subject, "Practical Reason and Faith," in *Proceedings of the American Catholic Philosophical Association* 57, ed. Daniel O. Dahlstrom, pp. 2-14. As in CMP, he continues to argue that Christian faith adds no new principles to what is naturally knowable (pp. 5, 7); and that the Pauline principle, requiring one not to do evil that good might arise, is apt to seem "unreasonable" without faith (p. 9).
3. On the aimless condition of fallen man, see CMP, p. 825.
4. Ibid., p. 122.
5. For recent articles by ethicians in the Grisez school of value theory, see John Finnis, "Human Good(s) and Practical Reasoning," and Joseph M. Boyle, "Practical Reasoning and Moral Judgment," both in *Proceedings of the American Catholic Philosophical Association* (see note 2 above).
6. On the use of these terms in Thomistic theory, see William A.

Wallace, "A Thomistic Philosophy of Nature," in *From a Realist Point of View: Essays on the Philosophy of Science,* 2nd ed. (Lanham, Md.: University Press of America, 1983), pp. 23-43.

7. The term "ethico-religious positivism" is borrowed from Vincent C. Punzo, "Theological Virtues in the Moral Life: A Critical Response." The paper was delivered in response to Grisez's paper (note 2 above). Punzo argues that Grisez's "failure to distinguish between the religious and moral dimensions of the theological virtues puts us on the slippery slope toward an ethico-religious positivism." He also notes that if adherence to the Pauline principle is unreasonable without faith, we should be all the more willing to admit that "such adherence is a religious rather than a moral matter." Punzo's paper was not printed in the *Proceedings,* and is quoted here with the permission of the author.

8. For a useful essay on why placing religion in the foundation will produce tensions within one's ethical theory, see Manfred Vogel "Kierkegaard's Teleological Suspension of the Ethical—Some Reflections From a Jewish Perspective," in *Georgetown Symposium,* pp. 19-48. Vogel distinguishes between a "type I" religion that has foundational status and a "type II" in which religion is constituted separately. Vogel argues that it is only by formulating the problem of religion and morality in the context of type I that the issue is interesting, and "indeed much more substantive and challenging" (p. 24).

9. John Locke, *Two Treatises of Government,* ed. Peter Laslett (New York: New American Library, 1965), 2.1.6, 2.5.31 (pp. 311, 332).

10. There is considerable debate over whether Locke gave his tongue to Hooker and his heart to Hobbes, and in general over the origin and role of his natural law theory. See Laslett's note, ibid., p. 310, and Leo Strauss's study of Hobbes and Locke on the subject in *Natural Right and History* (Chicago: University of Chicago Press, 1953), pp. 165-221. See also John Rawls, *A Theory of Justice,* p. 132.

11. In particular see Spinoza *Ethics* (Appendix to Part 1) and Spinoza, *Theologico-Political Treatise* (chap. 5).

12. CMP, p. 613.

13. Aquinas *Summa theologiae* 2.2 q.81, a.5.

14. Ibid., aa. 3, 4.

15. The giving of sacrifice to God is one of the laws of nature and of right reason. See Aquinas *Summa theologiae* 2.2 q. 85, aa.1-3.

16. For a study of the architectonic role of the natural virtue of religion in Aquinas, see Dom Odon Lottin, *Aux Sources De Notre Grandeur Morale* (Editions, De L'Abbaye Du Mont Cesar, 1956).

17. Aquinas *Summa theologiae* 2.2 q. 81, a. 5.

18. CMP, p. 124.

19. Aquinas *Summa theologiae* 1.2 q. 82, a. 3. On the role of final causality in Aquinas's moral theory, see R. Garrigou-Lagrange's study of the first fifty-four questions of the *prima-secundae*, *Beatitude: A Commentary on St. Thomas' Theological Summa*, trans. Patrick Cummins (St. Louis: Herder, 1956). One of the main problems in Aquinas's account of natural religion and ethics (in *Summa theologiae* 1.2, qq. 1-54, and in 2.2, q. 81) is that although demonstrations concerning the existence and attributes of God, and a philosophical anthropology, are presupposed, it is not clear how much knowledge of God is required for the operation of the natural virtue of religion. Clearly, his treatment of the virtue of religion presupposes some knowledge concerning God, and the fourth and fifth "ways" appear especially important for his moral reasoning in *Summa theologiae* 1.2 and 2.2. In *Summa contra gentiles* 3.1.38.5, he states that the virtue requires at least a "true opinion" [*opino vera de Deo*]; and in *Summa theologiae* 1.2 q. 104, a. 1, ad. 3, he suggests that it requires "reason informed by faith" [*ratio fide informata*].

20. Aquinas *Summa theologiae* 2.2 q. 104, a. 1, ad. 1. The section is on his discussion of the virtue of obedience.

21. Augustine *On the Trinity*, 10.5.7.

22. Aquinas *Summa theologiae* 1 q. 82, a. 2; Aquinas *Summa contra gentiles* 1.3.17, 19.

23. Bloch, the Marxist, understands that this necessary ordination to God is the decisive feature of Aquinas's natural law theory. See Ernst Bloch, *The Principle of Hope*, p. 1320. See also Robert Sokolowski's appendix on "Thomas Aquinas and the Christian Sense of the Good," in his *Moral Action: A Phenomenological Study* (Bloomington, Ind.: Indiana University Press, 1985), pp. 201-07. Sokolowski likewise emphasizes that the final end does not fall under choice. He correctly points out that it is necessary to show why the subordinate goods should not "melt away" in light of the transcendent good. This, I would suggest, requires careful attention to Aquinas's metaphysics of *esse* and the various uses of analogical reasoning, which allow at least a minimal philosophical understanding of participation and ordination on the one hand, while leaving open the specific disclosure of revelation on the other hand. Both the philosophical and theological facets allow, as Sokolowski puts it, a certain "distance" between the goods with which we are ordinarily familiar and the *finis ultimus*. Insofar as Aquinas has what we would today call a philosophy of religion, and to the extent that it bears upon his moral theory, the following elements are crucial: (1) God, is, by nature, the *finis ultimus* not only of human beings, but of all

created being; (2) religion arises because of this dependence upon and ordination to God; (3) the natural virtue of religion requires, minimally, some recognition of this dependence and ordination in the order of being, and as a virtue it governs acts of gratitude. We have underscored the term "minimal," but a full-scale study of Aquinas on this subject would show the massive amount of philosophical work necessary to establish this minimal toehold regarding the natural virtue of religion. Anyone who is doing work not only in natural law theory, but in theological ethics as well, will have to decide for himself or herself whether this minimal toehold is important, and whether he or she is willing to engage in all of the preliminary metaphysics necessary to secure it. Obviously, neither Grisez nor Finnis is willing (they do not see the need) to make the effort. Our analysis is meant to indicate what price is paid by refusing to do so.

24. Henry B. Veatch, *Human Rights: Fact or Fancy?*, pp. 67f.

25. Bruce R. Reichenbach has argued that a divine command theory is reconcilable with, and defensible in terms of, a natural law theory that stresses the objective good in divine creation. Nevertheless, Reichenbach contends that it is dubious that such a framework will be of much specific help in resolving concrete moral issues, such as the just distribution of scarce resources. See Bruce R. Reichenbach, "The Divine Command Theory and Objective Good," in *Georgetown Symposium*, pp. 219–33. There is some merit to Reichenbach's reservation, for even if a natural law theory were able to resolve the merely conjectural *convenientia* of Finnis, it would not imply that prudence must give way to a list of divine commands which have already determined what one is to do in each and every case. Yet it would make a considerable difference, not only in having the means for avoiding fideism, but more generally in establishing a philosophical framework that is conducive to, and not abrogated by, moral theology. In other words, it would constitute a foundational horizon in which moral principles and particular cases would be seen in a rather different light than if it were absent. Finnis wishes to reserve this horizon of implicational consideration; Grisez relies entirely upon theology once this issue is broached.

26. The problem of philosophical foundations and theological implications spurred the controversy which led to the papal encyclical *Humani Generis* in 1950. At least in part, the controversy was over Henri de Lubac, *Surnaturel: Etudes historiques* (Paris: Aubier, 1946), in which de Lubac examined Aquinas's argument that no natural desire can be in vain, and that human desire is necessarily ordained to God as the *finis ultimus*. From this, he concluded that man is not a thing of nature (*"l'homme n'est pas chose naturelle"*)

and cannot be understood except in relationship to divine life (p. 247). Thomists argued that this interpretation suggests that the supernatural cannot prove gratuitous, for in giving grace sufficient for beatitude, God would only be giving man what is his due by creation. The Thomists won the battle but probably lost the war in this controversy, for many Catholic philosophers and theologians (including, I suspect, Germain Grisez) came to view the debate as philosophically insoluble and virtually a tar pit. In any event, the raft of literature occasioned by *Humani Generis* represents the last serious debate over man's final end and natural law theory. Any recovery of natural law thinking will have to return to this tar pit and regroup the issues for consideration. For an excellent summary of the debate, see Philip J. Donnelly, "Current Theology," *Theological Studies* 8 (1947): 485ff.; and "Discussions on the Supernatural Order," *Theological Studies* 9 (1948): 216ff. For what is perhaps the clearest presentation of the Thomistic side in the controversy, see Anton Pegis, "Nature and Spirit: Some Reflections on the Problem of the End of Man," in the *Proceedings of the American Catholic Philosophical Association* 23 (1949), pp. 52ff.

27. Again, see RRM, p. 20, where Grisez and Finnis insist that even if Aquinas brought speculative conclusions to bear upon practical issues, such a move is not immediately relevant to the foundation of practical rationality.

28. John F. Wipple, *Metaphysical Themes in Thomas Aquinas* (Washington, D.C.: Catholic University Press of America, 1984), p. 240.

29. R. Garrigou-Lagrange, *Beatitude*, p. 100. In an article entitled "Natural Law, Human Action, and Morality," in *Georgetown Symposium*, pp. 82–87, Alan Gewirth brushes over any distinction between finality and providence and concludes that Thomistic natural law cannot be abstracted from its broader theological context. Like Grisez, he suggests that the proofs concerning nature require theology. Furthermore, he argues that because there is a smaller gap between action and goods than between nature and goods, a consistent ethic is more tenable by shifting from nature to human agency. Gewirth, however, not only fails to treat directly the substantive issue of whether there is a philosophically tenable distinction between finality and providence, but more seriously he does not address Aquinas's argument in the first five questions of the *prima secundae* that, objectively, the good of man ultimately cannot consist in any good of the soul. If Aquinas can make good on that claim, there is nothing to gain by undertaking the shift advocated by Gewirth. Like so many other ethicians, including those who would defend Aquinas, Gewirth treats Thomistic natural law theory as though it begins with

question 90—well after Thomas makes his most important claims concerning teleology and the goods. It is interesting that in the same volume of essays, Alan Donagan takes care to note that Aquinas's treatment of happiness in the first five questions of the *prima secundae* is crucial. Donagan argues that it is in these questions that Aquinas conceives of a "non-producible good" that can establish a point of correlation between Thomistic and Kantian ethics. See Alan Donagan, "Teleology and Consistency in Theories of Morality as Natural Law," in *Georgetown Symposium*, p. 93. Although Donagan is a neo-Kantian, he stands out from the rest of the crowd in seeing that it is possible to read backward profitably from question 90 in the *Summa theologiae*.

30. Alan Donagan, *The Theory of Morality*, p. 26.

31. J. L. Mackie, *Ethics: Inventing Right and Wrong* (Harmondsworth: Penguin, 1977), pp. 39–42.

32. Josiah Royce, *The Philosophy of Loyalty*, p. 1008.

33. See Mark C. Taylor's excellent study, *Kierkegaard's Pseudonymous Authorship: A Study of Time and the Self* (Princeton, N.J.: Princeton University Press, 1975), pp. 237–340.

34. John William Miller, *The Philosophy of History* (New York: W. W. Norton, 1982), p. 174. Stoicism lends itself to aphoristic remarks, but one of the most insightful is Ernst Bloch's observation that the Stoics tended "to preach wine and drink water"; for, having praised happiness and virtue, they were left with a one-dimensional virtue. See Ernst Bloch, *Natural Law and Human Dignity*, p. 6. This notion of preaching wine and drinking water seems like an apt characterization of the Grisez-Finnis version of the Fpm. In *After Virtue*, pp. 168ff., MacIntyre provides some important remarks on why Stoicism is a perennial temptation in the history of Western ethics.

35. Bloch, *Natural Law and Human Dignity*, p. xiii.

36. Bloch, *The Principle of Hope*, p. 1327.

37. Royce, *The Philosophy of Loyalty*, p. 977.

38. Ibid., p. 1008.

39. For a study of Kant's practical and historical antinomies, see Yirmiahu Yovel, *Kant and the Problem of History* (Princeton, N.J.: Princeton University Press, 1980), particularly the Epilogue, pp. 271ff. Besides being an excellent study of Kant's theory of practical reason, Yovel makes a persuasive case that the problems of speculative rationality cannot be deferred to what we have called the implicational approach.

40. NLNR, pp. 380f.

41. Ibid., p. 374.

42. MacIntyre's discussion of this in chapter 15 of *After Virtue* is worth considering.

43. Ibid., pp. 260, 272ff.

CONCLUSION

1. Henry B. Veatch, *Human Rights: Fact or Fancy?*, p. 50.
2. Alan Donagan, *The Theory of Morality*, p. 27.
3. Alasdair MacIntyre, *After Virtue*, pp. 183ff.
4. Aristotle *Nicomachean Ethics* 1.7 (1097e-1098a).
5. In this regard, see Harry V. Jaffa, *Thomism and Aristotelianism: A Study of the Commentary by Thomas Aquinas of the Nicomachean Ethics* (Chicago: University of Chicago Press, 1952), esp. pp. 187-92. MacIntyre refers to it as an "unduly neglected minor modern classic." It is an early work by Jaffa, but our interest in it is based upon Jaffa's claim that Aquinas transgresses the boundary between philosophy and theology by inventing virtues (particularly, the virtue of religion) which are not to be found, *secundum naturam*, in the Aristotelian system. Unfortunately, Jaffa was led astray by Frederick Copleston's contention that Aquinas invents new "natural virtues" by illicitly bringing theological data to bear upon morality. See Frederick Copleston, *A History of Philosophy*, vol. 2, pt. 2 (New York: Doubleday & Co., 1962 reprint), pp. 130f. Here one should reconsider notes 19, 23, and 29 in the previous chapter of this book. Aquinas's natural virtue of religion depends upon the employment of a philosophy of nature that goes well beyond the boundaries set by Aristotle—in particular (and just for starters), his understanding of how God can be both an *efficient* and final cause of participated *esse*. Thus, when Aquinas proceeds *ex suppositione naturae*, he quite clearly goes further than Aristotle in terms of what is capable of demonstration, and what applications can be made in other areas, such as moral conduct. This does not imply, however, that he is inventing "new natures." Both Jaffa and Copleston leap too quickly to the judgment that the incongruity between Aristotle and Aquinas is due to the faith-reason dilemma, and, correlatively, to philosophy-theology problems in the area of method. Nor is the problem simply one of the difference between the cultural and narratival horizons marking a fifth-century Athenian from a thirteenth-century Christian. The decisive point is that Aquinas has a broader view of what can be treated *secundum naturam*. It is a case in point regarding the manner in which philosophy proper shapes and determines the boundary of moral theory. One need not dismiss the important cultural and religious contexts, but is is important to resist the temptation to account for disagreements in moral theory simply by reducing the terms of disagreement to extraphilosophical matters.
6. Percy tends to view the problem exclusively in terms of the science versus self issue. In a recent article entitled "The Diagnostic Novel," *Harpers* (June 1986), pp. 39-45, Percy observes that the choice facing the intellectual today is whether he or she will be a

pathologist who comments upon what the patient died of, or, hopefully, a diagnostician who examines the illness and judges whether it is acute or chronic, fatal or treatable. Percy insists that the chronic illness of contemporary man is that he has forgotten that science can only deal with what is capable of generalization, whereas the human self is particular and eludes such generalizations. Our point in this regard is simply that insofar as ethicists today wish to play the role of diagnostician, one thing persistently seems to slip through the diagnostic nets: namely, the possibility that the chronic illness is a symptom of an inability to generalize about what is true, good, and noble, as well as a supine willingness to allow an emaciated science to go uncontested. Until this is directly addressed, the intellectual as diagnostician strikes us as contributing to the death of the patient. For a recent work that has set a different course in this area, see William Barrett, *Death of the Soul* (New York: Doubleday, 1986). Barrett has broken with the existentialist diagnostics, and has readdressed the problem of the nature of the soul.

7. Stanley Hauerwas, *The Peaceable Kingdom*, p. 17.

8. Ernst Bloch, *Natural Law and Human Dignity*, p. xxix.

9. Ibid., pp. 25, 39. As Bloch points out, this relative natural law theory requires something like the embryo seed model of sequential mediation and architectonic hierarchy (p. 7), and, however relative it is, it still requires a philosophical theory of hierarchy (p. 42).

10. Karl Barth insisted that the *analogia entis* is "*the* invention of Anti-Christ," but he went on to say that "I concede that all the other reasons one can have for not becoming a Catholic are shortsighted and frivolous." See Eberhard Busch, *Karl Barth: His Life from Letters and Autobiographical Texts*, trans. John Bowden (Philadelphia: Fortress Press, 1976), p. 215. We cite this remark to indicate that Barth himself saw very clearly that before matters of theological ethics can be settled, it is necessary to determine the status of natural theology, which in turn involves all of the theoretical tools implicated in natural law theory—the principal one being the *analogia entis*. The manner in which Barth and his main interlocutors (Erich Przywara and Hans Urs Von Balthasar) were able to sustain this debate during the 1930s has been lost—but it is worth retrieving. The main question for Barth and his Catholic critics was whether or not Christian revelation (and the first commandment in particular) is protected or undermined by natural theology. Today, ethicists lurch into questions of practical reason so quickly that the fundamental differences between Catholic and Protestant viewpoints scarcely come into conflict.

BIBLIOGRAPHY

I. *GERMAIN GRISEZ AND JOHN FINNIS: PUBLICATIONS*

Boyle, Joseph M., Grisez, Germain, and Tollefsen, Olaf. *Free Choice: A Self-Referential Argument.* Notre Dame, Ind.: University of Notre Dame Press, 1976.

Finnis, John. *Natural Law and Natural Rights.* Oxford: Clarendon Press, 1980.

———. *Fundamentals of Ethics.* Washington, D.C.: Georgetown University Press, 1980.

———. "Human Good(s) and Practical Reasoning." In *Proceedings of the American Catholic Philosophical Association* 58 (1984): 23-36.

Grisez, Germain. "Kant and Aquinas: Ethical Theory." *Thomist* 21 (1958): 44-78.

———. *Contraception and the Natural Law.* Milwaukee: Bruce Publishing Co., 1964.

———. "The First Principle of Practical Reason: A Commentary on the *Summa Theologiae,* Question 94, Article 2." *Natural Law Forum* 10 (1965): 168-201.

———. "Methods of Ethical Inquiry." In *Proceedings of the American Catholic Philosophical Association* 41 (1967): 160-68.

———. *Abortion: The Myths, the Realities, and the Arguments.* New York: Corpus Books, 1970.

———, and Shaw, Russell. *Beyond the New Morality.* Notre Dame, Ind.: University of Notre Dame Press, 1974; rev. ed. 1980.

———. *Beyond the New Theism: A Philosophy of Religion.* Notre Dame, Ind.: University of Notre Dame Press, 1975.

———. "Against Consequentialism." *American Journal of Jurisprudence* 23 (1978): 21-72.

———. "Christian Moral Theology and Consequentialism." In *Principles of Catholic Moral Life,* edited by William E. May. Chicago: Franciscan Herald Press, 1981.

———, and Finnis, John. "The Basic Principles of Natural Law: A

Reply to Ralph McInerny." *American Journal of Jurisprudence* 26 (1981): 21–31.

————. *The Way of the Lord Jesus.* Vol. 1, *Christian Moral Principles.* Chicago: Franciscan Herald Press, 1983.

————. "Practical Reasoning and Christian Faith." in *Proceedings of the American Catholic Philosophical Association* 58 (1984): 2–14.

II. *WORKS BY OTHER AUTHORS: BOOKS*

Allan, George. *The Importances of the Past: A Meditation on the Authority of Tradition.* Albany: SUNY Press, 1986.

Anscombe, Elizabeth. *The Collected Philosophical Papers.* Vol. 3, *Ethics, Religion and Politics.* Minneapolis: University of Minnesota Press, 1981.

Aquinas, Thomas. *Summa theologica.* Translated by the Fathers of the English Dominican Province. 3 vols. New York: Benziger Brothers, 1947–48.

————. *Summa theologiae.* Rome: Editiones Paulinae, 1962.

————. *On the Truth of the Catholic Faith: Summa Contra Gentiles.* Translated by James F. Anderson, Vernon J. Bourke, Charles J. O'Neil, and Anton C. Pegis. 5 vols. 1955–57. Reprint. Notre Dame, Ind.: University of Notre Dame Press, 1975.

————. *Summa Contra Gentiles: Seu De Veritate Catholicae Fidei.* Taurini: Marietti, 1937.

————. *In Decem Libros Ethicorum Aristotelis ad Nicomachum.* Taurini: Marietti, 1934.

Aristotle. *Nicomachean Ethics.* Translated by H. Rackham. Cambridge, Mass.: Loeb Classical Library, Harvard University Press, 1926.

Augustine. *City of God.* Translated by Marcus Dods. New York: Modern Library, 1950.

Barrett, William. *Death of the Soul: From Descartes to the Computer.* New York: Doubleday, 1986.

Barth, Karl. *Epistle to the Romans.* Translated by Edwyn C. Hoskyns. Oxford: Oxford University Press, 1933.

————. *Protestant Theology in the Nineteenth Century.* Translated by Brian Cozens. London: SCM Press, 1972.

————. *The Knowledge of God and the Service of God according to the Teachings of the Reformation.* The Gifford Lectures of 1937–1938. Translated by J. L. M. Haire and Ian Henderson. 1939. Reprint. New York: AMS, 1979.

Bloch, Ernst. *Natural Law and Human Dignity.* Translated by Dennis J. Schmidt. Cambridge, Mass.: MIT Press, 1986.

———. *The Principle of Hope.* 3 vols. Translated by Neville Plaice, Stephen Plaice, and Paul Knight. Cambridge, Mass.: MIT Press, 1986.

Busch, Eberhard. *Karl Barth: His Life from Letters and Autobiographical Texts.* Translated by John Bowden. Philadelphia: Fortress Press, 1976.

Calvin, John. *Institutes of the Christian Religion.* Translated by Ford Lewis Battles. Philadelphia: Westminster Press, 1960.

———. *The Catechism of the Church of Geneva.* Translated by J. K. S. Reid, Vol. 22 in the *Library of Christian Classics.* Philadelphia: Westminster Press, 1954.

Collins, James. *The Emergence of Philosophy of Religion.* New Haven, Conn.: Yale University Press, 1967.

Copleston, Frederick. *Mediaeval Philosophy.* Part I of Vol. 2 of *A History of Philosophy.* New York: Doubleday, 1962, reprint.

Descartes, Rene. *The Philosophical Works of Descartes.* 2 vols. Translated by E. S. Haldane and G. R. T. Ross. Cambridge: Cambridge University Press, 1931.

Dewey, John. *A Common Faith.* New Haven: Yale University Press, 1934.

Donagan, Alan. *The Theory of Morality.* Chicago: University of Chicago Press, 1977.

Feuerbach, Ludwig. *Lectures on the Essence of Religion.* Translated by Ralph Manheim. New York: Harper & Row, 1967.

Galston, William A. *Kant and the Problem of History.* Chicago: University of Chicago Press, 1975.

Garrigou-Lagrange, Reginald, O.P. *Beatitude: A Commentary on St. Thomas's Theological Summa.* Translated by Patrick Cummins, O.S.B. St. Louis: Herder, 1956.

Geach, Peter. *God and the Soul.* New York: Schocken Books, 1969.

Hauerwas, Stanley. *Truthfulness and Tragedy.* Notre Dame, Ind.: University of Notre Dame Press, 1977.

———. *The Peaceable Kingdom.* Notre Dame, Ind.: University of Notre Dame Press, 1983.

———. *Character and the Christian Life: A Study in Theological Ethics.* San Antonio, Tex.: Trinity University Press, 1975.

Hegel, G. W. F. *Early Theological Writings.* Translated by T. M. Knox. Philadelphia: University of Pennsylvania Press, 1977.

Heine, Heinrich. *Religion and Philosophy in Germany.* Translated by Dennis J. Schmidt. Albany: SUNY Press, 1986.

Hildebrand, Dietrich von. *Ethics.* Chicago: Franciscan Herald Press, 1953.

228   Bibliography

Jaffa, Harry. *Thomism and Aristotelianism: A Study of the Commentary by Thomas Aquinas on the Nicomachean Ethics.* Chicago: University of Chicago Press, 1952.

Kant, Immanuel. *Critique of Practical Reason.* Translated by Lewis White Beck. Indianapolis: Bobbs-Merrill, 1956.

———. *Religion Within the Limits of Reason Alone.* Translated by Theodore M. Greene and Hoyt H. Hudson. New York: Harper & Row, 1960.

———. *Perpetual Peace and Other Essays.* Translated by Ted Humphrey. Indianapolis: Hackett Publishing, 1983.

Kierkegaard, Soren. *Kierkegaard's Writings.* Vol. 6, *Fear and Trembling.* Translated by Howard V. Hong and Edna H. Hong. Princeton, N.J.: Princeton University Press, 1983.

Lee, Martin A., and Bruce Shlain. *Acid Dreams.* New York: Grove Press, 1985.

Locke, John. *Two Treatises of Government.* Critical Edition by Peter Laslett. New York: New American Library, 1965.

de Lubac, Henri. *Surnaturel: Etudes historiques.* Paris: Aubier, 1946.

Lottin, Odon. *Aux sources de notre grandeur morale.* Editiones, De L'Abbaye Du Mont Cesar, 1956.

McCormick, Richard A. *Notes on Moral Theology: 1981–1984.* Lanham, Md.: University Press of America, 1985.

McInerny, Ralph. *Ethica Thomistica.* Notre Dame, Ind.: University of Notre Dame Press, 1982.

MacIntyre, Alasdair. *After Virtue.* 2d ed. Notre Dame, Ind.: University of Notre Dame Press, 1984.

Mackie, J. L. *Ethics: Inventing Right and Wrong.* Harmondsworth: Penguin Books, 1977.

Marcel, Gabriel. *Homo Viator: Introduction to a Metaphysic of Hope.* Translated by Emma Craufurd. Chicago: Henry Regnery, 1951.

Mill, John Stuart. *On Liberty.* Indianapolis: Hackett Publishing, 1978.

Miller, John William. *The Philosophy of History.* New York: W. W. Norton, 1981.

Niebuhr, H. R. *Christ and Culture.* New York: Harper & Row, 1951.

Owens, Joseph. *Human Destiny.* Washington: Catholic University of America Press, 1985.

Pegis, Anton. *At the Origins of the Thomistic Notion of Man.* New York: Macmillan, 1963.

Porreco, Rocco, ed. *The Georgetown Symposium on Ethics: Essays in Honor of Henry Babcock Veatch.* Lanham, Md.: University Press of America, 1984.

Rahner, Karl. *Hearers of the Word.* Translated by Michael Richards. New York: Herder, 1969.

Rawls, John. *A Theory of Justice*. Cambridge, Mass.: Belknap Press, 1971.

Reichley, A. James. *Religion in American Public Life*. Washington, D.C.: Brookings Institute, 1985.

Royce, Josiah. *The Basic Writings of Josiah Royce*. Vol. 2, *The Philosophy of Loyalty*. Edited by J. J. McDermott. Chicago: University of Chicago Press, 1969.

Schleiermacher, Friedrich. *On Religion: Speeches to Its Cultured Despisers*. Translated by John Oman. New York: Ungar, 1955.

Smith, W. C. *The Meaning and End of Religion*. New York: Macmillan, 1963.

Sokolowski, Robert. *Moral Action: A Phenomenological Study*. Bloomington, Ind.: Indiana University Press, 1985.

Spinoza, Benedict. *The Ethics and Selected Letters*. Translated by Samuel Shirley. Indianapolis: Hackett Publishing, 1982.

––––––. *A Theologico-Political Treatise*. Translated by R. H. M. Elwes. New York: Dover Publications, 1951.

Strauss, Leo. *Natural Right and History*. Chicago: University of Chicago Press, 1953.

Taylor, Mark C. *Kierkegaard's Pseudonymous Authorship: A Study of Time and the Self*. Princeton, N.J.: Princeton University Press, 1975.

Veatch, Henry B. *Human Rights: Fact or Fancy?* Baton Rouge, La.: Louisiana State University Press, 1985.

Wallace, William A. *From a Realist Point of View: Essays on the Philosophy of Science*. 2d ed. Lanham, Md.: University Press of America, 1983.

Wipple, John F. *Metaphysical Themes in Thomas Aquinas*. Washington, D.C.: Catholic University of America Press, 1984.

Yovel, Yirmiahu. *Kant and the Problem of History*. Princeton, N.J.: Princeton University Press, 1980.

III. *WORKS BY OTHER AUTHORS: ARTICLES, ESSAYS, AND UNPUBLISHED MATERIAL*

Anscombe, Elizabeth. "Modern Moral Philosophy." *Philosophy* 33 (1958): 1–19.

Boyle, Joseph M. "Practical Reasoning and Moral Judgment." In *Proceedings of the American Catholic Philosophical Association* 58 (1984): 37–49.

Bourke, Vernon J. "The Background of Aquinas's Synderesis Principle." In *Graceful Reason: Essays in Ancient and Medieval Philos-*

ophy Presented to Joseph Owens, edited by Loyd P. Gerson.
Toronto: Institute for Mediaeval Studies, 1983: 345–60.

———. "The Synderesis Rule and Right Reason." *Monist* 66
(January 1983): 70–82.

———. Review of *Natural Law and Natural Rights,* by John Finnis.
American Journal of Jurisprudence 24 (1981): 243–47.

Donnelly, Philip J. "Current Theology." *Theological Studies* 8
(1947): 471–91.

———. "Discussion on the Supernatural Order." *Theological Studies*
9 (1948): 213–49.

Fortin, Ernest. "The New Rights Theory and the Natural Law."
Review of Politics 44 (October 1982): 590–612.

Hittinger, F. Russell. "When It Is More Excellent to Love Than to
Know: The Other Side of Thomistic 'Realism.'" *Proceedings of
the American Catholic Philosophical Association* 57 (1983):
171–79.

———. Review of *After Virtue. The New Scholasticism* 56, no. 3
(Summer 1982): 385–90.

McInerny, Ralph. "The Principles of Natural Law." *The American
Journal of Jurisprudence* 25 (1980).

Pegis, Anton. "Nature and Spirit: Some Reflections on the Problem
of the End of Man." *Proceedings of the American Catholic Philosophical Association* 23 (1949): 62–79.

Punzo, Vincent. "Theological Virtues and the Moral Life: A Response." Delivered at the 1984 National Conference of the
American Catholic Philosophical Association. Unpublished.

INDEX

Allan, George: 226
Anscombe, Elizabeth: 2ff., 97, 200,
   211, 226, 229
Anselm: 47
Aquinas: 2f., 5, 8f., 13f., 17, 20, 27,
   30f., 33ff., 46, 53f., 70f., 83f.,
   86, 91, 100, 159f., 169-75, 185,
   192, 194, 197, 202-6, 214, 217ff.,
   226
Aristotle: 1, 17, 68ff., 76, 151, 169,
   193, 216, 223, 226
Augustine: 17, 20, 27, 83, 133, 169,
   172, 215, 219, 226

Barrett, William: 226
Barth, Karl: 96, 104, 127, 196,
   210ff., 226
Bloch, Ernst: 3f., 37, 179f., 196f.,
   200, 203, 222, 224, 227
Bourke, Vernon: 202, 204, 206, 229
Boyle, Joseph M.: 229
Busch, Eberhard: 227

Calvin, John: 227
Cicero: 147
Collins, James: 93, 155., 169, 210f.,
   217, 227
Copleston, Frederick: 227

deLubac, Henri: 228
Derrida, Jacques: 168
Descartes, Rene: 209, 227
Dewey, John: 95f., 113, 115
Donagan, Alan: 2, 4, 29, 31, 76, 96f.,
   175, 185, 190ff., 194, 200, 202,
   211, 222f., 227

Feuerbach, Ludwig: 47, 95. 118,
   211, 227
Fortin, Ernest: 202, 205, 207, 230
Freud, Sigmund: 47, 95

Galston, William: 227
Garrigou-Lagrange: 175, 221, 227
Geach, Peter: 214, 227
Gifford, Lord: 94f.

Hauerwas, Stanley: 3f., 80, 187, 192,
   196f., 200, 208, 224, 227
Hegel, G. W.F.: 93, 210, 227
Heine, Heinrich: 227
Herbert, Lord, of Cherbury: 94
Hildebrand, Dietrich Von: 227
Hittinger, Russell: 230
Hooker, Richard: 169
Hume, David: 47, 95, 156, 169
Huxley, Aldous: 95, 111

Jaffa, Harry: 228
Janssens, Louis: 69

Kant, Immanuel: 2, 7, 12, 27ff., 55,
   69, 82, 102, 130, 142, 147, 154ff.,
   159, 161, 169, 176ff., 181f., 185,
   195, 211, 213, 222, 228
Kierkegaard, Soren: 72, 134, 177,
   215, 218, 228

Lee, Martin A.: 228
Locke, John: 169, 218, 228

231